Making the Invisible Real

Making the Invisible Real

Practices of Seeing in Tibetan Pilgrimage

CATHERINE HARTMANN

OXFORD
UNIVERSITY PRESS

OXFORD
UNIVERSITY PRESS

Oxford University Press is a department of the University of Oxford. It furthers the University's objective of excellence in research, scholarship, and education by publishing worldwide. Oxford is a registered trade mark of Oxford University Press in the UK and in certain other countries.

Published in the United States of America by Oxford University Press
198 Madison Avenue, New York, NY 10016, United States of America.

Library of Congress Cataloging-in-Publication Data
Names: Hartmann, Catherine, author.
Title: Making the invisible real : practices of seeing in Tibetan pilgrimage / Catherine Hartmann, Assistant Professor of Religious Studies, Department of Philosophy and Religious Studies, University of Wyoming.
Description: New York, NY, United States of America : Oxford University Press, 2025 | Includes bibliographical references and index. |
Identifiers: LCCN 2024055851 (print) | LCCN 2024055852 (ebook) |
ISBN 9780197791554 (hardback) | ISBN 9780197791561 |
ISBN 9780197791578 (epub) | ISBN 9780197791585
Subjects: LCSH: Buddhist pilgrims and pilgrimages—Tibet Region.
Classification: LCC BQ6450.T53 H37 2025 (print) | LCC BQ6450.T53 (ebook)
| DDC 294.3/43509515—dc23/eng/20250211
LC record available at https://lccn.loc.gov/2024055851
LC ebook record available at https://lccn.loc.gov/2024055852

DOI: 10.1093/9780197791585.001.0001

Printed by Marquis Book Printing, Canada

FSC
www.fsc.org
MIX
Paper | Supporting responsible forestry
FSC® C103567

Contents

Acknowledgments vii
A Note on Translations and Transliterations ix

Introduction 1

1. Introduction to Pilgrimage in Buddhism 23
2. How to See on Pilgrimage 47
3. One Thing, Many Appearances: Perception and Reality in the Controversy over Kailash 69
4. Opening Doors to Sacred Realms: Chökyi Drakpa's Visionary Transformation 96
5. How Pilgrimage Guides Use Language and Landscape to Cultivate Co-Seeing 120
6. Khatag Zamyak's Co-Seeing 143

Conclusion: A Glimpse of the Mandala 166

Appendix 1: Full Translation of Guidebook to Gyangme: Vajradhāra's Feast 171
Appendix 2: Translation of Khatag Zamyak's Nyindeb, *pages 166–174* 179
Bibliography 185
Index 203

Acknowledgments

This book would not exist without the support of many people and institutions. Thank you for lighting each step along the path.

I would like to extend special thanks for the financial assistance provided by institutions that support research in the humanities. The Robert H. N. Ho Family Foundation in Buddhist Studies Global, in cooperation with the American Council of Learned Societies, generously provided a year of funding to support my writing as a graduate student, established my position at the University of Wyoming, and held writing workshops where I shared dissertation chapters and book manuscript drafts. Thank you as well to the Harvard's Graduate School of Arts and Sciences, the Jefferson Scholars Foundation, the Victor Fung Family Foundation, the South Asia Institute at Harvard, the Woodenfish Foundation, the Fairbank Center for Chinese Studies, the Foreign Language and Area Studies Program, the Center for Global Studies at the University of Wyoming, the Wyoming Institute of Humanities Research, and the National Endowment for the Humanities, who funded travel, fieldwork, and writing time. Thank you to hosting institutions, including Rangjung Yeshe Institute, Sichuan University, the Tibetan Library of Works and Archives, and the Dunhuang Research Academy; each hosted me and enabled me to develop my research. Thank you to Theo Calderara of Oxford University Press for supporting this project. Finally, thank you to *History of Religions*, in which a previous version of Chapter 5 was published.

To list all the people who helped me write this book would be impossible, but I want to give particular thanks to my teachers. My Harvard doctoral advisors: Janet Gyatso, Charles Hallisey. Anne Monius, Leonard van der Kuijp, and James Robson. Teachers at the University of Chicago and the University of Virginia: Christian Wedemeyer, Dan Arnold, Bruce Lincoln, Wendy Doniger, Matthew Kapstein, Steve Collins, Kurtis Schaeffer, David Germano, John Nemec, and Karen Lang. My Tibetan teachers: Tsetan Chonjore, Karma Ngodrup, Naga Sangye Tendar, and Lobsang Shastri, as well as those who read with me in Kathmandu, including Champa Lhundrup, Sonam Sherpa, and Nyangsham Gyal. The nuns of Khachoe Drubling Monastery in Karsha. Scholars who took the time to advise me outside any institutional context: Jay Garfield, Reiko Ohnuma, Don Lopez, James Dobbins, Andy Quintman, Geoff Barstow, Berthe Jansen, Jason Protass, Frances Garrett, and too many others to name. Thank you as well to people I have never even met, but who have taught me so much. These include scholars whose work inspired me and two anonymous OUP reviewers whose suggestions improved the final work. Thank you to all these people who taught me new ways to see. I hope my teaching and my support of other scholars live up to your example.

I also relied heavily on friends, colleagues, and family while writing this. Thank you to Greg Clines, Ian MacCormack, Liz Angowski, Rory Lindsay, Justin Fifield, Davey Tomlinson, Jason Smith, Sarah Griffis, Joie Chen, Arya Moallem, Seth Powell, Nabanjan Maitra, Shoko Metaka, Sun Penghao, Francesca Chubb-Confer, Andy Taylor, Jue Liang, Sara Swenton, Becky Bloom, and others. Thank you to my University of Wyoming colleagues, who welcomed me to my new home (and in one case, literally sold me a house). And to my family: Mom, Dad, George, Delia, Aaron, Little Man, and Zhimi. Thank you, thank you.

Making the Invisible Real

Making the Invisible Real

Practices of Seeing in Tibetan Pilgrimage

CATHERINE HARTMANN

OXFORD
UNIVERSITY PRESS

OXFORD
UNIVERSITY PRESS

Oxford University Press is a department of the University of Oxford. It furthers the University's objective of excellence in research, scholarship, and education by publishing worldwide. Oxford is a registered trade mark of Oxford University Press in the UK and in certain other countries.

Published in the United States of America by Oxford University Press
198 Madison Avenue, New York, NY 10016, United States of America.

Library of Congress Cataloging-in-Publication Data
Names: Hartmann, Catherine, author.
Title: Making the invisible real : practices of seeing in Tibetan pilgrimage / Catherine Hartmann, Assistant Professor of Religious Studies, Department of Philosophy and Religious Studies, University of Wyoming.
Description: New York, NY, United States of America : Oxford University Press, 2025 | Includes bibliographical references and index. |
Identifiers: LCCN 2024055851 (print) | LCCN 2024055852 (ebook) |
ISBN 9780197791554 (hardback) | ISBN 9780197791561 |
ISBN 9780197791578 (epub) | ISBN 9780197791585
Subjects: LCSH: Buddhist pilgrims and pilgrimages—Tibet Region.
Classification: LCC BQ6450.T53 H37 2025 (print) | LCC BQ6450.T53 (ebook) | DDC 294.3/43509515—dc23/eng/20250211
LC record available at https://lccn.loc.gov/2024055851
LC ebook record available at https://lccn.loc.gov/2024055852

DOI: 10.1093/9780197791585.001.0001

Printed by Marquis Book Printing, Canada

MIX
Paper | Supporting responsible forestry
FSC® C103567
FSC www.fsc.org

Contents

Acknowledgments

This book would not exist without the support of many people and institutions. Thank you for lighting each step along the path.

I would like to extend special thanks for the financial assistance provided by institutions that support research in the humanities. The Robert H. N. Ho Family Foundation in Buddhist Studies Global, in cooperation with the American Council of Learned Societies, generously provided a year of funding to support my writing as a graduate student, established my position at the University of Wyoming, and held writing workshops where I shared dissertation chapters and book manuscript drafts. Thank you as well to the Harvard's Graduate School of Arts and Sciences, the Jefferson Scholars Foundation, the Victor Fung Family Foundation, the South Asia Institute at Harvard, the Woodenfish Foundation, the Fairbank Center for Chinese Studies, the Foreign Language and Area Studies Program, the Center for Global Studies at the University of Wyoming, the Wyoming Institute of Humanities Research, and the National Endowment for the Humanities, who funded travel, fieldwork, and writing time. Thank you to hosting institutions, including Rangjung Yeshe Institute, Sichuan University, the Tibetan Library of Works and Archives, and the Dunhuang Research Academy; each hosted me and enabled me to develop my research. Thank you to Theo Calderara of Oxford University Press for supporting this project. Finally, thank you to *History of Religions*, in which a previous version of Chapter 5 was published.

To list all the people who helped me write this book would be impossible, but I want to give particular thanks to my teachers. My Harvard doctoral advisors: Janet Gyatso, Charles Hallisey. Anne Monius, Leonard van der Kuijp, and James Robson. Teachers at the University of Chicago and the University of Virginia: Christian Wedemeyer, Dan Arnold, Bruce Lincoln, Wendy Doniger, Matthew Kapstein, Steve Collins, Kurtis Schaeffer, David Germano, John Nemec, and Karen Lang. My Tibetan teachers: Tsetan Chonjore, Karma Ngodrup, Naga Sangye Tendar, and Lobsang Shastri, as well as those who read with me in Kathmandu, including Champa Lhundrup, Sonam Sherpa, and Nyangsham Gyal. The nuns of Khachoe Drubling Monastery in Karsha. Scholars who took the time to advise me outside any institutional context: Jay Garfield, Reiko Ohnuma, Don Lopez, James Dobbins, Andy Quintman, Geoff Barstow, Berthe Jansen, Jason Protass, Frances Garrett, and too many others to name. Thank you as well to people I have never even met, but who have taught me so much. These include scholars whose work inspired me and two anonymous OUP reviewers whose suggestions improved the final work. Thank you to all these people who taught me new ways to see. I hope my teaching and my support of other scholars live up to your example.

I also relied heavily on friends, colleagues, and family while writing this. Thank you to Greg Clines, Ian MacCormack, Liz Angowski, Rory Lindsay, Justin Fifield, Davey Tomlinson, Jason Smith, Sarah Griffis, Joie Chen, Arya Moallem, Seth Powell, Nabanjan Maitra, Shoko Metaka, Sun Penghao, Francesca Chubb-Confer, Andy Taylor, Jue Liang, Sara Swenton, Becky Bloom, and others. Thank you to my University of Wyoming colleagues, who welcomed me to my new home (and in one case, literally sold me a house). And to my family: Mom, Dad, George, Delia, Aaron, Little Man, and Zhimi. Thank you, thank you.

A Note on Translations and Transliterations

This book is primarily based on Tibetan-language sources. My goal is that both people who do not know Tibetan and Tibet scholars can both benefit from it. This can be difficult because, even when transliterated into Roman script, Tibetan spelling and pronunciation can be inscrutable to those who do not know the language. Meanwhile, English translations or phonetic transliterations make it hard for Tibet scholars to know precisely what Tibetan term is meant. Throughout, I have tried to balance these concerns by giving English translations and phonetic transliterations in the main body of the text, with precise Tibetan spellings given in the Wylie system in parentheses after first use, in notes, and in the Bibliography. At times, I also give glosses in multiple relevant languages. When I do, I note whether the term is Tibetan (T), Sanskrit (S), or Pali (P). All translations are my own, unless otherwise noted.

For Sanskrit and Tibetan terms that occur in English dictionaries (i.e., karma, mandala), I omit diacritics. All words that do not occur in English dictionaries are italicized. Names and place-names are generally left untranslated. Often, Tibetan thinkers may be known by multiple names or titles. For texts that are cited frequently, I provide an English translation of the title. The transliteration for all phonetically spelled Tibetan names and translated titles of texts may be found in the Index. I have also provided the Buddhist Digital Resource Center (BDRC) identifiers for texts where possible.

Introduction

The Fault Lies with the Blind Man

Śāriputra is suffering from doubt. His teacher, the Buddha, proclaims that the world is perfectly pure, but his own senses tell him the world is rotten and ugly. How can the wondrous world the Buddha describes be real, when the world Śāriputra experiences is so full of pain and suffering? Śāriputra's moment of doubt, told in *The Holy Teachings of Vimalakīrti*, frames a problem familiar to religious traditions the world over: How can ordinarily invisible beings and landscapes feel *real* to people when they cannot be seen or felt directly?

In the story, the Buddha immediately intuits Śāriputra's doubts and asks him:

> "What do you think, Śāriputra? Are the sun and the moon impure? Is that why the blind man fails to see them?"
>
> Śāriputra replied, "No, Lord. It is not so. The fault lies with the blind man, and not with the sun and moon."
>
> The Buddha declared, "In the same way, Śāriputra, it is the failings of living beings that prevent them from seeing the marvelous purity of the land of the Buddha, the Tathāgatha. The Tathāgatha is not to blame. Śāriputra, this land of mine is pure, but you do not see it."
>
> At that time one of the Brahma kings with his conch-shaped tuft of hair said to Śāriputra, "You must not think that this Buddha land is impure. Because to my eyes, Śākyamuni's Buddha land is as pure and spotless as the palace of the highest deities."
>
> Then Venerable Śāriputra said, "When I look at this land, I see this great earth, with its highs and lows, its thorns, its precipices, its peaks, and its abysses, as if it were entirely filled with excrement . . .
>
> Thereupon the Buddha pressed his toe against the earth, and immediately it was transformed into a huge mass of precious jewels, a magnificent array of many hundreds of thousands of clusters of precious gems, until it resembled the Buddha Ratnavyūha's Jeweled Land of Immeasurable

Making the Invisible Real. Catherine Hartmann, Oxford University Press. © Oxford University Press 2025.
DOI: 10.1093/9780197791585.003.0001

Blessings. All the members of the great assembly sighed in wonder at what they had never seen before, and all saw that they themselves were seated on a throne of jeweled lotuses.

The Buddha said to Śāriputra, "Śāriputra, now do you see the marvelous purity of this Buddha land?"

Śāriputra replied, "I see it, Lord! Something I have never seen before, and never even heard of—now all the marvelous purity of the Buddha land is visible before me!"

The Buddha said, "Śāriputra, my Buddha land has always been pure like this. But because I wish to save those persons who are lowly and inferior, I make it seem to be impure and spoiled by many faults, that is all . . . living beings see the splendors of this Buddha land according to their own degrees of purity."[1]

According to the text, Śāriputra's glimpse of the perfect world awakens *bodhicitta*, the spirit of awakening, which sets him on the path toward Buddhahood.[2] No longer doubtful, he is convinced of the reality of the world the Buddha describes, and he is motivated to move forward in his practice. The story resolves Śāriputra's doubts magically, but absent this kind of divine intervention, how might Śāriputra or anyone else learn to see this suffering world as perfect and pure? Or, even if one cannot see it for oneself, how can someone experience this unseen world as real?

This passage from *The Holy Teachings of Vimalakīrti* frames two key questions that drive this book. First, how can people learn to see the world differently? Śāriputra sees the world as rotten but wants to see it as beautiful. How can he change? Buddhist traditions offer one way to approach this broad question because, like many religious traditions, Buddhism seeks to change how people see the world. Appeals to transform the ordinary, deluded way we see the world run throughout Buddhist traditions, which claim that we humans operate from egotistical delusions that process everything in terms

[1] Translated from *Dri ma med par grags pas bstan pa'i mdo*, in *Bka' 'gyur (dpe bsdur ma)*, BDRC W1PD96682 (Beijing: Krung go'i bod rig pa'i dpe skrun khang, 2006–2009), Vol. 60, 472.4–474.20. All translations are my own, unless otherwise noted. In this case, the translation largely follows that of *The Holy Teaching of Vimalakīrti: A Mahāyāna Scripture*, trans. Robert A. F. Thurman (Philadelphia: The Pennsylvania State University Press, 1976), 18–19.

[2] Literally, *bodhicitta* refers to the "awakening mind," usually interpreted to mean the mind that aspires to awaken for the sake of all beings. In his notes on this passage, Thurman writes that the moment of awakening bodhicitta (*bodhicittotpāda*) involves recognizing the inadequacy of ordinary consciousness, thinking that it is "possible, desirable, and essential" that he abandon this ordinary consciousness, and conviction that other beings must also be awakened. Ibid., 113.

of what we like or what we hate. These delusions prevent us from really seeing the world around us, as well as the deep ways we are connected to other beings, and this makes us all suffer. A large part of the Buddhist project, then, is to disrupt this habitually self-centered way of perceiving the world. As a consequence, Buddhist traditions have developed many practices to accomplish this transformation of perception. Most famously, Buddhists may meditate[3] or engage in philosophical inquiry[4] to uproot habitual thought patterns and cultivate new ways of seeing the world. However, Buddhists may also visualize a pure land or a particular chosen deity,[5] construct temples or other works of visual art that depict extraordinary ways of seeing,[6] tell narratives that thematize the faults of ordinary perception,[7] and perform rituals, all of which change the way people see and engage with the world.

Buddhist approaches to perception challenge how people typically think about seeing. Ordinarily, people think of perception, if they think of it at all, as passive and automatic, something that gives them more or less unmediated access to the world. *The Holy Teachings of Vimalakīrti*, however, complicates this notion. In it, the Buddha, the Brahma king, and Śāriputra are all looking at the same thing, and yet they see it in different ways. The Buddha claims this is because perception is constructed by the perceiver, but he holds out the possibility that Śāriputra—and by extension the rest of us—might someday transform that flawed perception to witness reality in its true purity and splendor.

Second, how can people experience that which is ordinarily invisible as real, vital, and present? At first, Śāriputra hears the Buddha describe the

[3] For a description of these practices, see Paul Griffiths, "Indian Buddhist Meditation," in *Buddhist Spirituality I*, ed. Takeuchi Yoshinori (New York: SCM Press, 1983), 34–66. For an analysis of how they work, see Karl Schmid, "Knowing How to See the Good: Vipaśyanā in Kamalaśīla's The Process of Meditation," in *Wilfrid Sellars and Buddhist Philosophy: Freedom from Foundations* (New York: Routledge, 2019), 200–218.

[4] For example, Malcolm David Eckel, *To See the Buddha: A Philosopher's Quest for the Meaning of Emptiness* (San Francisco: Harper San Francisco, 1992).

[5] For description and discussion of these practices, see Chris Hatchell, "Buddhist Visual Worlds II: Practices of Visualization and Vision," *Religion Compass* 7, no. 9 (2013): 349–360, as well as Eric M. Greene, "Visions and Visualizations: In Fifth-Century Chinese Buddhism and Nineteenth-Century Experimental Psychology," *History of Religions* 55, no. 3 (January 26, 2016): 289–328.

[6] For example, Julie Gifford, *Buddhist Practice and Visual Culture: The Visual Rhetoric of Borobudur* (New York: Routledge, 2011), Eugene Yuejin Wang, *Shaping the Lotus Sutra: Buddhist Visual Culture in Medieval China* (Seattle: University of Washington Press, 2007), Jacob Kinnard, *Imaging Wisdom: Seeing and Knowing in the Art of Indian Buddhism* (Richmond, Surrey: Curzon, 1999), and Wen-shing Chou, *Mount Wutai: Visions of a Sacred Buddhist Mountain* (Princeton, NJ: Princeton University Press, 2018).

[7] For example, see Andy Rotman, *Thus Have I Seen: Visualizing Faith in Early Indian Buddhism* (Oxford: Oxford University Press, 2009), and David McMahan, *Empty Vision: Metaphor and Visionary Imagery in Mahāyāna Buddhism* (New York: RoutledgeCurzon, 2002).

purity of the world, and maybe he even assents to it in an abstract and intellectual way, but it does not feel real to him. And so he doubts and cannot move forward. When the Buddha reveals the world for him to see directly with his own eyes, he develops the conviction that will carry him through the long path of practice toward buddhahood. Though this example comes from *The Holy Teachings of Vimalakīrti*, it illustrates an important question about religious traditions more broadly. As Robert Orsi puts it, "How do the gods and other special beings—and, more broadly, how does the world, visible and invisible, as the world is said to be within a particular religious culture—become as real to people as their bodies, as substantially there as the homes they inhabit"?[8] In different ways and in different contexts, Buddhist traditions describe features of the world—sacred landscapes, past lives, spirits, karmic connections—that are ordinarily invisible but that nonetheless form the world within which Buddhist practice makes sense. Scholars of Buddhism have sometimes assumed that people in Buddhist communities take the worldviews communicated in Buddhist texts as unquestionably obvious. However, it is not obvious to Śāriputra, and we should not assume that it is obvious to people in Buddhist communities.

This book will explore those broad questions by examining Tibetan Buddhist pilgrimage to holy mountains.[9] The tradition of mountain pilgrimage in Tibet is grounded in the claim that the mountain is a wondrous palace for an enlightened deity, or in other words, a mandala. Tradition maintains that most people cannot ordinarily see this reality; it is visible only to the most spiritually advanced practitioners. Still, the tradition challenges pilgrims to learn to see the mountain as a sacred palace through

[8] Robert Orsi, "Material Children: Making God's Presence Real through Catholic Boys and Girls," in *Religion, Media and Culture: A Reader*, ed. G. Lynch, J.P. Mitchell, and A. Strhan (London: Routledge, 2012), 147–158, 147. I also draw on the category of the real as it is used in Tanya Luhrmann, *How God Becomes Real: Kindling the Presence of Invisible Others* (Princeton, NJ: Princeton University Press, 2020).

[9] Tibetans of the non-Buddhist Bön school also undertake pilgrimage to holy mountains. These pilgrimages share many features with Buddhist pilgrimage, but while there is much to say on this subject, consideration of Bön materials is unfortunately outside the scope of the present work. Those interested in Bön pilgrimage should consult the work of scholars Samten Karmay and Charles Ramble listed in the Bibliography. A good place to start is Charles Ramble, "Gaining Ground: Representations of Territory in Bon and Tibetan Popular Tradition," *The Tibet Journal* 20, no. 1 (1995): 83–124. Note that Ramble describes various aspects of the Bön literature on sacred landscapes that have analogies in the Buddhist literature that will be discussed in the rest of the book, including ideas that non-human beings dwell in the landscape (86), that multiple invisible or "subtle" landscapes can exist in one physical place (89–93), that sacred places are said to be subdued by an advanced master (96–99), that places are conceptualized as mandalas (100), that sacred places must be "opened" (101), and that advanced masters can see sacred places as divine palaces (106). These are all features that have been noted across Bön and Buddhist pilgrimage literature.

the transformation of their perception. Pilgrims who could not see this extraordinary vision for themselves—which was generally held to be the large majority—still gained merit and blessings from their pilgrimage. However, their practices took place in a context that valorized those who could see the divine reality of the mountain. In effect, pilgrimage is an embodied, ritualized practice of transforming how people see the world. In pilgrimage, pilgrims restage for themselves the realization that the Buddha catalyzed in Śāriputra: the way that the world *appears* is not the way that the world *is*. Much of this tradition was transmitted through pilgrimage texts, both written and oral, of various genres. These texts mediate between pilgrims' experience and expectations, shaping how pilgrims experience their journeys. And throughout this literature, we find evidence of people trying to see ordinarily invisible realities.

While historians, philologists, and anthropologists have studied Tibetan pilgrimage, how the pilgrimage tradition connects to the fundamental questions of transforming perception and making invisible worlds real has yet to be explored. This is not to say that scholars have not already noted the central dynamic of the mountain appearing one way to ordinary people and another way to advanced masters—I am not the first to note this or many other features of Tibetan pilgrimage. My contribution to the field lies not in identifying novel features of Tibetan pilgrimage, but in providing an interpretation of the tradition, based on a variety of prescriptive materials, theoretical debates, and autobiographical accounts that illuminate questions of interest to scholars of Buddhism and other religious traditions.

This book thus brings together a range of textual sources to address these two driving questions about transforming perception and making the invisible real. These texts date from 1220 to 1950, and they are often previously untranslated and unstudied. Broadly speaking, the sources fall into three main groups: texts about how pilgrimage should be practiced, guidebooks written for pilgrims as guides to a particular place, and texts written by pilgrims about their own pilgrimage experiences. This diverse set of materials, which spans genres and time periods, allows me to explore how and why Tibetan pilgrimage texts attempt to transform pilgrims' perception during pilgrimage, what specific practices they advocated, and how those practices structured pilgrims' experiences at the holy mountain. These texts also address the general question of how religious traditions create and maintain shared worlds of extraordinary experience.

Practices of Seeing

To introduce some of the key analytical terms that will recur throughout the book, it will be helpful to illustrate them with a concrete example drawn from Toni Huber's *The Cult of Pure Crystal Mountain.* This groundbreaking book on Tibetan pilgrimage explores the traditions surrounding Tsari, a mountain in southeast Tibet. Tsari is a major pilgrimage mountain in Tibet, and it is often said to be a mandala with the tantric deity Cakrasaṃvara at its center.[10]

Mandalas are highly significant in tantric Buddhism, and they consist of a geometric configuration of deities in a divine palace, with the most important figure at the center preaching the dharma. The mandala palace is often analogized to the entire universe, with the central figure perched at the top of the cosmic mountain Meru. In the pilgrimage context, holy mountains are often said to be mandalas. However, tradition maintains that most pilgrims will not be able to see the mountain as a mandala directly. Just as Śāriputra's delusions prevented him from seeing the pure land, pilgrims' ordinary perception prevents them from seeing the mandala, which is the true nature of the mountain and which lies beyond ordinary perception. This pilgrimage tradition thus constructs an opposition between two understandings of reality: one, the ordinary reality pilgrims see every day, and the other, the deeper, extraordinary reality that pilgrimage texts (and Buddhist texts more broadly) claim lies beyond illusory ordinary perception.

To help us keep these different ways of seeing and types of reality straight, I will use the following sets of terms. First is a distinction used in Tibetan pilgrimage texts themselves[11] between the ordinary (*thun mong*) and the extraordinary (*thun mong ma yin pa*). The ordinary is what average people can see on an everyday basis, and the extraordinary is anything that lies outside of that everyday experience, including the wondrous and fantastic

[10] Tsari is associated with the mind of Cakrasaṃvara. Kailash and Lapchi are said to be the body and speech of Cakrasaṃvara, respectively. See Toni Huber, *The Cult of Pure Crystal Mountain: Popular Pilgrimage and Visionary Landscape in Southeast Tibet* (New York: Oxford University Press, 1999), 39–57. Note as well that Huber mentions many of the features of the pilgrimage tradition that will be further developed in this work, including sacred places as having multiple layers perceptible to people of different abilities (13), the importance of literary representations for shaping pilgrims' experiences (58–62), the benefits of pilgrimage to animals (147), the idea of the sacred place as a mandala (48–51) or stupa (54–56), and of visualization practices performed at mountains (74–76). As stated above, this book does not claim to identify these aspects of Tibetan pilgrimage for the first time, but instead to explore how they can help us understand how religious traditions attempt to transform perception and make ordinarily invisible worlds real.

[11] This distinction is most explicitly proposed in the work of Chödrak Yeshe, examined in Chapter 3, but it can be seen throughout the corpus of Tibetan pilgrimage literature.

descriptions of pilgrimage places. Pilgrims try to cultivate the ability to engage in extraordinary perception, and they use their imagination as a tool in that process. When I say that they visualize imagined and extraordinary worlds, I do not mean to imply that these worlds are not real. For pilgrims, both ordinary and extraordinary worlds are real, but they are real in different senses and different contexts. Ordinary perception is real in an everyday sense, but according to the pilgrimage tradition, the wondrous extraordinary vision of the mountain as mandala is *more* real. In describing the wondrous reality claimed by the pilgrimage tradition, I will thus speak of a more-than-real reality.[12] One key question for this book is how pilgrimage traditions get the extraordinary and more-than-real to *feel* real to pilgrims who cannot see it, in the sense that they feel it to be present, responsive, and alive in a direct rather than abstract and conceptual way.

To illustrate what I mean by these terms, let us turn to Huber's description of pilgrims to Tsari looking for the so-called Sexed Rocks of Tibet (*bod rdo mtshan can*). The "Sexed Rocks" are a rock formation said by pilgrimage guides to be the phallus of Maheśvara, a tantric deity, and a vulva that manifested itself to spiritual masters who first visited the site.[13] While it is relatively rare that Tibetan pilgrimage is about trying to see sexual organs in rocks, pilgrimage traditions frequently identify features of the ordinary, visible landscape as having a hidden significance or meaning. Within the overall challenge to see the mountain as a mandala, there are smaller invitations to see the extraordinary, hidden reality of smaller features at the mountain.

Huber provides accounts from two different pilgrims that show how they interacted with the sexed rocks. The two accounts are quite different—one is a written account by a high-ranking Bhutanese Drukpa monk who visited the site in 1782, and the other is an oral account by an unschooled farmer from Kongpo who visited it in 1958—but they share important similarities. It is worth quoting their accounts in full.

The Drukpa Lama's account reads as follows:

> On the eleventh day of the ninth month of the water-male-tiger year (1782), I arrived at the Sexed Rocks of Tibet within the né of Tsaritra, the powerful Khachö. Previously, when Kyewo Yeshé Dorje came to first open the door to

[12] In using this term, I draw on David Shulman, *More Than Real: A History of the Imagination in South India* (Cambridge, MA: Harvard University Press, 2012).
[13] Huber, *The Cult of Pure Crystal Mountain*, 75, with note on 244.

> this né, he was met here by the five long life sisters. In the middle of a mixed thicket of sang plants there was a flat rock with a checkered pattern. . . . I expected to see the Sexed Rocks as a phallus or a vulva, but instead they appeared to resemble thighs pressed together. I knew there were symbols which look like thighs, explained as the twenty-four symbols, including the symbol that looks like thighs and the symbol that looks like a phallus, in [Tantric] commentaries about the twenty-four countries. Today anyone, the wise and the foolish, going to see the site will all agree it resembles thighs pressed together, no matter how much time you spend above it. From another position it suddenly seems to be placed exactly like a stone phallus. There, it appeared recognizable as Sexed Rocks, and it is only this view that accounts for it as [one of] the twenty-four Sexed Rocks.[14]

Ngodrup, the farmer from Kongpo, says this:

> When my brother and I went to Tsari, our village neighbors had explained the route beforehand; they told us of the Sexed Rocks, saying it was an important place where a lama opened Tsari, the only rocks like this in Tibet, where you made prayers and could get empowerment, and drink the fertility water. When we got there we were disappointed, as we thought the genital shapes would be bigger and more obvious; we couldn't make them out really. My brother thought he found them, but we didn't know if it was correct. Lamas can see them, but none was present. So we left, and went on to Chikchar.[15]

Despite the differences in time and social status, these two pilgrims have strikingly similar experiences at the Sexed Rocks. They arrive at the site with expectations of seeing rocks resembling sex organs, based on textual sources or oral accounts. However, they are somewhat surprised, and in Ngodrup's words, "disappointed," that they cannot themselves see the rocks in the way they are described. They experience a disjunction between the extraordinary description of the site as a manifestation of tantric power and what they can see with their ordinary perception. In response, neither is content to know that the site is special in an abstract way—they want to see the extraordinary vision for themselves. The Drukpa Lama's account suggests that he moved

[14] Ibid., 76, with note on 244.
[15] Ibid., 76–77.

around and looked "from another position" until he suddenly sees the rocks in a new way, one that fits into the textual schema. Ngodrup's account also indicates that he moved around to look, but he says that "We couldn't make them out really." While Ngodrup seems confident that someone more qualified, such as a lama, would be able to see the rocks as sex organs and thereby enable him to see it, no such person is around, and so he and his brother eventually move on. In both cases, there is a conscious and active *looking* to attempt to reconcile the disjunction between descriptions given in guidebooks or oral tradition and that which pilgrims saw with their own eyes.[16]

Their attempts to resolve the disjunction between what they see and what they want to see exemplify what I will call practices of seeing. In trying to see the Sexed Rocks, Ngodrup and the Drukpa Lama both closely and actively examine the material world as seen in their ordinary perception to be able to see a deeper, more-than-real reality they believe to be hidden from that ordinary perception. Their accounts are very short and do not go into detail on their practices, but in future chapters we will explore a range of practices of seeing outlined by the pilgrimage tradition. These practices of seeing cultivate what I will call co-seeing—the state of seeing the site both in the mind's eye and with ordinary perception at once. Both Ngodrup and the Drukpa Lama have the extraordinary vision of the Sexed Rocks in their mind's eye, and when they see the site, they imagine the stories about Maheśvara attached to the site. However, with their ordinary perception, the rocks stubbornly look like rocks. The tension between these two ways of seeing prompts the pilgrims to try and resolve the tension through various practices of seeing, drawing their attention back and forth from the material world they can see with their eyes to the extraordinary world they imagine. The Drukpa Lama seems to resolve the tension in this instance, while Ngodrup does not, but both experience co-seeing. We do not get a sense from the passages whether these activities make the extraordinary nature of Tsari feel real to the pilgrims, but the passages demonstrate the types of practices that Tanya Luhrmann has characterized as "real-making" and that help make invisible worlds feel real.[17]

[16] Huber notes this, writing that "both high lama and farm-boy had to put a conscious effort into their acts of interpretation to make the site fit with what was expected." Ibid., 77.
[17] Luhrmann, *How God Becomes Real*, x–xi.

Central Argument

To address our two driving questions about changing perception and making the invisible real, this book will make one central argument, broken into three steps. The first step is a general claim about seeing and the role it plays in religious traditions. Whereas perception is often conceptualized as the passive reception of sense data from the external world, I argue that Tibetan pilgrimage materials show that perception is active and malleable. Vision bridges the internal world of language, imagination, and affect with the external, physical world. It is therefore a major site of religious traditions' attempts to reshape human experience of the world. In particular, religious traditions cultivate specific ways of looking at or seeing certain kinds of objects that have long-lasting effects for how practitioners experience and operate in the world. The study of vision and ways of seeing is thus a key component of the study of religion.

The next step in this argument is an interpretive account of how Tibetan pilgrimage texts mediate the encounter between pilgrims and the landscape to produce meaningful pilgrimage experiences. To do so, I highlight my Tibetan sources' sophisticated differentiation of different types of seeing and show how they understand perception to mediate between the internal world of imagination and the external material world and recommended techniques by which the pilgrim works *with* the material world. Such techniques, which I refer to as "practices of seeing," include a highly specialized form of reading the landscape for signs, practices of writing and reading, and an imaginative juxtaposition of physical and idealized landscapes. These practices facilitate what I will call "co-seeing," a state in which the pilgrim sees the site in two ways at once; that is, they see it in one way with their ordinary perception and in another quite different way in their mind's eye. Practices of seeing thus facilitate significant and potentially transformative religious experiences that arise from the interaction of physical reality, visionary reality, and the pilgrim who adopts these practices.

Finally, the last step of my argument is that these practices of seeing make a wondrous vision of the landscape real for pilgrims. By juxtaposing ordinary and imaginative perception, these practices of seeing interweave the world of the wondrous pilgrimage place with the ordinary physical world in the experience of the pilgrim, such that the pilgrim comes to experience the extraordinary world as interpenetrating the ordinary world at the pilgrimage site. The pilgrim can materially experience this extraordinary world, even if they cannot see it directly. Thus, practices of seeing enable the creation and maintenance of a shared place-world that is invisible but nonetheless experienced as *real* by the community of pilgrims. This, in turn, shows that seemingly fantastical religious worldviews are not simply believed or taken for granted, but actively constructed and reconstructed for new generations of practitioners.

I should also make it explicit what I am *not* arguing. First, I am not arguing for or against the reality of the visionary worlds described in pilgrimage texts. As a historian and textual scholar, I do not presume to have access to the capital-R Real. Instead, I am interested in how human communities create and sustain sacred landscapes that feel real and that orient people in the world. Second, I am not making a claim about how pilgrimage traditions developed or changed over time. Instead, I focus on the structural aspects of pilgrimage practice that exist throughout the tradition, to think about how they structure pilgrimage experiences. Third, I am not arguing that Tibetan scholars or pilgrims during the times these texts were written would have interpreted their own practices in the way I interpret them. I approach Tibetan materials with a set of questions and analytical language that differs from emic approaches with those materials, and it does not aim to supplant those emic approaches. Throughout this book's scholarly engagement with Tibetan texts, we should not forget that these texts, practices, and places are not a matter of merely academic concern to Tibetans, both in China and in exile, who are often restricted from visiting holy sites, and who face immense challenges to preserving their language and culture.

Textual Sources

To make this argument, I have brought together a variety of textual sources stretching from a dispute about a particular mountain's holiness from the 1230s to a pilgrim diary written in the 1950s. These sources comprise a variety of genres, perspectives, and historical periods. More will be said about each of these sources, their authors, and the historical contexts from which they emerged in the chapters dealing specifically with these materials, but for now a sense of the general nature of these sources will suffice. Broadly speaking, the sources used fall into three main groups: texts about how pilgrimage should be practiced, guidebooks written for pilgrims as guides to a particular place, and texts written by pilgrims about their own pilgrimage experiences.

First, I examine a few representative texts that make an argument for how pilgrimage *should* be practiced. That is, they articulate and defend a specific vision for how pilgrims should undertake pilgrimage practice and how they should *not* undertake pilgrimage practice. Some argue against pilgrimage entirely, and others contest the legitimacy of particular mountains. These normative statements can be found in several genres. For instance, songs or letters of advice offer guidance for potential pilgrims. Examples of such texts were written by such figures as Drakpa Gyeltsen (1147–1216),[18] Taranatha (1575–1634),[19] Karma Chagmé (1613–1678),[20] Jigmé Lingpa (1730–1798),[21] Kathog Situ Panchen (1880–1924),[22] and they are contained in their respective collected works (*gsung 'bum*). We also find instructions about how to do pilgrimage embedded in pilgrimage guides written by figures such as Pema Karpo (1527–1592)[23] and Jamgön Kongtrül (1813–1899).[24] Some normative statements about pilgrimage were also made in genres that were not directly addressed to pilgrims. For instance, because tantric texts such as the *Cakrasaṃvara Tantra* or *Hevajra Tantra* instruct tantric practitioners to go practice at certain holy places (S. *pītha*), commentaries written in both India and Tibet on these tantric texts will often discuss these pilgrimage practices and make arguments for how they should or should not be performed. We find such arguments in texts written by Naropa (c. eleventh century?)[25] and

[18] Grags pa rgyal mtshan, *Gnas bstod kyi nyams dbyangs*, in *Sa skya gong ma rnam lnga'i gsung 'bum dpe bsdur ma las grags pa rgyal mtshan gyi gsung*, BDRC W2DB4569, 5: 344–347 (Beijing: Krung go'i bod rig pa dpe skrun khang, 2007).

[19] TA ra nA tha, *Las stod kyi gnas skor ba 'dra la gdams pa*, in *Collected Works of TA ra nA tha*, BDRC W1PD45495, 3: 79–80 (Beijing: Krung go'i bod rig pa dpe skrun khang, 2008).

[20] Karma chags med, *Gnas mjal ba'i tshul*, in *Collected Works of Karma chags med*, BDRC W22933, 43: 637–638 (Chengdu: Si khron zhing chen mi rigs zhib 'jug su'o bod kyi rig gnas zhib 'jug khang, 1999).

[21] 'Jigs med gling pa Mkhyen brtse 'od zer, *Gnas bskor ba la spring ba'i gtam*, in *Collected Works of 'Jigs med gling pa Mkhyen brtse 'od zer*, BDRC W27300, 4: 575–579 (Gangtok: No publisher, 1985).

[22] KaH thog si tu Chos kyi rgya mtsho, "Gnas skor pa rab 'bring mtha' gsum gyi rnam dbye," in *Gnas yig phyogs bsgrigs*, BDRC W20828, 1–2 (Chengdu: Si khron mi rigs dpe skrun khang, 1998).

[23] 'Brug chen Kun mkhyen Pad+ma dkar po, *Gnas chen tsa ri tra'i ngo mtshar snang ba pad dkar legs bshad*, in *Collected Works of Padma dkar po*, BDRC W10736, 4: 215–282 (Darjeeling: Kargyud sungrab nyamso khang, 1973–1974).

[24] 'Jam mgon Kong sprul Blo gros mtha' yas, *Thugs kyi gnas mchog chen po de bI ko TI tsA 'dra rin chen brag gi rtog pa brjod pa yid kyi rgya mtsho'i rol mo*, in *Rgya chen bka' mdzod*, BDRC W21808, 11: 489–558 (Paro: Ngodup, 1975–1976).

[25] Naropa, *Rdo rje'i tshig gi snying po bsdus pa'i dka' 'grel* (S. *Vajrapādasārasaṃgraha*), in *Bstan 'gyur (dpe bsdur ma)*, BDRC W1PD95844, 2: 914–1137 (Beijing: Krung go'i bod rig pa'i dpe skrun khang, 1994–2008).

Vajragarbha (?)[26] that are contained in the Tibetan Tengyur, as well as in Tibetan commentaries and subcommentaries written on these texts.[27]

Second, I examine texts written for pilgrims about a particular place. Such texts are often classified as *néyik* (*gnas yig*), a term literally meaning writing (*yig*) about a holy place (*gnas*), but may also be called *néshé* (*gnas bshad*, explanation of a holy place), *nétö* (*gnas bstod*, holy place praise, also sometimes *sa bstod*, praise of the place), *lamyik* (*lam yig*, itinerary),[28] *karchak* (*dkar chag*, inventory),[29] or *logyü* (*lo rgyus*, history).[30] These texts generally praise a particular holy place (*gnas*), often a holy mountain or temple complex, relate the site's history, describe the benefits that will accrue to pilgrims who visit the site, and exhort audiences to visit the site on pilgrimage. Pilgrimage guides often adopt the voice of a tour guide (indeed, there is evidence that at least some written pilgrimage guides are derived from the oral traditions of human pilgrimage guides),[31] leading the potential pilgrim through the sites and describing individual objects that the pilgrim will see so that the pilgrim will fully appreciate them.

Third, I explore texts written by pilgrims about their own pilgrimage experiences. Again, there are several ways in which this type of writing occurred. Often, Tibetan writing about pilgrimage exists as part of larger autobiographies in which authors described pilgrimage in the larger context of their lives. Some pilgrims, such as Khatag Zamyak, a Tibetan merchant

[26] Vajragarbha, *Rdo rje snying po'i 'grel pa* (S. *Hevajrapiṇḍārthaṭīkā*), in *Bstan 'gyur (dpe bsdur ma)*, BDRC W1PD95844, 1: 940–1144 (Beijing: Krung go'i bod rig pa'i dpe skrun khang, 1994–2008).

[27] See, for example, Rang byung rdo rje, *Dgyes pa rdo rje'i brtag pa gnyis pa'i 'grel pa dri ma med pa'i 'od*, in *Collected Works of Rang byung rdo rje*, BDRC W30541, 8: 497–636 (Zi ling: Mtshur phu mkhan lo yag bkra shis, 2006). There are several other Tibetan commentaries on Tantric texts and commentaries, but a full investigation of such sources is outside the scope of this project.

[28] This term literally means path text or path writing. It can be used to refer to an itinerary for pilgrims to follow, a text in which someone writes an account of their travels, or a passport-type document signed by a local official that allows the holder to pass through a particular area. See Sam van Shaik and Imre Galambos, *Manuscripts and Travelers: The Sino-Tibetan Documents of a Tenth-Century Buddhist Pilgrim* (Berlin: Walter de Gruyter, 2011).

[29] This genre title can refer to lists of texts in a particular collected works (*gsung 'bum*), the items held in a library, or in the case of famous places, the texts, images, and other features found at the site. These inventories can range from simple lists of items without any commentary to detailed accounts that not only list the items and where they can be found but also relates the history and significance of the items.

[30] This term literally means account or history, and it is more frequently found in historiographical works, but it is sometimes used to talk about the history of a particular place.

[31] Dkon chog bstan 'dzin Chos kyi blo gros, for example, mentions consulting caretakers at pilgrimage sites when he is compiling his written pilgrimage guide. Elena de Rossi Fillibeck, *Two Tibetan Guide Books to Ti se and La phyi* (Bonn: VGH Wissenschaftsverlag, 1988), 84.

who went on pilgrimage to central Tibet and Kailash from 1944 to 1956,[32] also kept diary accounts of their pilgrimage journeys. Others describe their dreams or visions when practicing at a particular place.[33] Advanced masters may also claim to have founded pilgrimage sites and to relate the story of how they did so.[34]

Theoretical and Methodological Touchstones

This book draws from varied textual sources, including texts written by different authors, for different purposes, over a long period of time. This diversity of sources grants multiple perspectives on pilgrimage, and thus onto our central questions. However, a project involving such diverse sources also requires sensitivity to the ways these sources talk about pilgrimage, and a methodological approach that takes varied textual projects into account. To that end, I present some of the theoretical and methodological touchstones that I return to throughout the book.

How people see is a complex product of practices, sensory objects, ideas, and aesthetic sensibilities, all of which are shaped by history and culture. Scholars of visual culture,[35] historians and anthropologists of the senses,[36]

[32] Kha stag 'dzam yag, *Bod dang bal po rgya gar bcas la gnas bskor bskyod pa'i nyin deb: Phyi lo 1944 nas 1956 bar: A Pilgrim's Diary: Tibet, Nepal & India 1944–1956* (Hereafter, *Nyin deb*), BDRC W1KG23814 (Dharamsala: Acarya Jamyang Wangyal, 1997).

[33] For example, Chos kyi grags pa, *Bye ri stag rtser zla gsang gi bsnyen sgrub zhig bgyis pa'i tshe 'khrul snang du byung ba bden par bzung nas bris pa* and *Brag dkar lha chur tshe sgrub bgyis dus mthong snang byung tshul*, in *Collected Works of Chos kyi grags pa*, BDRC W22082, 1: 469–478 and 525–530 (Kulkhan: Drikung Kagyu Institute, 1999).

[34] For example, Bzhad pa'i rdo rje, *Ltal chung mkha' 'gro'i dga' tshal gyi gnas sgo gsar du phye ba'i lam yig* and *Gsal dwangs ri bo che'i gnas zhal gsar du phye ba'i lo rgyus*, in *Collected Works of Bzhad pa'i rdo rje*, BDRC W22130, 9: 213–229 and 237–262 (Leh: T. Sonam and D. L. Tashigang, 1983–1985). Chos kyi grags pa, *Rgyang me'i gnas yig rdo rje 'dzin pa'i dga' ston*, in *Collected Works of Chos kyi grags pa*, BDRC W22082, 2: 457–477 (Kulkhan: Drikung Kagyu Institute, 1999).

[35] See volumes such as Marita Sturken and Lisa Cartwright, ed., *Practices of Looking: An Introduction to Visual Culture* (New York: Oxford University Press, 2009); Nicholas Mirzoeff, ed., *An Introduction to Visual Culture* (London: Routledge, 1999); Birgit Meyer, *Aesthetic Formations: Media, Religion, and the Senses* (New York: Palgrave Macmillan, 2009); Birgit Meyer, "Picturing the Invisible: Visual Culture and the Study of Religion," *Method & Theory in the Study of Religion* 27, no. 4–5 (2015): 333–360; David Morgan, *The Embodied Eye: Religious Visual Culture and the Social Life of Feeling* (Berkeley: University of California Press, 2012); and David Morgan, *The Sacred Gaze: Religious Visual Culture in Theory and Practice* (Berkeley: University of California Press, 2005).

[36] See, for example, Susan Ashbrook Harvey and Margaret Mullett, *Knowing Bodies, Passionate Souls: Sense Perceptions in Byzantium* (Washington, DC: Dumbarton Oaks Research Library and Collection, Trustees for Harvard University, 2017); Wietse de Boer and Christine Göttler, *Religion and the Senses in Early Modern Europe* (Leiden: Brill, 2013); Susan Ashbrook Harvey, *Scenting Salvation: Ancient Christianity and the Olfactory Imagination* (Berkeley: University of California Press, 2006); David Le Breton, *Sensing the World: An Anthropology of the Senses*, Sensory

and Buddhist philosophers all push against the common notion that seeing is a simple act of receiving sense data from the outside world. Instead, social and cultural practices shape what sorts of images get produced, how we pay attention, what we see, how we see it, and how we make meaning out of images. What and how people see are influenced by imagination, language, and expectation.[37] Images, in turn, shape the people who view them. They construct a world of meaning that orients how people move about in that world. This is not to say that vision is entirely *determined* by culture, but rather that acts of seeing and meaning-making take place in a culturally conditioned framework. When we recognize how seeing is embedded within other cultural processes, we can reexamine assumptions about the ordinary boundaries of perception.

Based on this touchstone, I treat pilgrimage as a visual practice embedded in a broader cultural framework. When Tibetan pilgrims see a holy mountain, they do not do so in a vacuum, but rather are influenced by culturally patterned ways of looking and ways of interpreting what they see. Pilgrimage is clearly not *only* a visual practice—much more could be said about the other senses or aspects of pilgrimage—but, in particular, I examine the practices, objects, concepts, and attitudes that affect how pilgrims visually engage with the mountain. This involves analyzing how pilgrimage materials promote certain types of vision, guide pilgrims' visual focus, create a mental image of the mountain, and valorize specific ways of seeing.

Humans encounter places as already thick with meaning, but the material world also pushes back against attempts to make it conform to ideological models. Scholars studying place have shown that places are never just bare material backdrops to human activity.[38] Instead, when a person visits a place, they encounter the stories associated with that place, memories about what happened there in the past, social expectations about how to behave

Studies Series (New York: Bloomsbury Academic, 2017); and Sarah Pink, "The Future of Sensory Anthropology/The Anthropology of the Senses," *Social Anthropology* 18, no. 3 (2010): 331–333. Note also that a recent volume of *Revue d'Etudes Tibétaines* focused on the senses. James Duncan Gentry, "Tibetan Religion and the Senses," *Revue d'Etudes Tibétaines* 50 (June 2019): 5–12.

[37] Tibetan philosophers developed sophisticated accounts of the mind but do not generally describe a *faculty* analogous to imagination. Instead, they use terms like "appearing before the mind" (*yid la snang ba, blo'i 'char*) or "emanations of the mind" (*yid kyis sprul pa*). Visualization texts instruct practitioners to "generate" (*bskyed*) or to "cultivate" (*bsgoms*) rather than terms specific to imagination like "imagine" or "visualize." Likewise, Tibetan accounts of pilgrimage do not refer to the imagination. Imagination is thus an etic term I am using to interpret Tibetan texts.

[38] See the work of Keith Basso, Edward Casey, and Henri LeFebrve.

there, and all sorts of other cultural factors that structure how people experience the place. Encounters with meaning-rich places—whether pilgrimage sites, temples, museums, or myriad other places—are thus part of how societies shape people and reproduce cultural models. Human societies construct places by telling stories about the place, performing rituals there, and depicting the place, but in turn those places shape people. In studying Tibetan mountain pilgrimage, then, I am conscious of how texts like pilgrimage guides help construct places as meaningful, and how the various meanings attached to pilgrimage sites shape how experience their pilgrimage.

However, even cultural meanings and discourses structure people's encounters with places, they do not *determine* how those encounters unfold.[39] As Janet Gyatso puts it, the "inchoate intractability of the material world"[40] often resists human discursive attempts to contain it. Though humans try to control, classify, or transform the material world, it stubbornly refuses to conform to our ideas of how it is supposed to be. In the Tibetan context, the pilgrimage tradition tells pilgrims that the mountain before them is really a mandala, but try though they might, pilgrims cannot see it this way. There is something *there* that pushes back against discursive formation. Although culture shapes the way people see and experience the world, it appears that the material world, and the human perception of it, is resistant to radical refiguration. In the past, some scholars have suggested that Tibetan people simply experience the world in a different way than people in our contemporary disenchanted world, and they have insisted that scholars bracket their ontological assumptions. However, noting how the texts I read depict pilgrims *failing* to see the mountain in the way the tradition tells them they should, I start with the assumption that the material world resists attempts to see mountains as mandalas.

Historical texts do not transparently tell us what happened and what people did. However, by reconstructing how people received and responded to these texts, historians can better understand how these texts structured people's interactions with the world. As an intellectual historian who works with texts, I want to dispense with the overly simplistic idea that texts grant transparent windows into the past. Rather, influenced by the work of Dominic LaCapra,

[39] I am influenced here by scholarship often called New Materialism, which includes scholars such as Bruno Latour, Jane Bennett, Diana Coole, Samantha Frost, and Anna Tsing. These scholars are united in their attempts to understand how the material world acts in meaningful ways outside of human intention or understanding.

[40] Janet Gyatso, *Being Human in a Buddhist World: An Intellectual History of Medicine in Early Modern Tibet* (New York: Columbia University Press, 2015), 195.

I recognize that texts have both "documentary" and "work-like" aspects. The documentary, he wrote, "situates the text in terms of factual or literal dimensions involving reference to empirical reality and conveying information about it," and the work-like "supplements empirical reality by adding to and subtracting from it . . . bringing into the world something that did not exist before."[41] To put it simply, the documentary describes how the world is, and the work-like tries to make the world into what it is not yet.

Following this logic, I am interested in *how* Tibetan pilgrimage texts attempted to work on audiences and elicit certain responses, and I draw on the work of Umberto Eco and other theorists of reader response. Eco distinguishes between the model reader and the empirical reader.[42] We will likely never know how an actual Tibetan pilgrim in the seventeenth century read these texts or performed pilgrimage—the empirical reader may read a text however they please. Nevertheless, careful attention to pilgrimage texts can still give us insight into the model reader that the text anticipates and tries to create. Such a reader is attentive to the various aspects of the text and participates in the itinerary of meaning laid out by the text.[43] Eco takes texts on their own as fundamentally *incomplete* insofar as the text "asks the reader to fill in a whole series of gaps." He continues, "Every text, after all (as I have already written), is a lazy machine asking the reader to do some of the work."[44] In deploying particular narrative strategies and eliciting this kind of participation, texts *structure* the way in which the model reader responds to them. In studying these texts, we are trying to understand the narrative strategies embedded in the text and how they structure the experience of the model reader or, in this case, the model pilgrim.

Mindful of the limits of textual study, and aware of how attempts at reconstruction can go awry, I sought out as many perspectives on pilgrimage

[41] Dominick LaCapra, *Rethinking Intellectual History: Texts, Contexts, Language* (Ithaca, NY: Cornell University Press, 1983), 30.

[42] According to Eco, empirical readers may pick up a text and read it in whatever way she pleases, regardless of how we might say that the text "ought" to be read. By contrast, Eco describes the "model reader" as the type of reader "whom the text not only foresees as a collaborator but also tries to create." Umberto Eco, *Six Walks in the Fictional Woods* (Cambridge, MA: Harvard University Press, 1994), 8.

[43] It may seem strange to speak of a text as a kind of agent, but Eco speaks of texts as having model authors that we can distinguish from the text's actual empirical author. The model author, for Eco, is the imagined creator of the narrative strategies embedded in the text. In the case of unsigned and undated pilgrimage guides, for example, we may still speak of the way in which the model author seeks to work on the model reader. Or, for ease of use, we may speak of the way that the text seeks to work on the model reader.

[44] Ibid., 3.

as I could find to guide my interpretations of historical texts. I draw on the work of anthropologists and art historians to benefit from their disciplinary approaches to pilgrimage, and on the work of other historians and textual scholars of Tibet. My own work is deliberately broad in scope, so I am especially indebted to the work of scholars who closely examine a single text or figure. I also read my texts alongside Tibetan scholars in Kathmandu, Cambridge, and Chengdu, and benefitted from their perspective. Finally, in the course of researching this book, I participated in pilgrimages in Zangskar, Leh, Bodhgaya, Wutai Shan, and Kathmandu. Political and visa concerns prevented me—like so many Tibetans—from visiting the major holy mountains in Tibet. My arguments are thus primarily based in my readings of historical texts, but they are contextualized by these other forms of engagement.

People do not automatically believe in invisible beings and landscapes, so religious traditions develop various means to make the extraordinary real for people. Scholars such as Tanya Luhrmann, Robert Orsi, Ann Taves, and Birgit Meyer have challenged the common assumption that religious people simply *believe* certain claims by virtue of their membership in a religious community, that religious practice flows from those beliefs, and religious objects express those beliefs. Instead, they point to the ways embodied practices and material objects mediate the experiences of religious people and communities to create and sustain a sense of the reality of ordinarily invisible beings and worlds.[45] The approach taken by these scholars prompts us to look at the chains of material, embodied, and sensory mediators through which a certain vision of reality is continually remade as real.

Luhrmann suggests various real-making practices that people and communities use to kindle a sense of the reality of nonhuman beings. These practices are always socially shaped and locally specific, but they have certain common features. These include imagining richly detailed worlds and engaging with those worlds by telling stories about them, training the inner senses through prayer and visualization, engaging outer senses through ritual and material objects, and examining ordinary experience for signs of response from these worlds. All these direct the attention to invisible beings and worlds, promote absorption into those worlds, and ultimately blur the boundaries between the imagined and ordinary such that extraordinary and

[45] See, for example, Luhrmann, *How God Becomes Real*; Orsi, "Material Children," 147–158; Ann Taves, *Religious Experience Reconsidered: A Building Block Approach to the Study of Religion and Other Special Things* (Princeton, NJ: Princeton University Press, 2009); and Meyer, "Picturing the Invisible," 333–360.

invisible beings feel real to people. These practices take work, and people can have more or less natural talent at them, but with training, people can learn to experience invisible beings and worlds as real. In identifying practices of seeing and thinking about how those practices make invisible worlds real, I draw on Luhrmann's ideas about real-making practices.

Some may object that while the modern secular West distinguishes between natural and supernatural, we should not assume that non-Western cultures do so. I agree that we should not assume that contemporary Anglophone assumptions about the boundaries between the natural and supernatural (or, following my language, ordinary and extraordinary) apply everywhere. However, that does not mean that Tibetan communities exist in an enchanted world where gods and spirits are understood to be real *in exactly the same way* as rocks and trees. Rather, we can see in Tibetan pilgrimage texts that the authors distinguish between ordinary, material reality and extraordinary perception, and grant each of them more or less weight in different contexts.[46] I do not doubt that many Tibetan communities understand the world to be filled with various nonhuman beings, but I am pointing to the ways these understandings are perpetuated through rituals and other practices that teach people how to pay attention to a world that lies outside ordinary perception.[47] These include many different types of practice, not just pilgrimage, but pilgrimage meaningfully participates in the construction and maintenance of an otherwise invisible world.

Chapter Outline

This book contains six chapters. They are split into two units, the first focusing on theoretical accounts of pilgrimage, and the second focusing on the practical question of how to transform perception on pilgrimage.

In Chapter 1, I provide a broad introduction to pilgrimage in Buddhist traditions, with a specific focus on the history of pilgrimage practices in Tibet. The chapter draws on a wide range of sources, including some of the earliest writings on pilgrimage in the Pali canon, as well as Mahayana and esoteric textual sources and contemporary ethnography. For readers

[46] In describing everyday reality, authors might refer to "the way things really are" (*dngos po'i gnas lugs*), "what is known in the world" (*'jig rten grags pa*), "seen in direct perception" (*mngon sum du mthong pa*), or "common perception" (*mthun snang*).

[47] See Luhrmann, *How God Becomes Real*, 13–17 for further discussion on this point.

unfamiliar with Buddhism or Tibet, it will provide an accessible introduction to pilgrimage that will ground the rest of the book. For readers more familiar with Buddhist pilgrimage, it will make the argument that seeing as a technique for making the Buddha's presence feel real runs throughout the history of Buddhist pilgrimage.

Chapter 2 delves into the question of what it means to see in Tibetan pilgrimage. While perception is often assumed to refer to passive reception of sense data from the external world, this chapter surveys Buddhist and Tibetan approaches to perception to argue for an understanding of vision as bridging the internal world of language, imagination, and affect with the external, physical world. Perception is an active and therefore malleable process that becomes an important tool for reshaping human experience of the world. The chapter demonstrates how Buddhists in various times and places have utilized that tool, developing practices that aim to replace or improve ordinary ways of seeing the world, thus situating Tibetan Buddhist pilgrimage within a long lineage of Buddhist thought and practice centered on vision.

Building on the themes developed in the first two chapters, Chapter 3 argues that issues of perception lie at the heart of Tibetan pilgrimage practice. It does so through an examination of a centuries-long debate about the authenticity of Kailash, a mountain in Western Tibet. Most Tibetans consider Kailash to be the famed Mount Himavat (and later associated with Meru),[48] described in glorious terms in Buddhist scriptures. Focusing mainly on two central texts in this debate—one by Sakya Paṇḍita (1182–1251) and one by Chödrak Yeshe (1453–1524)—I show that the main issue fueling debate is the gap between fantastic descriptions of the wonders of pilgrimage places and the mundane way those same places appear to ordinary perception. While Sakya Paṇḍita takes mundane ordinary perception as evidence that Kailash is not legitimate, Chödrak Yeshe articulates an account of how a single object can appear to different people in different ways. He separates the ordinary perception possessed by most humans from the extraordinary perception possessed by gods and masters and related in scripture. Ordinary pilgrims cannot see the extraordinary vision of Kailash and must instead imagine its presence at the pilgrimage site.

In the second half of the book, I transition from broad theoretical accounts of pilgrimage to texts that attempt to transform perception. The three

[48] The nature of this identification will be discussed in Chapter 3.

chapters in this section examine three different genres of Tibetan pilgrimage literature and ask how they approach the goal of transforming vision. One source examines how someone creates the possibility for a place to be experienced as real; another explores how pilgrimage texts maintain this sense of reality for pilgrims; and the third type shows how an individual pilgrim puts this into practice for himself.

Chapter 4 focuses on an idealized account of how to transform perception by the Drikung master Chökyi Drakpa (1595–1659). In it, he tells the story of how he "opened the doors" (*gnas sgo phye ba*) of a holy mountain by directly seeing the mountain as a divine mandala, an event that transforms both him and the mountain. I examine Chökyi Drakpa's account of how he transformed his ordinary perception through skilled practices of reading signs in landscape and cultivating the ability to see past surface appearances. I also theorize how this act of vision is understood to permanently alter the sacred place. I suggest Chökyi Drakpa's visionary activities forge a lasting interpenetration between the primordial realm of the deity and the temporal realm of the present day. This interpenetration allows future pilgrims, even those who cannot see the mountain as the mandala or sacred abode of the tantric deity Cakrasaṃvara, to benefit from the connection between the worlds, and it allows some fortunate pilgrims to reenact Chökyi Drakpa's vision of the mountain as Cakrasaṃvara's mandala.

In Chapter 5, I explore the genre of pilgrimage guides (*gnas yig*), which aim to instruct pilgrims how to see the pilgrimage place. I identify the literary strategies by which pilgrimage guides direct the reader's attention. I develop an account of how the language of these guide texts facilitates co-seeing by functioning as a kind of extended metaphor. In other words, language creates for pilgrims a fantastic vision of the hidden worlds of the pilgrimage place. Meanwhile, the guides constantly draw pilgrims' attention to their ordinary perception of the physical world in front of them. The effect is to juxtapose that fantastic vision of the site with the pilgrims' ordinary perception of it. In so doing, the texts themselves create the conditions for pilgrims to see the mountain as the divine palace that such guides say it truly is.

Next, in Chapter 6, I consider an ordinary pilgrim's practices of seeing and how they shape his experience of pilgrimage. The chapter focuses on the pilgrim diary of Khatag Zamyak (1896–1961), a merchant who traveled across Tibet in the 1940s. Centered on his experience at Kailash, I show how Khatag Zamyak employs a variety of practices of seeing, including what I call close looking (*zhib mjal*), visualizing (*gsal btab*), reading the landscape (*sa dpyad*), recognizing particular sites (*ngo 'phrod*), identifying signs (*rtags*), and reading narratives of particular masters who traveled to the site or histories of the site itself. These practices mean that Khatag Zamyak both sees the landscape in its ordinary form with his physical eyes and also sees the wondrous landscape depicted in scriptures, guides, and narratives with his mind's eye. By going on pilgrimage, Khatag Zamyak is constantly drawing his focus back and forth between ordinary perception and imaginative vision, a process I refer to as "interweaving worlds." These practices culminate in Khatag Zamyak reporting a visionary experience, where he claims to have seen the face of the legendary saint Milarepa.

The Conclusion brings together the themes of the preceding chapters to reaffirm the main thesis of the book and to make a broader case for why these practices matter. I suggest that Tibetan pilgrimage practices participate in a broader religious phenomenon of world-building and real-making. Though the pilgrimage practices described in this book can seem small, and below the lofty concerns of Buddhist philosophy, practices like these help construct a world in which Buddhist practice makes sense. They orient people in a world beyond the ordinary concerns of everyday life, in which radically new possibilities emerge.

1

Introduction to Pilgrimage in Buddhism

Prostrating to Lhasa

The 2015 film *Kang Rinpoche*[1] opens with a shot of two women walking and prostrating themselves on a desolate asphalt road. Mountains stretch up behind them, with only a corner of gray sky visible. Snow blankets the peaks, and scrubby vegetation grows in patches. The only color comes from the older woman's bright-red head wrap and the younger girl's faded pink hooded sweatshirt. She appears to be no more than ten or eleven. The two figures walk down the road, stopping every few steps to clap the wooden blocks they wear on their hands and lay their bodies on the asphalt before rising, taking a few steps, and repeating the process. It is clearly exhausting, and the older woman sits for a moment to rest, but the younger girl urges her onward. The camera lingers on these two for almost a minute, which feels like an eternity in a ninety-second film trailer. The camera then pulls back to show that these women are part of a larger group of pilgrims all walking and prostrating themselves on the ground, now in gently falling snow. Without indicating anything further about the plot, the trailer ends. Nonetheless, these lingering shots raise the question of what these people are doing. Where are they going, and why go there in such a difficult way?

The film features Tibetan Buddhist pilgrims going to Kailash, but we could ask these same questions of Buddhist pilgrims more generally. Pilgrimage practices exist across Buddhist communities, from local pilgrimages to small shrines to massive national processions. These pilgrimages take many forms, but the earliest versions seem to date back to the early centuries after the Buddha's death. Pilgrims may undergo great hardship and travel great distances to visit pilgrimage sites. But why?

This chapter will introduce pilgrimage in Buddhism generally and in Tibet specifically to provide background for chapters. It draws from sources

[1] Chinese: 冈仁波齐, Pinyin: Gāng Rénbōqí, Tibetan: *Gangs rin po che*, released in English as *Paths of the Soul* (He Li Chen Guang International Culture Media, Beijing).

Making the Invisible Real. Catherine Hartmann, Oxford University Press. © Oxford University Press 2025.
DOI: 10.1093/9780197791585.003.0002

spanning from the Pali canon to contemporary ethnographies to lay out the variety of pilgrimage traditions across Buddhist cultures.

Pilgrimage in Early Buddhist Scripture

As with much about early Buddhist communities, the origins of pilgrimage practices are unclear. However, the Buddhist tradition attributes it to the Buddha himself. According to the *Mahāparinibbāṇa Sutta*, which is preserved in the Pali canon,[2] Ananda, the Buddha's chief disciple, mourns the imminent death of his beloved teacher. He reminisces about how monks used to travel to see (P. *dassanāya*) the Buddha after the rainy season, and he wonders what will happen when this is no longer possible. The Buddha responds:

> Ananda, there are four places the sight of which should arouse emotion in the faithful. Which are they? "Here the Tathāgata was born" is the first. "Here the Tathāgata attained supreme enlightenment" is the second. "Here the Tathāgata set in motion the Wheel of Dhamma" is the third. "Here the Tathāgata attained the Nibbāna-element without remainder" is the fourth.[3] And, Ananda, the faithful monks and nuns, male and female lay-followers will visit those places. And any who die while making the pilgrimage to these shrines with a devout heart will, at the breaking-up of the body after death, be reborn in a heavenly world.[4]

In other words, the Buddha suggests that monks can visit locations associated with the Buddha's life. Though he does not command it, he clearly encourages it. The Buddha anticipates a future when his followers could no longer see or access him directly, and so suggests an alternate way to access him. Pilgrims who travel to those places will be able to say to themselves, "*Here* the Buddha was born" or "*Here* the Buddha gained enlightenment."

[2] There are several parallel versions of this text which have slightly different readings. Here I focus on the Pali version, but those interested in different readings in different Sanskrit versions should consult Gregory Schopen, *Bones, Stones, and Buddhist Monks: Collected Papers on the Archaeology, Epigraphy, and Texts of Monastic Buddhism in India*, Studies in the Buddhist Traditions (Honolulu: University of Hawai'i Press, 1997), 115–118.

[3] These locations are generally interpreted to refer to Lumbinī, Bodhgaya, Sarnath, and Kuśinagar in present-day north India and Nepal.

[4] Maurice Walshe, *Long Discourses of the Buddha: A Translation of the Digha Nikaya* (Somerville, MA: Wisdom Publications, 2005), 263.

Thus, these sites serve as a reminder of the Buddha's presence, offering a way for devotees to access him indirectly.

This passage highlights three key aspects of pilgrimage. First, seeing these places can evoke powerful emotion in visitors. It uses the term *saṃvega*, which conveys agitation, excitement, and intensity. In early Buddhism, *saṃvega* characterizes the realization of the reality of life, including old age, sickness, and death, when someone realizes the reality of life in a human body. *Saṃvega* is unpleasant but can be valuable insofar as it breaks people out of the lull of everyday life and motivates them to Buddhist practice. The idea is that visiting the sites associated with the Buddha's life generates a powerful sense of agitation, reminding pilgrims of the Buddha's past presence and current absence. Implicitly, the Buddha seems to be suggesting that physically traveling to these places and seeing them arouses urgency that hearing or thinking about them alone cannot achieve. Something about *seeing* (P. *dassanīyāni*) these places—particularly when imagining stories of the Buddha being there—generates urgency in an especially powerful way. It is as though this helps elide the difference between the narrative world of the Buddha and the materially present world of the pilgrim, bringing the former into the latter, as though the Buddha is really present. This agitation can then motivate pilgrims to redouble their own efforts in practice.

Second, the passage links pilgrimage to faith and devotion (P. *saddhā*).[5] It twice describes visitors as faithful (*saddhasa*) and adds that those with a heart of devotion (*passanacittā*) will be born in heavenly realms if they die on pilgrimage.[6] The Buddha acknowledges that not all pilgrims will have a heart of devotion, but he promises that those who do adopt the appropriate devotional attitude toward the site will gain merit and a good rebirth. Pilgrims cannot simply go through the physical motions but should instead engage emotionally with the pilgrimage site.

Third, the passage highlights the sense of vision. Ananda's initial question asks what monks will do when they can no longer *see* the Buddha, and in response, the Buddha names four places they should *see*. In all, Ananda

[5] The text describes pilgrims as *pasādika*, that is, as having *pasāda*, meaning clarity, serene confidence, or faith. We should note that Buddhist texts often pair *pasāda* with *saṃvega*, the term discussed above. *Pasāda* prevents *saṃvega* from turning into despair and hopelessness. With both urgency and clear-eyed confidence, practitioners will be motivated and able to do the work necessary to practice effectively.

[6] The Pali terms *saddhā*, *prasāda*, and *passana* are closely connected, and each conveys this sense of faith or devotion. See Andy Rotmann, *Thus Have I Seen: Visualizing Faith in Early Indian Buddhism* (New York: Oxford University Press, 2008), 127.

uses seeing-related terms three times, and the Buddha uses seeing-related terms six times. This emphasis on seeing is subtle in the original passage, and the later history of pilgrimage does not always thematize vision. However, it is worth noting—given this book's emphasis on vision—that Tibetan pilgrimage picks up on themes present from the earliest references to Buddhist pilgrimage.

These three themes present in the *Mahāparinibbāṇa Sutta* will continue to play an important role throughout this book. Pilgrimage to sacred sites generates an involuntary emotional reaction (*saṃvega*) but also requires pilgrims to adopt a devotional attitude (*saddhā*), and it engages the senses, especially vision. All of these, moreover, relate to the desire to connect with a version of Buddhism that is alive, present, and *real*.

Pilgrimage in Early Indian Buddhism

While the *Mahāparinibbāṇa Sutta* claims that pilgrimage began with the Buddha, some scholars question this account and suggest that passages about pilgrimage were added later to legitimize existing pilgrimage practices.[7] As result, scholars have turned to other historical sources, including other early Buddhist texts, accounts written by Chinese pilgrims to India,[8] inscriptions dating back to the time of Emperor Aśoka, and archeological excavations of old monastic or pilgrimage sites, in order to reconstruct the history of pilgrimage.[9]

Based on these sources, it seems various pilgrimage traditions developed in the centuries after the Buddha's death. Some of them were preexisting practices of honoring local deities Buddhists adapted, while others

[7] Scholars have found at least four versions of the paragraph of the *Mahāparinibbāṇa Sutta* that discusses pilgrimage, as well as parallels to the *Mahāparinibbāṇa Sutta* that do not discuss pilgrimage at all. For discussion of these different versions, see John S. Strong, "The Beginnings of Buddhist Pilgrimage: The Four Famous Sites in India," in *Searching for the Dharma, Finding Salvation*, ed. Christoph Cueppers and Max Deeg (Lumbini: Lumbini International Research Institute, 2014), 50–54. See as well André Bareau, "La Composition et les Étapes de la Formation Progressive du Mahàparinirvânasûtra Ancien," *Bulletin de l'Ecole Française d'Extrême-Orient* 66, no. 1 (1979): 45–103.

[8] The most important of these pilgrims were Faxian, who traveled in India from 399 to 412; Xuanzang, who traveled in India from 629 to 645; and Yijing, who studied at Nalanda in north India from 675 to 685. For an overview of these pilgrims as well as a list of additional sources, see T. Sen, "The Travel Records of Chinese Pilgrims Faxian, Xuanzang, and Yijing," *Education About Asia* 11, no. 3 (2006): 24–33.

[9] One particularly useful source that gathers much of the scholarship on this question is Strong, "The Beginnings of Buddhist Pilgrimage," 49–63.

were newly created by growing Buddhist communities. Pilgrims visited various sites, including *stūpas* believed to contain the Buddha's relics,[10] the Bodhi tree and other kinds of sacred tree, shrines, images in monasteries, monasteries themselves, and numerous places important to the life of the Buddha. Somewhat later, Chinese pilgrims describe extended processional rituals in which devotees venerated the Buddha's "sacred traces."[11] *Stūpas* were particularly important, and pilgrims donated, made offerings, or walked clockwise around them. Pilgrimage was thus not a unitary phenomenon, nor was it solely tied to the four major places mentioned by the *Mahāparinibbāṇa Sutta*. Instead, it involved diverse expressions of devotion. These differences, moreover, do not seem to be tied to different Buddhist sects but were shared across multiple schools.

As Buddhism spread, the network of sites associated with events in the Buddha's life also grew, and it eventually expanded far beyond the area where the Buddha lived. Buddhist texts from the first millennium contain a variety of formulations about places to go on pilgrimage. The most prominent are the four sites of the Buddha's birth, awakening, first teaching, and death mentioned by the *Mahāparinibbāṇa Sutta*. However, texts also sometimes describe the "eight great places" (P. *aṭṭhamahāṭhānāni*), which also includes four places where the Buddha performed miracles, or formulations involving ten, thirty-two, or even more sites. In addition, the particular sites included could vary widely from time and place. Toni Huber refers to this variability as "the shifting terrain of the Buddha."[12] In other words, Buddhist pilgrimage sites were not fixed, and they varied across different eras or geographic boundaries as different communities recognized different places as holy.

Alongside practices of traveling to earthly locations, Indian Mahayana Buddhists also developed practices of imagining pure lands.[13] Pure

[10] The *Mahāparinibbāṇa Sutta* also describes how, after the Buddha's death, his body was cremated, and his relics were divided into eight portions that were entrusted to eight kings. These kings promised to erect earthen mounds called *stūpas* to hold the remains, and to hold festivals in the Buddha's honor. The *Mahāparinibbāṇa Sutta* thus suggests multiple types of pilgrimage sites: places where important events in the Buddha's life occurred and places said to contain the Buddha's relics. See Walshe, *Long Discourses of the Buddha*, 275–277.

[11] See Todd Lewis, "A History of Buddhist Ritual," in *The Buddhist World*, ed. John S. Strong (New York: Routledge, 2016), 318–337, 332.

[12] Toni Huber, *The Holy Land Reborn: Pilgrimage and the Tibetan Reinvention of Buddhist India* (Chicago: University of Chicago Press, 2008), 17–24.

[13] The term "pure land" itself was likely coined in China (淨土; pinyin: *jìngtǔ*) rather than in India. The equivalent Sanskrit term is *buddhakṣetra*, but this was not used in the early texts now considered to be the precursors of pure land traditions. However, I follow scholars such as Jan Nattier in using "pure land" to refer to early Sanskrit texts focused on Amitābha, Akṣobhya, and other celestial buddhas. See Jan Nattier, "The Realm of Akṣobhya: A Missing Piece in the History of Pure

lands, as described in popular texts such as the *Pure Land Sutra* (S. *Sukhāvatīvyūhasūtra*), were created by bodhisattvas as wondrous places free of suffering where the Buddha continuously preaches the dharma. By visualizing or praying for rebirth in the pure land, practitioners hoped they could be reborn there and then attain enlightenment quickly. Interpretations of pure land texts varied, with some considering it a kind of heaven attainable upon death, others regarding it as a physical place in this world, and others viewing it as existing only in the mind. Although these practices were not directly related to pilgrimage in early Buddhism, they would become important for later Buddhist pilgrimage practices.

Indian Tantric Pilgrimage

Tantric Buddhism developed distinctive pilgrimage practices, which differed from those shared among other Indian Buddhist schools. Tantra, also known as esoteric Buddhism or Vajrayāna, resists definition because it encompasses diverse ritual and intellectual formations.[14] Its origins are unclear, with many possible antecedents, but scholars believe that tantra emerged around the sixth century and thrived until the twelfth century in India. During this time, initially simple rituals and chants for protection and good fortune developed into complex ritual practices and sophisticated philosophical systems codified in texts such as the *Cakrasaṃvara Tantra*. Tantric Buddhism claimed to offer an accelerated path to spiritual powers and enlightenment for advanced practitioners by means of a variety of practices, including the use of mandalas, special sounds and incantations known as mantras and *dharanis*, special hand gestures known as *mudras*, deity visualizations, and manipulations of subtle anatomy. By understanding the nonduality and inherent purity of all phenomena and transforming their body and mind, tantric adherents could rapidly progress toward awakening.

Land Buddhism," *Journal of the International Association of Buddhist Studies* 23, no. 1 (2000): 71–102, 73–75.

[14] For an overview of the history of the category of tantra, see Christian K. Wedemeyer, *Making Sense of Tantric Buddhism: History, Semiology, and Transgression in the Indian Traditions* (New York: Columbia University Press, 2013), as well as Ronald M. Davidson, *Indian Esoteric Buddhism: A Social History of the Tantric Movement* (New York: Columbia University Press, 2002).

Pilgrimage was one of these practices, as tantric texts identified a network of sacred sites.[15] These sites are considered special for different reasons across texts and traditions but are often associated with fierce battles between tantric buddhas and fearsome demons, and to consequently hold numinous power.[16] However, these places are also said to correlate with locations in the human body and to participate in a subtle anatomy of special winds, channels, and nodes that practitioners can learn to manipulate to gain rapid spiritual attainments. By visiting external sites that correspond to this internal network of subtle anatomy, pilgrims can gain control over their internal sacred landscape.[17]

Pilgrimage in the Broader Buddhist World

As Buddhism spread from India throughout Asia, pilgrimage networks expanded. Pilgrims came to India from places like China and Tibet in search of texts and places associated with the Buddha. Outside of India, Buddhist communities established their own conceptions of sacred geography in their own regions. Initially, Buddhist communities in places like China, Tibet, Japan, and Southeast Asia regarded themselves as on the edges of the Buddhist world, but as their distinctive Buddhist cultures developed, they began to see themselves as inhabiting a sacred geography with its own set of powerful sites. These sites often had prior associations with local deities or religious traditions but were adopted or "converted" by Buddhist narratives

[15] These texts describe twelve kinds of pilgrimage site: *pīṭha* (T. *gnas*), *upapīṭha* (*nye ba'i gnas*), *kṣetra* (*zhing*), *upakṣetra* (*nye ba'i zhing*), *chandoha* (*tsha ndho ha*), *upachandoha* (*nye ba'i tsha ndho ha*), *melāpaka* (*'du*), *upamelāpaka* (*nye ba'i 'du*), *veśma* (sometimes *pīlava*, *'thung spyod*), *upaveśma* (sometimes, *upapīlava*, *'thung spyod*), *śmaśāna* (*dur 'khrod*), and *upaśmaśāna* (*nye ba'i dur 'khrod*). Texts then identify particular sites as being different kinds of *pītha* sites, often with two or three specific places being identified with each type, resulting in counts of twenty-four or thirty-two sites. Sometimes an additional five places—often the four continents and Mount Meru—are added to the total to make thirty-seven. These places generally include familiar names such as Jalendra, Oddiyana, Devikota, or Kalinga, but there is also huge variation, even between texts in the same lineage, about what places are matched with what categories. Notably, these lists of places generally do not include familiar sites of mainstream Buddhist pilgrimage such as Bodhgaya, Amaravati, or Lumbini.

[16] For more information about tantric formulations of pilgrimage sites, and debates about the number and identity of sites, see Vesna Wallace, *The Inner Kalacakra: A Buddhist Tantric View of the Individual* (New York: Oxford University Press, 2001), 77–86. See also David Snellgrove, *The Hevajra Tantra: A Critical Study* (London: Oxford University Press, 1959), 68–70, especially 69, no. 2; and Davidson, *Indian Esoteric Buddhism*, 206–211.

[17] Some theorists of tantric practice—both in India and Tibet—advocated travel to these external sites, while others took the external sites to *really* indicate internal sites, such that pilgrimage to the external sites is not necessary. See Hartmann, "Against Pilgrimage," *Revue d'Etudes Tibétains* 65 (2022): 127–158, especially 134–138.

and veneration. It is important to remember, however, that what we might call Buddhist pilgrimage is actually a diverse set of different practices and meanings, often drawing on or existing alongside local pre- or non-Buddhist forms of engagement. Buddhist pilgrimage, then, encompasses a rich array of different practices, motivations, and understandings.[18]

Tibetan Buddhist Pilgrimage

> Kailash is like a king's throne,
> With smaller mountains circled around like ministers.
> In the eyes of worldly and ignorant,
> It has that outer appearance.
>
> To students of the path, however,
> Kailash, king of snow mountains,
> Is the palace of Cakrasaṃvara,
> Like an outer body with a mandala inside.
>
> —Pilgrimage guide to Kailash[19]

Buddhist pilgrimage in Tibet adapts Indian Buddhist pilgrimage traditions but also incorporates aspects of pre-Buddhist Tibetan practice. As such, while I may refer to Tibetan pilgrimage, this term is a broad category encompassing varied practices with overlapping logics yet significant differences. This book focuses primarily on the visual aspects of pilgrimage to holy mountains, but we should remember that this is only one part of a complex and multifaceted set of practices.

Pilgrimage practices of all sorts were and are widely popular across all strata of Tibetan society. Pilgrimage was broadly accessible to laypeople, as it required no textual expertise or elite empowerments. Pilgrimage was not, however solely a "low" practice that might be contrasted with the "high" practices of monastic study and tantric practice; monks and religious leaders

[18] For more introduction to the varieties of Buddhist pilgrimage, see Kevin Trainor, "Pilgrimage," in *Encyclopedia of Buddhism*, ed. Robert E. Buswell, Vol. 2 (New York: Macmillan Reference USA, 2003), 651–655.

[19] *Ti se rgyal po gdan bzhugs la / ri phran blon pos bskor pa 'dra / 'jig rten byis pa'i snang ngo la / phyi ru de 'dra'i rnam pa yod / lam la slob pa gang zag la / ti se gangs kyi rgyal po de / bde mchog 'khor lo'i gzhal yas khang / phyi nang lus kyi dkyil 'khor bzhin.* Dkon chog bstan 'dzin chos kyi blo gros, *Gangs ri chen po ti se dang mtsho chen ma dros pa bcas kyi sngon byung gi lo rgyus*, in Dge 'dun chos 'phel, ed., *Gnas yig phyogs bsgrigs*, 151.

at all ranks also went on pilgrimage, as we can see in the biographies of nearly any prominent religious figure. These figures may have interpreted their practices in different ways, but the practices themselves were widespread.

The Tibetan term for pilgrimage is *nékorwa* (*gnas skor ba*) or *néjelwa* (*gnas mjal ba*). This literally means circling (*bskor*) sacred places, known as *né* (*gnas*), or meeting/seeing (*mjal*) these sacred places. The act of circling these places in a clockwise direction shows respect and generates good karma, while meeting/seeing them indicates encountering a highly respected object. *Né* refers to ta place charges with numinous power that can grant good fortune, purification, spiritual blessings, enhanced life force, karma, or social status.[20] *Né* can include sacred mountains, monasteries, lakes, caves, and sometimes even holy people.

Destinations in Tibetan Pilgrimage

Among the various *né* that Tibetan Buddhists visited on pilgrimage, one of the most well-known is holy mountains. The veneration of these mountains likely predates the arrival of Buddhism, although the lack of written historical records makes it difficult to say for sure. Tibetans have long understood the natural world to be teeming with various powerful beings.[21] These include *naga* spirits living under the ground (*klu*), earth spirits dwelling in fields or in mountains (*sa bdag, gzhi bdag*), deities living in mountains (*yul lha*), and various types of demons (*gdon*). These beings can be either benevolent or malevolent, and so humans have developed various ways of cohabitating with these beings, including soothing them or protecting against them. The belief that the Tibetan landscape is inhabited by powerful beings can be seen in early Tibetan legends that cast the land itself as a large demoness that needed to be pinned down by monasteries.[22] In addition, early Tibetan

[20] For a more extensive discussion of the term *gnas*, see Toni Huber, "Putting the Gnas Back into Gnas-Skor: Rethinking Tibetan Pilgrimage Practice," in *Sacred Spaces and Powerful Places in Tibetan Culture: A Collection of Essays*, ed. Toni Huber, 77–104 (Dharamsala: The Library of Tibetan Works and Archives, 1999). While some pilgrimage benefits refer to Buddhist ideas such as karma, others such as blessings or life force are deeply rooted and cannot be easily reduced to Buddhist concepts.

[21] For more on Tibetan demonology, see René de Nebesky-Wojkowitz, *Oracles and Demons of Tibet: The Cult and Iconography of the Tibetan Protective Deities* (Graz: Akademische Druck-u Verlagsanstalt, 1975).

[22] See Janet Gyatso, "Down with the Demoness: Reflections on a Feminine Ground in Tibet," *The Tibet Journal* 12, no. 4 (1987): 38–53.

emperors in the eighth and ninth centuries seem to have had a mountain cult related to the emperor.[23]

Practices around holy mountains may stem from the belief that powerful beings dwell in mountains (*gnas* can mean "abode"). Some mountains are held to be the residence of autochthonous place deities (often a *yul lha* or *gzhi bdag*) that are powerful but primarily concerned with this-worldly benefits and harms, such as granting blessings, influencing local weather, or ensuring crop health. These deities may have been converted to Buddhism and now exist as protectors, but they are not connected to other-worldly Buddhist goals like attaining enlightenment. However, some mountains house world-transcending tantric buddhas that defeated demons in cosmic battle to convert the land to Buddhism. For instance, Kailash is considered the residence of the Buddhist tantric deity Cakrasaṃvara. Such deities can offer this-worldly benefits and can also aid pilgrims in progressing toward enlightenment. The type of being residing in the mountain affects the site's importance and practices performed there. Major transregional sites typically identify with tantric deities, whereas smaller local sites associate with territorial gods. However, in practice this distinction is blurry, and it is unclear how salient this difference was to pilgrims.

The lore around mountain pilgrimage in Tibet suggests that many mountains were "converted" to Buddhism. This reflects Tibetan accounts of history that describe Tibetan land and people as demonic until being "tamed" by Buddhism, but some scholars also think it reflects the historical development of pilgrimage practices at these mountains. As Buddhism spread across Tibet, mountains that were already the focus of indigenous mountain cults and believed to be the residence of local deities were converted (Buffetrille uses the term "Buddhicized," Huber speaks of "mandalization") into Buddhist mountains. This involved converting the deities into protectors of the dharma, reinterpreting the landscape in Buddhist terms, and framing pilgrims' practices at the mountain as Buddhist, even if the practices themselves had not changed much. Consequently, scholars often reject attempts

[23] See Toni Huber, *The Cult of Pure Crystal Mountain: Popular Pilgrimage and Visionary Landscape in Southeast Tibet* (Oxford: Oxford University Press, 1999), 25. For more information on the mountain cult at the time of the Tibetan Empire, see Samten Gyaltsen Karmay, "The Cult of Mountain Deities and Its Political Significance," in *The Arrow and the Spindle: Studies in History, Myths, Rituals and Beliefs in Tibet*, ed. Samten Gyaltsen Karmay (Kathmandu: Mandala Book Point, 1998), 432–450, as well as the essays in Anne-Marie Blondeau, Ernst Steinkellner, and Österreichische Akademie der Wissenschaften. Philosophisch-Historische Klasse, *Reflections of the Mountain: Essays on the History and Social Meaning of the Mountain Cult in Tibet and the Himalaya* (Wien: Verlag de Österreichischen Akademie der Wissenschaften, 1996).

to interpret pilgrimage solely in Buddhist doctrinal terms, for there are rich layers of significance to these practices, and Buddhist frameworks for interpreting pilgrimage are not always the most relevant.[24]

The notion that holy mountains are residences for gods or buddhas seems to have developed into the related notion that these mountains have an outer appearance visible to ordinary people and an inner reality that is visible only to a few advanced pilgrims. The quotation from the pilgrimage guide to Kailash that opened this section exemplifies this phenomenon when it declares that the "worldly and ignorant" see its "outer appearance" and that "students of the path" see that it is truly the "palace of Cakrasaṃvara" and a mandala.[25] In this same vein, the pilgrimage tradition often claimed that mountains appeared one way, but on a deeper level existed in a different and better way. Pilgrims could and should aspire to see the deeper, inner reality of the mountain rather than the outer appearance visible to those of lowly merit

The power of these mountains, and of the beings dwelling in them, also makes them fundamentally *wild*, so while they are potentially fruitful places for practice, they are initially too dangerous for most people. Hostile spirits, demons, and *dakinis*, attracted by the site's numinous power, dwell there and threaten visitors. However, according to lore, if a spiritually advanced master comes to the mountain and ritually overpowers the various belligerent spirits residing at the place, he can convert them into fierce protectors of the dharma. Often, as part of ritually overpowering the demons, the advanced master must also see the mountain as the mandala the tradition claims that it truly is. Ordinarily, the mountain appears as made of rocks and snow, but advanced masters with extraordinary ability can see it as the palace of the tantric Buddha who dwells there. At this point, the master is said to have "opened the doors" (*sgo phye*) of the mountain so ordinary people can visit the mountain without harm. It is not clear where this notion of opening the

[24] See, for example, Katia Buffetrille, "Reflections on Pilgrimages to Sacred Mountains, Lakes and Caves," in *Pilgrimage in Tibet*, ed. Alex McKay, 18–34 (London: Curzon Press, 1998); Katia Buffetrille, "The Pilgrimage to Mount Kha Ba Dkar Po: A Metaphor for Bardo?" in *Searching for the Dharma, Finding Salvation—Buddhist Pilgrimage in Time and Space: Proceedings of the Workshop "Buddhist Pilgrimage in History and Present Times" at the Lumbini International Research Institute (LIRI), Lumbini, 11–13 January 2010*, ed. Christoph Cueppers and Max Deeg, 197–220 (Lumbini: Lumbini International Research Institute, 2014), as well as Huber, *The Cult of Crystal Mountain*, 7–10 and 25–30.

[25] Dkon chog bstan 'dzin chos kyi blo gros, *Gangs ri chen po ti se dang mtsho chen ma dros pa bcas kyi sngon byung kyi lo rgyus*, 151.

doors of the holy place originates. It seems to be a Tibetan idea,[26] and it is not found in discourse about pilgrimage elsewhere in South Asia.[27]

These aspects of the pilgrimage tradition emerged between the twelfth to the fifteenth centuries. During this time, esoteric tantras of the supreme yoga class (*nirūttarayoga*) were introduced to Tibet, and tantric masters such as Marpa (eleventh century) and Milarepa (mid-eleventh to early twelfth century) developed a following. Milarepa, in particular, is important for Tibetan pilgrimage traditions. He was said to practice at the sacred mountains of Tsari, Lapchi, and Kailash, and tantric masters like Jigten Gonpo (1143–1217) consequently sent disciples to practice there.[28] Later histories and pilgrimage guides describe how pilgrimage mountains were "opened" during this time, contributing to the development of the cult of holy mountains. Although it is unclear how this interest among virtuosic tantric practitioners affected popular pilgrimage practices, but they were certainly important for developing the lore around holy mountains.

I have thus sketched out a broad overview of Tibetan mountain pilgrimage, but within this category, there are a number of subtypes of holy mountains. For instance, there are major mountains that are nationally famous as sites of transregional pilgrimage, there are smaller local pilgrimage sites, and there are mountains somewhere in between. In addition, certain mountains came to prominence at different times in Tibetan history.

The most famous holy mountains—Kailash (also known as Tise, *ti se*) in southwestern Tibet; Lapchi (*la phyi*) in southern Tibet, and Tsari (*tsA ri*) in southeastern Tibet—are identified as the body, speech, and mind of the tantric deity Cakrasaṃvara. These mountains were known throughout Tibetan cultural areas as places where famous masters achieved spiritual realizations and where tantric masters still practiced. Pilgrims traveled great distances to

[26] One indication that the idea of opening the doors of the holy place is an indigenous Tibetan idea is that there are so many ways in which it is spelled. One finds *sgo phye*, *sgo dbye*, *sgo 'byed*, and *sgo phyes*. The second syllable of these compounds all have similar meanings of "to open," to differentiate," or "to separate," but the nonstandardized spelling may indicate that this is not a concept being translated from Sanskritic sources.

[27] The metaphor of doors does exist in South Asian sources, but not in connection with sacred places. For instance, humans are said to have "three doors"—body, speech, and mind—(S. *tridvāra*), which are the means by which they interact with the world. The five external senses are also referred to as five doors and require protection. Mandalas have doors at their cardinal points, and tantric ritual practices involve generating the features of the mandala palace, including the doors and the wrathful deities that guard them, before entering through the doors. However, none of these sources talk about opening these doors, to my knowledge.

[28] See Dan Martin, "Jikten Gonpo Rinchen Pel," Treasury of Lives, accessed December 12, 2019, http://treasuryoflives.org/biographies/view/Jigten-Gonpo-Rinchen-Pel/2899.

visit these sites and to partake in their power and blessings. Especially large numbers of pilgrims gathered every twelve years according to the Tibetan calendar—the monkey year for Tsari and the horse year for Kailash—on auspicious dates where blessings were said to be multiplied.[29]

Kailash was sometimes identified with Indic lore around Mount Meru, the cosmic mountain at the center of the world.[30] Lore about Meru varies, but it can be found in early Buddhist, Hindu, and Jain texts. Meru is the home of the god Śiva and is surrounded by four continents, with humans living on the southern continent of Jambudvipa.[31] Meru, which may also be called Himavat ("possessing snow"), Himālaya ("abode of snows"), Kailāsa, or several other names,[32] is mentioned in important Buddhist texts like the *Abhidharmakośa* of Vasubandhu. While Indian Buddhism did not consider Meru a destination for pilgrimage—the mountains were held to be bitterly cold and impassable, suitable only for gods and hardcore yogis—Tibetans identified present-day Kailash in western Tibet as the mountain described in early Buddhist texts and venerated it as such. Although Kailash's identification as Meru/Himavat was debated among Tibetan intellectuals, it contributed to Kailash's status as the most famous Tibetan holy mountain.

Another important mountain for Tibetans is Wutai Shan in Shanxi province, known to Tibetans as "Five-Peak Mountain" (*ri bo rtse lnga*) or "Mount Clear and Cool" (*ri bo dwangs bsil*). Although it is located outside the Tibetan cultural area, Tibetan pilgrims have been traveling there since at least the seventh century. Wutai Shan was considered the seat of the bodhisattva of wisdom, Manjuśrī, by Chinese Buddhists since the fifth century, and it became a famous site for international pilgrims from India, Tibet, Mongolia, China, and Manchuria. Pilgrims came in hopes of catching a glimpse of Manjuśrī, who was believed to appear in various guises to fortunate pilgrims. Wutai Shan became particularly important for Tibet during

[29] Huber's *The Cult of Pure Crystal Mountain* is the best source about pilgrimage to Tsari. For more about Kailash (also known as Tise), see Toni Huber and Tsepak Rigzin, "A Tibetan Guide for Pilgrimage to Ti-Se (Mount Kailas) and MTsho Ma-Pham (Lake Manasarovar)," in *Sacred Spaces and Powerful Places in Tibetan Culture*, ed. Toni Huber, 125–153 (The Library of Tibetan Works and Archives, 1999); Alex McKay, *Kailas Histories: Renunciate Traditions and the Construction of Himalayan Sacred Geography* (Leiden: Brill, 2015); Elena De Rossi Filibeck, *Two Tibetan Guide Books to Ti Se and La Phyi* (Bonn: VGH Wissenschaftsverlag, 1988).

[30] There is debate about when this identification occurred. See McKay, *Kailas Histories*, 273–338.

[31] Śiva is more famously associated with Hinduism, but since Buddhist texts assume the same Indic cosmological framework that Hinduism does, Buddhist texts also reference Śiva, albeit sometimes under the name Iśvara.

[32] Confusingly, these different names sometimes apply to different mountains, and they can sometimes apply to whole mountain ranges rather than individual mountains.

the period from the seventeenth to the twentieth century under the Chinese Qing dynasty, when Wutai Shan became a cosmopolitan center of multicultural interaction.[33]

While national pilgrimage sites receive most of the scholarly attention, there are also regionally important pilgrimage mountains such as Amye Machen (*a myes rma chen*)[34] in Amdo and Khawa Karpo (*kha ba dkar po*)[35] in Kham that are equally significant in their respective regions. At an even more local level, there are mountains that only receive visits from pilgrims in nearby villages and may be unknown to those outside those areas.[36] These local pilgrimage mountains served as more frequent and accessible destinations for those who could not afford the time and expense required to travel to distant mountains like Kailash. Strikingly, many of these smaller mountains still claim affiliation with major mountains like Kailash by proclaiming themselves a second Kailash (T. *ti se gnyis pa*). So even small, local mountains frame themselves as part of broader conceptions of sacred geography.

Features of the natural landscape like caves and mountains can also be destinations for pilgrimage. Caves are often where famous meditators like Milarepa lived while engaging in advanced meditative practice away from society, and so they bear the karmic traces and blessings left by these masters. Lakes are most often associated with holy mountains, with the lake imagined to be the female-coded consort to the male-coded mountain.[37] Lakes can also be sites of divination, where specialized interpreters gaze into the lake for help in determining future courses of action.

Pilgrims also visited human-built places like holy cities or monasteries. The city of Lhasa, in particular, was a significant destination for pilgrims

[33] For more on Tibetan pilgrimage to Wutai Shan, see David Germano, ed., "Wutai Shan and Qing Culture," special issue of the *Journal of the International Association of Tibetan Studies*, no. 6 (2011), particularly the introductory article by Karl Debreczeny, "Wutai Shan: Pilgrimage to Five-Peak Mountain," *Journal of the International Association of Tibetan Studies*, no. 6 (2011): 1–133. See also Wen-shing Chou, *Mount Wutai: Visions of a Sacred Buddhist Mountain* (Princeton, NJ: Princeton University Press, 2018).

[34] See, for example, Katia Buffetrille, "The Great Pilgrimage of A Myes rMa-Chen: Written Traditions, Living Realities," in *Mandala and Landscape*, ed. A. W. Macdonald, 75–132 (New Delhi: D.K. Printworld, 1997).

[35] See Buffetrille, "The Pilgrimage to Mount Kha Ba Dkar Po."

[36] Anthropologists have studied a number of these local sites. See, for example, Katia Buffetrille, "The rTsib Ri Pilgrimage: Merit as Collective Duty?," in *Nepalica-Tibetica: Festgabe for Christoph Cüppers*, ed. Franz-Karl Ehrhard and Petra Maurer (Andiast: International Institute for Tibetan and Buddhist Studies, 2013), 1:37–64, as well as Nakza Drolma, "Pilgrimage to Drakar Dreldzong: The Written Tradition and Contemporary Practices among Amdo Tibetans," (M.Phil., University of Oslo, 2008).

[37] Huber, *The Cult of Pure Crystal Mountain*, 51, explains this at greater length.

due to its numerous temples and monasteries, notably the Jokhang temple, which houses the renowned Jowo image, said to have been brought by the seventh-century Chinese princess who helped convert the Tibetan emperor to Buddhism. Lhasa contains multiple circumambulation routes for pilgrims to travel, including the inner route inside the Jokhang, the middle route around the temple, and the outer route around the city. It is also the cite of important monasteries that pilgrims visited to prostrate before the holy images contained there, to make donations to monks living there, circumambulate the entire structure, or participate in a holy day or festival. Similar practices took place at monasteries outside Lhasa, albeit at a smaller scale.

While they are not pilgrimage destinations in the usual sense, it is also important to mention hidden lands (*sbas yul*). The most famous is Pemakö (*pad + ma bkod*), although there are many others. These earthly paradises in Tibet are believed to be filled with stunning natural features and serve as a safe refuge in times of peril. Most of the time, ordinary people cannot access or even *see* these places. Like holy mountains, they must have their "doors opened" (*sgo phye*) by an advanced tantric master so that ordinary people can visit them. Then, when danger arises, people can follow written guides (*gnas yig, lam yig*) to find these places. Although hidden lands are not sites of regular pilgrimage, they do figure importantly in Tibetan conceptions of sacred geography.[38]

Tibetan practitioners of tantra also visited tantric pilgrimage sites, following in the footsteps of their Indian predecessors. As discussed above, Indian Buddhist tantric texts outlined sets of places where practitioners could manipulate their subtle anatomy to rapidly attain advanced spiritual states. These texts were later translated into Tibetan and adapted by Tibetan practitioners. At first, Tibetan tantric thinkers assumed that the network of tantric sacred sites were in India, but eventually, Tibetans began to see the land around them as the sacred sites described in Tantric texts.[39] For

[38] For more on these hidden lands, including analyses of guides written about these places, see Abdol-Hamid Sardar-Afkhami, "The Buddha's Secret Gardens: End Times and Hidden-Lands in Tibetan Imagination" (PhD Diss., Harvard University, 2001), as well as Frances Garrett, Elizabeth McDougal, and Geoffrey Samuel, eds., *Hidden Lands in Himalayan Myth and History: Transformations of* Sbas Yul *through Time* (Leiden: Brill, 2020).

[39] Tibetan interest in tantric *pīthas* in Tibet did not necessarily translate to an interest in traveling to the complete set of *pīthas* in South Asia. While Tibetan access to the tantras advocating for travel to the twenty-four pīthas dates to the eleventh century, there is no record of Tibetan practitioners attempting to visit all these external sites at that time. It is not until the thirteenth century that wandering Tibetan yogis recorded attempts to visit all the *pīthas*, and even then, they imagined the *pīthas* to all be in a relatively small area in northwest India. Then, after the thirteenth century, there is no evidence of Tibetans attempting to visit these sites in India. See Huber, *The Holy Land Reborn*, 100–101.

example, holy mountains in Tibet were identified with tantric *pīthas.* Kailash was identified as Himavat or Himālaya, Tsari was identified as either Caritra or Devikota, and Lapchi was identified as Godavari. Many sacred sites were assumed to remain in India, but Tibetans began to see Tibet itself as part of broader tantric geography.

Tibetan remapping of tantric holy sites onto Tibet only accelerated over time. The tantric texts that had outlined these holy sites described them as specific locations in South Asia but also suggested that they were a movable map that could exist anywhere. Thus, the twenty-four sacred places could be in India, Tibet, or even a single city.[40] Tibetan thinkers then remapped these sacred sites onto their own landscape in various ways, resulting in at least eight different places in Tibet said to be Devikota.[41] While most Tibetan pilgrims were not visiting the places identified as tantric holy sites as part of dedicated tantric practice, these identifications increased the importance of Kailash, Tsari, and Lapchi, even for nontantric pilgrims.

Tibetan pilgrims also sometimes visited the holy land of India, including sites of significance such as those associated with the life of the Buddha, and to access teachers and texts where the dharma originated. However, it is unclear how many Tibetans made this journey. While there were likely trade routes linking Tibet with Nepal and Kashmir during the imperial period (eighth to early ninth century), there is little evidence that Tibetans traveled to Buddhist pilgrimage sites in India at that time.[42] Tibetans did translate Sanskrit and Chinese texts, but partnerships between Tibetan and South/Central Asian scholars seem to have been the primary means of obtaining these texts. In the eleventh to twelfth century, however, Tibetans began to travel to India to visit pilgrimage sites and obtain teachings from Buddhist universities like Nalanda.[43]

By the end of the thirteenth century, however, Buddhism had declined and disappeared from India, causing Tibetan interest in visiting Buddhist pilgrimage sites to diminish. Tibetans continued to think of India as a holy land, but fewer Tibetans went there, and those who did rarely went to places where pilgrimage sites had been, as they were now controlled by people Tibetans considered to be heretics. This lack of interest persisted for five centuries until

[40] See Naropa, *Rdo rje'i tshig gi snying po bsdus pa'i dka' 'grel* (S. *Vajrapādasārasaṃgraha*), 979: *rnal 'byor ma rnams kyi rigs sum cu rtsa drug ni grong khyer gcig tu yang gnas.* Huber also discusses this idea in Huber, *The Holy Land Reborn*, 121.

[41] Ibid., 121.

[42] Huber, *The Holy Land Reborn*, 45–47.

[43] Ibid., 58–84.

the nineteenth and twentieth centuries when Buddhist modernist reformers like Anagarika Dharmapāla and the Archaeological Survey of India began rediscovering and promoting sites like Bodhgaya, and Tibetans once again began traveling to India.[44] This situation has been further complicated by the political situation of Tibetans. In recent times, Tibetans in exile who can no longer access holy places in Tibet have increased their focus on Indian pilgrimage sites, while those in China may not be able to access Indian sites.

This survey of different pilgrimage destinations demonstrates the variety of reasons why sites may be considered holy and worth visiting. Monasteries and sacred cities, for instance, are part of the built environment and are visited by pilgrims to hear from important teachers, see sacred objects, and attend rituals. In contrast, sacred mountains, lakes, and caves are part of the natural environment. They are often located far away from human communities and are considered holy due to their association with deities or holy masters. They may have monasteries built nearby, but their holiness is primarily based on their identification as the residence for a deity. Pilgrimages to India are motivated by a desire to obtain authentic teachings or visit sites significant to the life of the Buddha, while pilgrimages to hidden lands are undertaken in times of crisis.

The goal of trying to see a pilgrimage place as fully pure or as a mandala operates across multiple types of pilgrimage, but it is particularly prominent in discussions of holy mountain pilgrimages. In accounts of pilgrimages to monasteries or India, the aspect of vision is not emphasized as much, and even if the place is said to be a mandala or a pure land, this seems secondary to other reasons for visiting the place. By contrast, because the rationale of why holy mountains are sacred is precisely their identification as the divine palace of a tantric buddha, the question of how to see the mountain is heavily thematized. While this book focuses primarily on pilgrimage to holy mountains, it is important to remember that this is one part of a complex set of pilgrimage practices.

The Power and Blessings of Pilgrimage Sites

I have referred to the power and blessings of pilgrimage sites, so it is fair to ask what that means and how it works. However, most Tibetan authors who

[44] Ibid., 83–84, and 251–290.

write about pilgrimage do not explicitly explain how pilgrimage sites benefit the pilgrim. It largely went without saying—texts do not have to explain what readers already know.[45] While the opponents of pilgrimage sometimes made explicit arguments against pilgrimage, because pilgrimage was such a ubiquitous practice, proponents of pilgrimage could count on their audiences' deeply engrained familiarity with the underlying logics of pilgrimage. Despite this, we can still attempt to reconstruct the basic logic (or, following Huber, the multiple overlapping logics) informing pilgrimage.

One central idea is that pilgrimage places are charged with *jinlap* (*byin brlabs*), which is often translated as "blessings" or "empowerments." This term comes from the full phrase *jingyi lap* (*byin gyis brlabs*), which literally means flooded (*brlabs*) by *jin* (*byin*), a term that can be translated as "power, magnificence, splendor, or blessings." This term is sometimes associated with Sanskrit terms,[46] but it also seems to have pre-Buddhist connotations. For instance, it was associated with the pre-Buddhist royal cult of divine kings, who were said to be characterized by *byin*. One also finds the term *jinlap* used in descriptions of tantric visualization practices; the practitioner first generates a visualized image of the appropriate deity and then visualizes the deity granting the practitioner *jinlap*, which grants efficacy to the whole ritual process. As such, Toni Huber argues that *jinlap* should be translated as "empowerment" instead of the common translation of "blessings," because it conveys the sacred power of the place that flows to pilgrims. However, this may be confusing as "empowerments" (*dbang*) are typically associated with tantric ritual initiations, and so I will continue to use the term "blessings."

What is the nature of these blessings and empowerments? Again, textual sources rarely explain this explicitly. However, Geshe Ngawang Dhargyey, a Geluk lama, offered the following explanation:

> All objects at power places (*gnas-chen*) have the empowerment (*byin-gyis-brlabs*) of the deities and great practitioners associated with that place. It is like [the effects of] water soaking into things, so it includes rocks, dirt, water, plants, trees; this is also called "empowerment of *gnas* (i.e. as residence)" (*gnas-kyi byin-brlab*), for example a Heruka place (*gnas*) has Heruka's empowerment, and a Guru Rinpoche place his empowerment. So this empowerment can be collected in the form of rocks, dirt, plant parts,

45 Huber, "Putting the Gnas Back into Gnas-Skor," 87.

46 Especially Sanskrit *adhiṣṭhāna*, which can be translated as "authority," "power," "benediction," "residence," "basis," or "abode."

and so on, and due to the Tibetans' great faith in the power of these things they do collect them.[47]

The blessings or empowerments of pilgrimage places thus flow from these places' connections with certain tantric deities or great masters. Pilgrimage places that have this *jinlap* are teeming with an almost electrical power that can be engaged by the pilgrim, and which grants benefits to the pilgrim both in this life and the next.[48]

Pilgrimage is also believed to purify the pilgrim's defilements (*sgrib*) and to enable them to accumulate merit (*bsod nams*).[49] The sixteenth-century writer Pema Karpo puts it clearly in his *Pilgrimage Guide to Tsari* that "Pilgrimage is the best method for purifying sins and defilements. By offering *torma*[50] and feast offerings, and by focusing on the tantric divinities assembled here, one delights those gods and perfects the accumulation of merit."[51] Thus by going on pilgrimage, the pilgrim will purify their sins and accumulate merit and blessings. The eighteenth-century writer Jigmé Lingpa concurs, writing that "Even for beings who have not entered into the path, this [pilgrimage practice], which must be supported by prudence, purifies the obscurations and accumulates merit—it is profound."[52] He suggests that pilgrimage, if it is done well and with care, accrues real benefits to the pilgrim.

Another logic that informs pilgrimage practice involves karmic connections, or *tendrel* (*rten 'brel*). The term *tendrel* has multiple connotations. As an abbreviation of the phrase *rten cing 'brel bar 'byung ba*, it refers to the general Buddhist concept of interdependent arising (S. *pratītyasamutpāda*) and thus refers to the fact that all phenomena come into existence based on multiple causes and conditions, and thus exist in an interconnected web. In more colloquial usage, however, the term takes on a somewhat different sense to mean auspicious connections or circumstances, often

[47] Ibid., 91–92.

[48] Ibid., 91 and 94.

[49] See Huber, "Putting the Gnas Back into Gnas-Skor," 90, for more discussion of *sgrib* and a list of secondary sources that have also explored this concept.

[50] Ritual cakes and dough balls usually made from roasted barley flour and butter. They may be dyed or decorated.

[51] *'Di bskor ba ni sdig sgrib sbyong ba'i thabs mchog yin pa dang / 'dir gsang sngags kyi lha tshogs la dmigs te / gtor ma / tshogs kyi 'khor lo phul bas / lha de dag mnyes / bsod nams kyi tshogs rdzogs pa yin la.* 'Brug chen Kun mkhyen Pad+ma dkar po, *Gnas chen tsa ri tra'i ngo mtshar snang ba pad dkar legs bshad*, 272.

[52] *Lam ma zhugs kyi skye bo la'ang / bag yod shugs la brten dgos pa'i / tshogs gsog sgrib sbyong 'di nyid zab.* 'Jigs med gling pa, *Gnas bskor ba la spring ba'i gtam*, 579.2.

presumed to have been caused by actions in a prior life.[53] For instance, if someone were to meet a friend unexpectedly on the road, they might attribute the run-in to *tendrel*. Or if a person were trying to explain why they picked a particular lama as their teacher, they might say that they have *tendrel* with that teacher. Pilgrimage places, as well, bear auspicious connections, and pilgrims describe going on pilgrimage to establish auspicious connections with a particular place or, by extension, others who have visited there.[54] The seventeenth-century writer Taranatha, for example, gave a teaching to pilgrims that emphasized the various karmic connections present in pilgrimage places and encouraged pilgrims to "seek out and understand the method for putting together auspicious connections. If you know how to put together (*sgrig*) the inner and outer auspicious connections, everything you need or want, as well as spiritual attainments, will fall like rain."[55] In other words, by going on pilgrimage, pilgrims were planting seeds that would bear fruit in future lives.[56]

These general logics inform pilgrimage, but the specifics vary according to local conditions and can also differ depending on who you ask. Different people within Tibetan society interpreted pilgrimage practices differently. For instance, some texts describe pilgrimage as providing benefits automatically to any being who goes there. They may even tell stories of dogs or pigs wandering unwittingly around these sites and being reborn in heaven. Such stories emphasize how the site is so powerful that even animals (assumed to lack intentionality, intelligence, or faith) benefit from it. Other texts, however, suggest that faithful pilgrims derive more benefit than careless ones, or that the benefits of a pilgrimage place come entirely from the pilgrim's faith and devotion, rather than from the place itself. Other texts state that ordinary pilgrims benefit, but those with a particular mindset or perception benefit even more. Still other texts praise wandering pilgrims like Shabkar or Milarepa who consider all places as equally holy. In other words, Tibetan views and approaches to pilgrimage are internally diverse.

[53] For a discussion of this term, see Janet Gyatso, *Apparitions of the Self: The Secret Autobiographies of a Tibetan Visionary: A Translation and Study of Jigme Lingpa's Dancing Moon in the Water and Ḍākki's Grand Secret-Talk* (Princeton, NJ: Princeton University Press, 1998), 179.

[54] For example, Chos kyi grags pa frequently speaks of "establishing connections" (*'brel pa bzhag*) at holy places example. See 'Bri gung chung tsang Rig 'dzin Chos kyi grags pa, *Rang gi tshul gyi rtogs pa brjod pa'i gtam rang bzhin brjod pa'i rgyan kho nas smras pa gsong po'i dga' ston*, in *Collected Works of Chos kyi grags pa*, BDRC W22082, 1: 19–264 (Kulhan: Drikung Kagyu Institute, 1999), for example, 228.

[55] *Rten 'brel ba sgrig lugs shes te 'tshal / phyi nang gi rten 'brel sgrig shes na / dgos 'dod dngos grub char ltar 'bab*. Tāranātha, *Las stod kyi gnas skor ba 'dra la gdams pa*, 80.

[56] Personal conversation with Lobsang Shastri, April 30, 2019.

Practices themselves vary, but explanations about how those practices work vary as well.

Social, Political, and Economic Dimensions of Pilgrimage

Pilgrimage in Tibet has important social, political, and economic dimensions. I focus on the visual dynamics of pilgrimage, and so I will often focus on intellectual history, but it is also important to keep in mind the material and social contexts in which these practices occurred.

For example, pilgrimage is a communal activity in which pilgrims often travel together in groups from the same village or family. They may travel with a few monks or lamas who provide information along the way. Although groups from different areas may interact and exchange news, they do not usually engage in extensive interaction.[57] Pilgrimage could also bolster the social status of pilgrims who could afford the time and cost of pilgrimage by making them pure and meritorious in the eyes of others.[58]

Pilgrimage is also gendered in important ways. Pilgrimage sites themselves may have gendered connotations, as with the example of "male" mountains paired with "female" lakes. There are also fierce female spirits called *dakinis* (T. *mkha' 'gro*, literally, sky-goer) imagined inhabiting pilgrimage sites and imagery such as the "sexed rocks of Tibet" discussed in the Introduction. Anthropologists have documented how pilgrimage sites exclude women from certain locations on the pilgrimage mountain on the grounds that their impurity will anger the local spirits.[59] More recently, anthropologists have also explored the way modern revitalization of pilgrimage in Tibet has affected gender dynamics,[60] and how female leaders in the past invoked the

[57] As such, while there is some mixing, the spirit of *communitas* as described by the theorist of pilgrimage Victor Turner is not generally relevant. See, for example, discussions in Katia Buffetrille, "The Evolution of a Tibetan Pilgrimage: The Pilgrimage to A Myes rMa Chen Mountain in the 21st Century," in *Symposium on Contemporary Tibetan Studies, 21st Century Tibet Issue, Collected Papers* (Taipei: Mongolian and Tibetan Affairs Commission, 2003), 2.

[58] Huber, "Putting the Gnas Back in Gnas-bskor," 96.

[59] The exclusion of women from certain parts of the mountain is rooted in the belief that they are of lower status (one word for "woman" in Tibetan is *skye dman*, meaning low birth) and that their bodies are impure. However, there are competing discourses about why women are excluded. See Huber, *The Cult of Pure Crystal Mountain*, 121–127. For more on women and pilgrimage, see Huber, *The Cult of Pure Crystal Mountain*, 90–92 and 120–127, as well as Toni Huber, "Why Can't Women Climb Pure Crystal Mountain? Remarks on Gender, Ritual, and Space in Tibet," in *Tibetan Studies: Proceedings of the 6th Seminar of the International Association for Tibetan Studies, Fagernes, 1992*, ed. Per Kvaerne (Oslo: Institute for Comparative Research in Human Culture, 1994), 350–371.

[60] Charlene Makley, "Gendered Practices and the Inner Sanctum: The Reconstruction of Tibetan Sacred Space in 'China's Tibet,'" *Tibet Journal* XIX, no. 2 (1994): 61–94.

authority of pilgrimage places to ground their own authority as religious teachers.[61]

The Tibetan state also sometimes participated or sponsored pilgrimage practice, most famously in the case of the Tsari Rongkor pilgrimage. The Tsari Rongkor Chenmo, meaning "the great ravine circuit of Tsari," occurred every twelve years on the monkey year in the Tibetan zodiac and attracted around twenty thousand pilgrims from across the Tibetan plateau. The route took them clockwise around Tsari, which involved traversing lowland jungle, high snowy passes, and territory controlled by the tribal Löpa people. From the early eighteenth century to the 1950s, the Central Tibetan government organized the Rongkor Chenmo, providing supplies and logistical support, appointing government officers to direct pilgrims, and negotiating payments to the non-Tibetan Löpa people so that they would allow the pilgrims to pass through their land.[62] This pilgrimage thus gave the state a platform to display political and symbolic authority.

Pilgrimage in Tibet was also deeply intertwined with economic activities. While some readers may assume that pilgrimage needs to involve "pure" religious motivations that are incompatible with economic activity, such assumptions were not shared by Tibetan pilgrims. We can see this in the pilgrim diary of Khatag Zamyak, which we will examine more closely in Chapter 6. Khatag Zamyak regularly engaged in commercial activities alongside pilgrimage activities and did not understand these types of activities to be in conflict. According to all historical and anthropological accounts, pilgrims regularly traveled with traders, brought valuable items to trade at pilgrim markets, or combined business travel with visits to sacred sites on the way to Lhasa. Sacred sites often had associated markets where pilgrims bought offerings, consecrated substances, or souvenirs like bamboo walking sticks from Tsari.[63] As such, pilgrimage sites—and the monasteries that controlled them—often generated substantial revenue from pilgrim donations and markets.[64] Disputes about pilgrimage thus had important economic stakes in addition to concerns about proper religious practice.[65]

[61] Hanna Havnevik, "On Pilgrimage for Forty Years in the Himalayas: The Female Lama Jetsun Lochen Rinpoche's (1865–1951) Quest for Sacred Sites," in *Pilgrimage in Tibet*, ed. Alex McKay, 85–107 (London: Curzon Press, 1998).

[62] For more on the Tsari Rongkor Chenmo, see Huber, *The Cult of Pure Crystal Mountain*, 128–174.

[63] Ibid., 196–218.

[64] Wim van Spengen, "On the Geographical and Material Contextuality of Tibetan Pilgrimage," in *Pilgrimage in Tibet*, ed. Alex McKay, 35–51 (London: Curzon Press, 1998).

[65] In this book, I take it as a given that pilgrimage and trade are inextricable but resist the reductive impulse to read pilgrimage solely in terms of its economic aspects.

Tibetan pilgrimage has also been deeply affected by modernity, globalization, and the Chinese occupation of Tibet. Tibetans in China are limited in their ability to travel or practice religion freely, and some pilgrimage routes have been shut down by authorities for long periods of time or require permits that are nearly impossible to get in practice.[66] Tibetans in exile are prevented from accessing traditional sacred sites and have consequently refocused attention on sites in India and Nepal. Meanwhile, the global popularity of Buddhism, and of Tibetan Buddhism in particular, has led to increasing tourist interest in pilgrimage sites such as Kailash, Wutai Shan, or Bodhgaya. It remains to be seen how Tibetan pilgrimage will continue to change in the future.

Conclusion

This overview of pilgrimage in Buddhism generally and Tibet specifically has had two main goals. The first is to give a sense of the wide variety of pilgrimage practices across Buddhist Asia. Throughout the history of Buddhism, people have traveled to special places, but how and why they do so vary across time and place, and even within particular times and places. Tibetan pilgrimage is equally diverse, drawing on a variety of logics, some that have antecedents in Buddhist textual traditions, and some that do not. Tibetans developed vibrant models of sacred landscape populated by heroes, demons, and various nonhuman beings, as well as a wide variety of practices for engaging this landscape. The full richness of this tradition can only be glimpsed in the textual record, which mostly documents the views of cultural elites. Within this broader pilgrimage tradition, the goal of seeing a holy mountain as a divine mandala is important, but certainly not the only goal or destination for pilgrims. Even for pilgrims to holy mountains, many likely saw the goal of seeing the mountain as a mandala as out of reach in their current birth. Nonetheless, they participated in a tradition that valorized those who could see in this way, and that considered such vision critical to allowing pilgrimage to happen at all. As such, as this book focuses on pilgrimage texts, we must remember that the practices of seeing

[66] Tsering Woeser, "Local Authorities Limit the Issuing of 'Border Permits,' Prohibit Tibetans to go on Pilgrimage to the Sacred Mountain," https://highpeakspureearth.com/local-authorities-limit-the-issuing-of-border-permits-prohibit-tibetans-to-go-on-pilgrimage-to-the-sacred-mountain-by-woeser/, accessed January 17, 2023.

thematized in this project are but one part of a larger and multifaceted tradition of Tibetan pilgrimage.

The second goal of this chapter was to highlight certain themes that recur throughout Buddhist pilgrimage traditions. In particular, the *Mahāparinibbāṇa Sutta* demonstrated an interest in seeing the holy places, as well as in what was required to see correctly (a faithful heart) and what that seeing would do to a pilgrim (arouse emotion). Pilgrimage has always been many things, but it has often involved recollecting the Buddha or other important figures, interacting with powerful but hidden landscapes, and trying to catalyze spiritual advancement. Tibetan mountain pilgrimage differs from many other forms of Buddhist pilgrimage, but it also draws on these recurring themes. With that in mind, we will next turn to visual perception, and specifically to the question of what, in a Tibetan context, it means to see on pilgrimage.

2
How to See on Pilgrimage

Introduction

How should pilgrims see the holy places they visit on pilgrimage? This may seem like a strange question, particularly if we understand the term "seeing" to indicate the passive reception of sense data from the external world. Pilgrims go to the holy place and, so long as their eyes are open and healthy, they will see it. While this account might seem attractive, two facts about the Tibetan pilgrimage tradition should give us pause. First, the tradition claims that different types of people will see the mountain in different ways. Some people see it as a pile of rocks, and some people see it in its pure form as a divine mandala. Second, pilgrimage texts use a range of terms for seeing, each with its own associated attitudes and actions. As such, we should pause to consider means to see a holy mountain and how pilgrims should see on pilgrimage.

Even in English, the verb "to see" can refer to a variety of actions. For example, we might glance, gaze, glimpse, or stare. We might see somebody's point or see where they are coming from. We might also see red or see something through. We might also see something in a dream or see a snake in the path that turns out to be a stick. We might see our favorite book characters vividly in the mind's eye. We say things like "What you see is what you get" but also write off strange experiences as just "seeing things." Tibetan and other classical Buddhist languages also recognize a variety of ways to see.

To understand what it means to see on pilgrimage, this chapter will approach the subject from three angles. First, we will survey general Buddhist ideas about perception. Next, we will zoom in on Tibetan words for perception. Finally, we will explore Tibetan advice texts about how to perform pilgrimage. Based on these three areas of analysis, I will argue for an understanding of perception as bridging the internal world of language, imagination, and affect with the external, physical world. I will show how Tibetan texts understand perception as an active and therefore malleable process that becomes an important tool for reshaping human experience of the world. The chapter further demonstrates how Buddhists in various times and places

Making the Invisible Real. Catherine Hartmann, Oxford University Press. © Oxford University Press 2025.
DOI: 10.1093/9780197791585.003.0003

have utilized that tool, developing practices that aim to replace or improve ordinary ways of seeing the world. I develop an account of these "practices of seeing," which include seeking out visual encounters with certain kinds of objects and adopting certain ways of looking. This chapter situates Tibetan Buddhist pilgrimage within a long lineage of Buddhist thought and practice centered on vision.

Buddhist Approaches to Vision

Interest in vision runs throughout Buddhist traditions, and it is thematized in metaphors, philosophical theories, narratives, and practices. Buddhists sought to understand how we ordinarily see, how seeing affects our actions, and how to change the way that we see, ultimately to cultivate insight into the nature of reality. Tibetan pilgrimage literature does not always explicitly draw on these ideas, or even map neatly onto them. However, since this book claims that Tibetan pilgrimage literature responds to fundamental Buddhist questions about perception, it is worth sketching out some of the major themes of Buddhist philosophy of perception. This will also educate our imaginations in ways that will be helpful for future chapters.

To start at the broadest level of analysis, vision takes on two seemingly contradictory roles in Buddhist thought: as a metaphor for true knowledge and as a prime example of ordinary delusion. In the former case, vision and visual terms illustrate what it means to be enlightened. For example, we might say that the very title of the Buddha as the "awakened one" entails a visual metaphor insofar as the person who is awake rather than asleep or dreaming has their eyes open. Similarly, early Buddhist texts describe those who hear the Buddha preach as having opened the "dharma eye,"[1] and they describe the middle way as "producing vision, producing knowledge."[2] In each example, the eye and vision produced are not ones that see ordinary physical reality,[3]

[1] The Pali suttas often describe people who hear the Buddha's teachings as having "the dustless, stainless dhamma eye" (P. *virajaṃ vītamalaṃ dhammacakkhuṃ*) arise within them. In other words, hearing the Buddha's teachings awakens a person's ability to see reality. In contrast to the ordinary eyes, which are tainted by conceptuality, habitual reactions, and cravings, this dharma eye is clear and undefiled.

[2] P. *cakkhukaraṇī ñāṇakaraṇī.*

[3] That said, Buddhist practitioners are said to be able to develop literal advanced sensory powers through meditation. Alongside these accounts of ordinary perception, we also find descriptions of higher perceptions that can be developed through advanced practice. For example, the Buddha is said to have five eyes, each of which grants a special type of extrasensory perception. Advanced meditators, too, can develop special powers such as the "divine eye" (P. *dibbacakkhu*), which grants

but instead see the truth of the Buddha's teachings and directly understand the nature of reality. The idea of seeing as a model for liberatory knowledge occurs throughout Buddhism,[4] which supports an understanding of enlightenment as "intimate, direct, and full knowledge" of reality unmediated by concepts.[5]

However, if Buddhists took vision as a central model for enlightenment, they also invoked vision as a common example of ordinary delusion. We have already seen, for example, how the *Holy Teachings of Vimalakīrti* suggests that ordinary perception is deluded. Like many Buddhist texts, it emphasizes the gap between ordinary appearance and reality to suggest that most people, most of the time, incorrectly perceive reality. Likewise, we find discussions about mistakenly perceiving the world, as when someone sees a rope and thinks it is a snake, or see unenlightened people said to have dust in their eyes. This fundamental misperception, according to the tradition, drives human sin and suffering.

In addition to thinking about vision in these two broad ways, Buddhist philosophers also developed sophisticated models for analyzing perception. One such model is that of the "five aggregates" (P. *khanda*, S. *skandha*). According to this model, human experience of the world is made up of five aggregates that are bundled together in a dynamic process. (1) Perceptual *contact* with form generates (2) *feeling* (positive, negative, or neutral), which in turn gives rise to (3) *recognition*, whereby one mentally labels the object with a particular concept, leading in turn to (4) *volition* in the sense of a habituated reaction to that kind of object, and finally (5) a *consciousness* that is aware of the perception.[6] This framework of the five aggregates primarily

clairvoyance. For the five eyes: P. *pañcacakkhu*, S. *pañcacakṣu*, T. *spyan lnga*. In Pali, for example, one commonly finds the formulation of fleshly eye (*mamsacakkhu*), divine eye (*dibbacakkhu*), wisdom eye (*paññacakkhu*), buddha eye (*buddhacakkhu*), and universal eye (*samanthacakkhu*). See Pali Text Society, *The Pali Text Society's Pali-English Dictionary* (Oxford: Pali Text Society, 1998), 259–260. One finds other slightly different presentations elsewhere. For example, see Robert E. Buswell and Donald S. Lopez, *The Princeton Dictionary of Buddhism* (Princeton, NJ: Princeton University Press, 2014), 216.

[4] For more on the root metaphor of "seeing is knowing" and its role in Mahāyāna thought, see David L. McMahan, *Empty Vision: Metaphor and Visionary Imagery in Mahāyāna Buddhism* (London: RoutledgeCurzon, 2002).

[5] Ibid., 65.

[6] Another basic account of perception can be found in the early Buddhist discourses preserved in the Pali canon. It is similar to the account given in the five aggregates and uses several of the same terms, but it also differs in certain respects. These accounts highlight how the perceiver thinks about (P. *vitakka*) the object perceived and then expands (P. *papañca*) upon it, spinning off conceptual elaborations about the object and eventually leading to craving and delusion. See Saracchandra, *Buddhist Psychology of Perception* (Colombo, Sri Lanka: Ceylon University Press, 1958), 4–12.

functions to demonstrate that humans lack a permanent self. However, it also provides a theory of perception suggesting that the apparently simple act of seeing is a multistep process with many of the steps outside conscious awareness. That process involves both the external object seen and the various factors internal to the perceiver, including their conceptual framework, their experiences, and their emotions.

Later Buddhist philosophers developed and expanded Buddhist philosophy of perception. They both wanted to understand how distorted perception might be rectified and how certain types of perception could yield reliable knowledge.[7] Certain issues emerged as points of debate among Buddhist philosophers, including the question of how perception becomes connected with concepts in order to yield usable knowledge about the world.[8] In each of these accounts, however, Buddhist philosophers affirmed that perception is a multistep process involving both internal and external factors, including emotional tone, conceptual categories, and habits engrained through past actions and experiences.[9]

As result of this understanding, many Buddhist texts emphasize the need to carefully guard vision from the wrong kind of external object. We find, for example, analogies comparing the person with unguarded sense faculties to a

[7] Abhidharma philosophers, for example, compiled lists of the various factors involved in the process of perception, including sense objects, sense faculties, and different sense consciousnesses, and debated the relative importance of various components. For an overview of Abhidharma approaches to the philosophy of perception, see Georges B. J. Dreyfus, *Recognizing Reality: Dharmakirti's Philosophy and Its Tibetan Interpretations* (New York: State University of New York Press, 1997), 331–336, as well as Bhikkhu K. L. Dhammajoti, *Abhidharma Doctrines and Controversy on Perception* (Hong Kong: Centre of Buddhist Studies, 2007).

[8] The early Buddhist philosophers Dignāga (c. sixth century) and Dharmakīrti (c. seventh century) articulated a notion of perception as nonconceptual and argued that this entails that perception yields direct, reliable information about the world. Their account, however, raised the question of how, if perception is nonconceptual and inexpressible, such perception can count as knowledge at all. If we cannot put perceptions into words, how can we have intentional thoughts and beliefs about what we perceive? See Dan Arnold, "Dharmakīrti and Dharmottara on the Intentionality of Perception: Selections from the *Nyayabindu*," in *Buddhist Philosophy: Essential Readings*, ed. Jay Garfield and William Edelglass (New York: Oxford University Press, 2009). Later Buddhist philosophers such as Dharmottara, Candrakīrti, Śantideva, Chaba, Sakya Paṇḍita, and Tsongkhapa each respond to this issue. For overviews of these debates, see Sonam Thakchöe, "Prāsaṅgika Epistemology in Context," in *Moonshadows: Conventional Truth in Buddhist Philosophy*, ed. Cowherds (New York: Oxford University Press, 2011), 53–54; and Dreyfus, *Recognizing Reality*, chaps. 21–24.

[9] It is worth noting that some Buddhists did question whether perception interfaces between the internal and external world. Some Buddhist idealist philosophers, for example, argued that mental phenomena are what most directly gives rise to episodes of perception, and as result, there is no need for us to posit an external reality at all, and that all perception might be like perception in dreams. While there is a vast literature on this topic, one useful resource is David Duckworth et al., *Dignāga's Investigation of the Percept: A Philosophical Legacy in India and Tibet* (New York: Oxford University Press, 2016).

fish able to be caught by temptation's hooks,[10] to a tortoise with outstretched limbs that makes easy prey for a jackal,[11] or to a poorly roofed house that lets rain inside and destroys the interior.[12] For ordinary people, perception is a vulnerable location that exposes them to external objects that can arouse lust, greed, or other dangers.[13]

As such, Buddhist texts praise monks for keeping their eyes downcast (P. *okkhitta cakkhu*). Buddhaghoṣa tells the story of a monk named Cittagutta who lived in a cave for sixty years. When some other monks come to visit him, they praise a lovely wall painting in the cave, but Cittagutta says, "For more than sixty years, friends, I have lived in the cave, and I did not know whether there was any painting there or not. Now, today, I know it through those who have eyes."[14] Cittagutta has guarded his vision so carefully that he spent sixty years in the cave without once looking up, to the point that he considers himself not to have eyes at all. By cutting himself off from looking at objects (such as paintings or women) that could arouse greed or lust, he is able to cultivate ethical discipline and mental tranquility.

Alternatively, if monks cannot entirely avoid looking at external objects, Buddhist texts recommend that they learn to control perception so that potentially corrupting objects no longer affect them. For example, Buddhaghoṣa tells the story of another monk who, when he sees a woman walking down the street, sees only a pile of bones.[15] Instead of lust, he feels

[10] "The Fisherman Simile," *Saṃyutta Nikāya* 35.230, Bhikkhu Bodhi, trans., *The Connected Discourses of the Buddha: A Translation of the Saṃyutta Nikāya* (Boston: Wisdom Publications, 2000), 1228.

[11] "The Simile of the Tortoise," *Saṃyutta Nikāya* 35.240, ibid., 1240–1241. See also SN 1.17, ibid., 96.

[12] Buddhaghoṣa, *The Path of Purification: Visuddhimagga*, trans. Bhikkhu Ñāṇamoli, 5th ed. (Kandy, Sri Lanka: Buddhist Publication Society, 1991), 37–38.

[13] One typical passage: "And how, friend, does one guard the sense-doors? In this a monk seeing an object with the eye, does not seize hold of either its general appearance or its details. Because anyone dwelling with the eye-faculty uncontrolled could be overwhelmed by cupidity and dejection, evil and unwholesome states of mind, therefore he practices to control the eye-faculty, guards it and gains control over it. So one guards the sense-doors." From "Sāriputta," *Saṃyutta Nikāya* 35.120, Bodhi, *The Connected Discourses of the Buddha*, 1193–1194.

[14] Buddhaghoṣa, *The Path of Purification: Visuddhimagga*, 38.

[15] Buddhaghoṣa describes a monk wandering down the road when he comes across a woman dressed up like a celestial nymph. The woman laughs at him, which catches the monk's attention and causes him to look up. What he sees, however, is not this beautiful woman, but rather her teeth. What is more, he sees those teeth as bones, and thus has the perception of foulness. The woman's husband comes up the road looking for her and asks the monk if he has seen a woman, and the monk replies that "Whether it was a man or woman / that went by I noticed not / But only that on this high road / there goes a group of bones." The monk does not see the beautiful woman as beautiful or even as a woman, but rather sees her as fundamentally the same as a rotten corpse. As such, the sight of her does not cause lust that would undermine his vows, but rather a further revulsion with the body that supports his dedication toward renunciation. The object of his perception is the same, but his

revulsion, awareness of death, and ultimately rededication to renunciation. This monk has cultivated his mind such that external objects cannot sway his virtue. In these two stories, we see seemingly impossible idealizations of monks guarding their perception. Both will be difficult for actual monks to realize, but both clearly express the ideal of guarding and purifying perception.

However, while some objects are harmful to perceive, other objects can benefit those who see them. Here, vision's status as an interface between internal and external is a good thing—vision becomes the locus where powerful objects can work on people. For example, Buddhist narratives repeatedly show how seeing the Buddha can provoke strong reactions in viewers. Buddhist literature repeatedly describes people seeing the Buddha and immediately developing faith (P. *prasāda*, S. *śraddhā*) in the Buddha's teachings or a devotion to a particular teacher.[16] Importantly, in many of these cases, the transformative power of the object is not dependent on the intention or agency of the viewer, but rather inherent in the visible object itself. The object transforms the person who sees it. This interest in powerful objects, which also includes images of buddhas and holy masters, monuments such as *stūpas*, temples, ritual implements, amulets, and more, recurs throughout the Buddhist world.[17]

Because certain objects can transform people who see them, Buddhist traditions have developed various practices of directing their attention to certain kinds of visual objects. For example, meditation texts describe meditation supports (P. *kasiṇa*) that can range from simple colored disks to the excellent qualities of the Buddha[18] to a decomposing corpse. These different visual objects can help focus attention, inspire awe, or cultivate repulsion for the body, all of which can help move people along the Buddhist path.

reaction—one presumably supported by practices of looking at decaying corpses and meditating on impermanence and foulness—is completely different. Ibid., 39.

[16] See Andy Rotman, *Thus Have I Seen: Visualizing Faith in Early Indian Buddhism* (Oxford: Oxford University Press, 2009).

[17] For more on Buddhist visual culture, see Jacob N. Kinnard, *Imaging Wisdom* (London: Curzon, 1999), and Cynthea J. Bogel, *With a Single Glance: Buddhist Icon and Early Mikkyō Vision* (Seattle: University of Washington Press, 2009).

[18] On the other hand, Buddhist texts have a pervasive interest in beauty and that which is pleasing to the eye. While Buddhist texts are at times wary of beauty that could corrupt virtue, this did not mean that Buddhist texts rejected or were disinterested in beauty. Far from it—texts go on at length to describe the beauty of the Buddha's body, of the sites where he preached, and the wonders of the heavens and pure lands. In both the case of dangerous beauty and good beauty, that which is pleasing to the eye seems to be regarded as inherently attractive and motivating.

Alongside practices of looking at visual objects, Buddhists also developed practices of generating images in the mind's eye even without an external visual support. These visualization practices can be found in early Buddhist texts,[19] but they found fuller expression in later (especially tantric) Buddhist traditions. Tantric Buddhists engaged in visualization practices often called deity yoga in which they attempted to build and sustain a mental image of the Buddha or some other deity. Other Buddhists experimented with cutting off sensory stimulation by sealing themselves inside a dark room for an extended period or gazing into the empty sky to generate visionary experiences.[20] In these cases, practitioners deliberately sought to cultivate new ways of seeing that were not determined by the external world but were actively generated by the perceiver.

This brief survey of Buddhist thought and practices surrounding perception can only gesture toward the full extent of this material, but it serves to highlight some key ideas that run throughout Buddhist treatments of perception. First, Buddhists thought and wrote about vision, and they developed various practices of looking. They did so because they thought that vision mattered as one moved along the Buddhist path. Next, perception was understood as a multistep process involving not only external objects but also internal factors such as concepts, emotional tone, and experience. As such, there are multiple points of intervention where one can try to change perception. Finally, perception is treated as an interface between internal and external such that perception itself is co-created by seers and by the things seen. There are thus certain actions that perceivers can take to change the way that they see, but there are also certain kinds of visual objects that transform the way people exist in the world, whether for good or ill. We should keep these in mind as we turn to Tibetan ideas about what it means to see.

Tibetan Terms for Visual Perception

As is the case in English, Tibetan has many words for seeing that convey different meanings. Here we will survey those terms to better frame discussions

[19] Bhikkhu Anālayo, "Visualization in Early Buddhism," *Mindfulness* 13, no. 9 (September 1, 2022): 2155–2161.

[20] For more on these practices, see Christopher Hatchell, *Naked Seeing: The Great Perfection, the Wheel of Time, and Visionary Buddhism in Renaissance Tibet* (Oxford: Oxford University Press, 2014).

in the rest of the book. This linguistic survey will yield a different picture from the one created by reviewing general Buddhist approaches to perception, because instead of proceeding by top-down conceptual analysis, it will explore the distinctions that emerge from a bottom-up analysis of language. However, familiar themes will arise.

To begin, let us start with the instrument of visual perception: *mik* (*mig*), or "eye." The term is defined[21] as "the looker" (*lta byed*), or the organ of perception (*snang ba'i dbang po*), and can either refer to the fleshly eye (*sha'i mig*) or the mind's eye (*blo mig*).[22] *Mik* can also mean an aperture (*i khung*) or hole (*bu ga*), which recalls early Buddhist conceptions of the eye as the orifice through which the external world comes into contact with a person's inner world. Tibetan also uses honorifics to indicate respect of high status, and so there are also honorifics for many of the words we will discuss. For instance, the honorific for *mik* is *chen* (*spyan*).[23]

Moving on to verbs, we find *ta* (*lta*), "to look."[24] *Ta* is a voluntary verb, meaning that it is an action that an agent takes, rather than something that just happens.[25] Tibetan dictionaries differentiate between looking and seeing, as in the example, "In the dark, although I looked, I did not see."[26] In other words, a person can actively *look*, but may not see the objection. Looking refers to an action, while seeing indicates that perception occurred. Many usages of *ta* involve ordinary physical perception, but the term can also be used in a more general way that might be rendered by the English "to

[21] Zhang Yisun, *Bod rgya tshig mdzod chen mo* (Beijing: Minzu Chubanshe, 1993). Hereafter, *Tshig mdzod chen mo*.

[22] The *Tshig mdzod chen mo* in turn defines this term as *sems mig gi gzugs su bkod pa or gnas lugs ji bzhin mthong ba'i blo mig gsal ba. Tshig mdzod chen mo*, 1923.

[23] Ibid., 1671. For example, one frequently finds references to the five eyes (*spyan lnga*). This notion goes back to early Buddhist materials. Lists in the Pali canon vary, but one commonly finds the formulation *mamsa, dibba, pañña, buddha, samantha*. See Pali Text Society, *Pali-English Dictionary*, 259–260. In Tibetan presentations, the five eyes include the *sha'i spyan, lha'i spyan, shes rab kyi spyan, chos kyi spyan*, and *sangs rgyas kyi spyan*. This presentation is likely influenced by that of the *Abhisamayālaṅkāra* (T. *Mngon rtogs rgyan*). See Maitreyanātha, *Abhisamayālaṃkāra with Vṛtti and Ālokā*, trans. Gareth Sparham (Fremont, CA: Jain Publications, 2006). The trope of the five eyes comes up multiple times, including in Vol. 1, 46–47.

[24] Additionally, classical Tibetan verbs have different conjugations in the four main tenses of past, present, future, and imperative. The verbal root often takes different spellings in these different tenses; for example, the root *lta ba* takes the different spellings *blta, lta, bltas, ltos* in the different tenses.

[25] Tibetan grammarians divide Tibetan verbs into two broad categories: voluntary (*tha dad pa*, literally meaning differentiated) and involuntary (*tha mi dad pa*, literally meaning nondifferentiated). Voluntary verbs are something that an agent does, while involuntary verbs are something that happens without an agent.

[26] *Mun nag gi nang du bltas kyang mi mthong. Tshig mdzod chen mo*, 1082.

consider" or "to analyze." *Ta* also functions as a noun meaning "viewpoint," or "philosophical position."

In contrast to the voluntary active verb *ta*, there is also the involuntary verb *tong* (*mthong*), meaning "to see" or "to perceive," which does not require an agent. It has the sense of ordinary sense perception which sees material forms, and again it is distinguished from *ta* in the example, "One who does not see the sun, even though they looked at it, is blind."[27] *Tong* also renders nonvisual conceptual understanding, as in the example of "clearly seeing the profound meaning."[28] For example, we find the term *lhaktong* (*lhag mthong*) used to render the Sanskrit *vipaśyanā*, or in English, "insight,"[29] and *tonglam* (*mthong lam*) used to render the Sanskrit *darśana-mārga*, "the path of seeing."[30] In both of these cases, *tong* refers to direct realization of certain abstract concepts or of the nature of reality that is explicitly nonconceptual.[31]

One honorific verb, *zig* (*gzigs*), covers both *ta* and *tong*. It can thus be used as an involuntary verb meaning "to see" or as a voluntary verb meaning "to look at." *Zig* can also be used as the honorific for "to realize" (*rtogs*),[32] indicating that, like *ta* and *tong*, *zig* renders both ordinary visual perception and conceptual understanding or realization.

The verb *jel* (*mjal*) is an honorific term primarily meaning "to meet," but it can also mean "to see" or "to encounter."[33] This matches the English usage of "to see" as in the sentence, "I went to see the doctor." In the context of Tibetan pilgrimage, when the pilgrim sees or encounters a holy place or image, they will generally use the honorific term *jel* rather than saying that they looked (*ta*) or saw (*tong*) the holy object. Indeed, one of the common terms for pilgrimage is *néjel* (*gnas mjal*), in the sense of seeing/encountering a holy place.

Another important term is *nang* (*snang*), which has a range of meanings and uses, both as a verb and as a noun. Primarily, it takes the involuntary

[27] *Nyin mor bltas kyang mi mthong long ba yin*. Ibid., 1219.

[28] *Zab don legs par mthong*. Melvyn C. Goldstein, ed., *The New Tibetan-English Dictionary of Modern Tibetan* (Berkeley: University of California Press, 2001), 517.

[29] This, along with *śamatha*, or calming meditation, is one of two major meditative modes found in Buddhist materials, and it indicates a set of practices by which one gains insight into the nature of reality by analyzing Buddhist doctrines and convincing oneself of their validity.

[30] This is the third of the so-called five paths that characterize an arhat or bodhisattva's spiritual progress. At this stage, the practitioner has a direct perception of the nature of reality without mediation by concepts. For more, see Buswell and Lopez, *Princeton Dictionary of Buddhism*, 217.

[31] *Tong* also translates the Sanskrit *darśana*. For more on the notion of *darśan* in Hindu contexts, see Diana Eck, *Darśan: Seeing the Divine Image in India*, 2nd ed. (New York: Columbia University Press, 1996).

[32] *Tshigs mdzod chen mo*, 2495.

[33] Ibid., 880.

verbal sense of "to appear." The moon can *nang*, bad omens can *nang*, and dreams or visions can *nang*—the term only indicates that something is appearing to the subject.[34] What appears may not truly exist, as indicated in the example, "It is difficult to be certain about something which merely appears to the eye."[35] One might be hallucinating or simply mistaken. *Nang* can also function as a noun indicating "that which appears," and it frequently appears in compound words. For example, we find the term *daknang* (*dag snang*) in pilgrimage literature. This term means "pure appearance" or "pure perception," and it refers to a state in which all phenomena appear to the subject in their pure and good aspects.[36] This state of pure perception, and the ability to cultivate such a state, is highly desirable for pilgrims and for Buddhist practitioners more generally.

In contrast to *nang*, which emphasizes appearance, the term *ngön sum* (*mngon sum*), meaning "actual" or "real," indicates that the person is seeing reality correctly without error or obscuration. In this sense, it translates the technical Sanskrit term *pratyakṣa*, or "direct perception,"[37] held to be one of the few sources of reliable knowledge.

Various Tibetan terms can translate "to visualize," in the sense of using the imagination to see something in the mind's eye.[38] These terms describe widespread practices of deliberately generating an image, often of a deity, in the mind of the practitioner.[39] These are active and controlled practices in which the practitioner tries, in effect, to *create* what they see.

[34] There are closely related terms *char* (*'char*) and *shar* (*shar*). These terms are closely related, and *shar* occurs as the past tense of *char*. They translate as "to appear," "to arise," "to dawn," or "to shine," with *char* often referring to the arising of thoughts or the arising of sensory phenomena. Ibid., 861 and 2838, respectively.

[35] *Mig la snang ba tsam gyis blo la nges dka'.* Ibid., 1589.

[36] The *Tshig mdzod chen mo* describes it as a state in which the entire world, animate and inanimate, appears as a pure land, or in which everything appears as the play of wisdom and the bodies of the Buddha. Ibid., 1237: *snang srid snod bcud thams cad dag pa'i zhing du snang ba ste sku dang ye shes kyi rol bar snang ba.*

[37] Ibid., 691. As a technical term, it indicates one of the means of knowledge (*anumāna*) recognized by Buddhist philosophers and indicates a direct and nonconceptual awareness of some object. Ibid., 691: *<pratyak + Sha> blo rig bdun gyi nang gses / rtog bral ma 'khrul ba'i shes pa / dper na / bum 'dzin dbang mngon dang / gzhan sems shes pa'i mngon shes dang / 'phags pa'i mnyam bzhag ye shes lta bu'o.*

[38] Indeed, as Eric Greene has pointed out, no single such term exists in Sanskrit either. Rather, there are several Sanskrit verbs that are frequently translated as "to visualize." When these verbs take an abstract cognitive object, scholars translate the verb as "contemplate," but when the verbs take an object with visual qualities, scholars translate the verb as "visualize," thus marking a difference that is not present in the Sanskrit verb. See Eric Greene, "Visions and Visualizations: In Fifth-Century Chinese Buddhism and Nineteenth-Century Experimental Psychology," *History of Religions* 55, no. 3 (January 26, 2016): 289–328.

[39] This whole process is framed in terms of two stages: the generation stage (*bskyed rim*), in which the image is generated, a process that necessarily involves artificial contrivance (*bcos pa*); and the perfection stage (*rdzogs rim*), in which the divine image is made real and uncontrived.

Finally, there are also terms that, strictly speaking, do not refer to sight or seeing but may nonetheless be translated as perception. Foremost among these is *dushé* (*'du shes*), a term which translates the Sanskrit *saṃjñā* and refers to the process of recognizing and mentally labeling some perceived object. That is, there is a moment where a subject comes into visual contact with an object and then a second moment where the subject recognizes that object *as* something. *Dushé* refers to that second moment.

Tibetan words for seeing thus both underscore themes we have already explored from the Buddhist treatments of perception—namely, the idea that perception is a multistep process—and introduces new distinctions. For example, Tibetan words for seeing can refer either to sensory perception ("I see the grass") or cognitive, nonsensory understanding ("I see what you mean"). This highlights that in Tibetan—much like in English or Sanskrit—there is a deep association between knowing and seeing. In addition, Tibetan highlights various degrees of *agency* of seeing. Some terms for seeing, like *ta*, cast seeing as an active, volitional verb, whereas some others, like *tong*, depict the passive, receptive, and nonvolitional aspect of seeing. Sometimes, seeing is something an agent *does*, and other times, seeing is something that *happens* to a patient.[40] This simple distinction can obscure the complex interplay between volitional seeing and nonvolitional seeing, for as we will see, a person can work very hard to cultivate a type of seeing that appears spontaneously. Nevertheless, we should track the distinction. Finally, Tibetan terms for seeing distinguish between appearance and reality. Terms such as *nang* emphasize the phenomenological character of the seeing, such that dreams or hallucinations can *nang*. Even when used in reference to external objects, *nang* refers to the fact of their appearing, and not necessarily to what they really are. By contrast, terms such as *ngön sum* generally imply direct perception of the way things actually are, with the implication being that they are seen correctly. As such, there is a distinction implied between the way objects appear to a particular subject and the way things really are. As we turn to Tibetan pilgrimage literature in future chapters, we will pay careful attention to how texts use different terms for seeing because it will help us understand how these texts prompt pilgrims to look at the pilgrimage place.

[40] As Wittgenstein points out in the *Philosophical Investigations*, a person cannot will themselves to see a leaf green. Ludwig Wittgenstein, *Philosophical Investigations*, trans. G. E. M. Anscombe (New York: Macmillan, 1953), 213. For further discussion of this point, see Colin McGinn, *Mindsight: Image, Dream, Meaning* (Cambridge, MA: Harvard University Press, 2004), 48.

Cultivating Body and Mind on Pilgrimage

One final way to think about what it means to see on pilgrimage is to consult advice texts written for pilgrims. These texts offer various pieces of advice to future pilgrims, but one theme that emerges is how seeing is intertwined with bodily and mental comportment. In other words, to do pilgrimage correctly, pilgrims should not just go through the motions of seeing the holy place, but should maintain the appropriate bodily discipline and mental attitude. We have already seen Buddhists treat perception as a multistep process that involves both the seer and the object seen. Following that logic, if pilgrims actively cultivate specific bodily and mental states, this will affect how they see on pilgrimage.

As a way into Tibetan advice literature, let us consider a representative poem of advice for pilgrims written by Kathog Situ Chökyi Gyatso (1880–1925).[41] In it, he identifies three different types of pilgrims—the best kind, the middling kind, and the worst kind—and discusses how they behave on pilgrimage. Throughout, he thematizes perception as exemplifying the divide between these different sorts of pilgrims.

> Without attachment or desire, without fixed or certain plans,
> Without selfishness, without lineage bias,[42]
> Wandering freely through the country for the sake of beings,—
> These are the activities of the best kind of pilgrim.
>
> Following holy masters without bias or fault,
> Requesting holy teachings without preference or contradiction,
> Gathering merit at holy places without partiality or grasping—
> These too are the activities of the best pilgrim.
>
> Their faith in the three supports unshaken by fatigue,[43]
> Gathering merit and pure perception (*dag snang*) without fighting or
>   irritation,

[41] Other authors that write at length on this subject include Jamgon Kongtrul ('Jam mgon kong sprul, *TsA 'dra rin chen brag gi rtog pa brjod pa yid kyi rgya mtsho'i rol mo*, see especially pages 537–543), Jigme Lingpa ('Jigs med gling pa, *Gnas bskor ba la spring ba'i gtam*), and Pema Karpo ('Brug chen Kun mkhyen Pad+ma dkar po, *Gnas chen tsa ri tra'i ngo mtshar snang ba pad dkar legs bshad*), 264–265.

[42] In previous translations, I rendered *gdul bya* here as "those to be trained," but now, seeing it alongside *ris med*, I am inclined to see it as referring to vinaya traditions, and thus to sectarian bias. However, both readings are possible.

[43] The various images and objects at a pilgrimage shrine are often said to be "supports" (*rten*) for body, speech, and mind. These physical objects give a material basis so that the pilgrim can encounter the enlightened body, speech, and mind of the Buddha.

At all of the hermitages, holy places, and monasteries—
These are the activities of the middling pilgrim.

First they promise to circumambulate the whole world,
Then whenever they see (*mthong*) an uphill, they stay in place.
Finally they fall into a mindset of "been there, done that"
(*byas lo song lo*)—
This the situation in which pilgrimage has no real meaning.

Not seeing (*mthong*) the virtues of the sangha, but seeing (*mthong*)
every flaw,
Not properly seeing (*mjal*) the images and scriptures, but looking from a
distance (*rgyang bltas*),
If someone is watching (*mthong*), they beg, but if they aren't watched
(*mthong*), they steal—
This is the second situation in which circling holy places is really
circling sin.

When they are tired, they have false views (*log lta*) towards the holy place,
Now they see (*mjal*) the temple, and now they forget it,
They consider their anger along the path to be heroic—
Renounce this "pilgrimage" which is a pointless endeavor!

—Kathog Situ Chökyi Gyatso (1880–1925),
"Division of the Three Kinds of Pilgrim"[44]

For Kathog Situ, the best pilgrim is defined by a series of lacks ("without," T. *med*). Specifically, the best pilgrim lacks attachment, desire, partiality, grasping, contradiction, fixed direction, certain plans, selfishness, and bias

[44] *Chags med zhen med gtad med nges med gnas / rang 'khris med pas gdul bya ris med la / phan byed 'gro don rgyal khams phyogs med byed / gnas skor rab kyi rnam thar pa'o // dam pa phyogs med sel med bsten pa dang / dam chos ris med 'gal med zhu ba dang / sgrub gnas phyogs med 'dzin med tshogs bsags pa / 'di yang gnas skor rab kyi rnam thar ro // rten gsum kun la dad pas ngal dub la / mi skyo dben gnas dgon sde thams cad du / 'gras med sun med dag snang tshogs byed / gnas skor 'bring gi rnam par thar pa'o // dang po khas len steng skor na bsam / bar du gyen re mthong na gnas re bzhag / tha ma byas lo song lo'i ngang du thal / gnas skor mdo don med pa'i ngang tshul gcig / dge 'dun yon tan mi mthong skyon re mthong / lha sku gsung rab mi mjal rgyang bltas byas / mthong na slong zhing ma mthong rku ba de / gnas skor sdig skor song ba'i ngang tshul gnyis / dka' chad byung dus gnas la log lta byas / lha khang da lta mjal ba da lta brjed / gnas skor lam du khong khro dpa' tu brtsi / gnas skor nga ba 'bras med ngang tshul dor.* "Gnas skor pa rab 'bring mtha' gsum gyi rnam dbye," in *Gnas yig phyogs bsgrigs.*

toward lineage.[45] This pilgrim visits holy places, and benefits by generating merit and receiving teachings there, but they do not become overly attached to the physical place nor to the personal benefits they will receive. Kathog Situ's portrayal of this directionless pilgrim suggests a concern—shared by many critics of pilgrimage in Tibet—that pilgrims might become overly attached to holy places or visit them for selfish reasons.[46] Instead, the best pilgrim does not seem to be concerned with the holy place at all—instead, they wander without direction from place to place, regarding all places as equally holy.[47] This is an ideal that most pilgrims would fail to fully realize, but one that shaped their pilgrimage nonetheless.

Kathog Situ contrasts this superior way of seeing with the selfish outlook of the bad pilgrim. The bad pilgrim begins with grand intentions for their pilgrimage, but when they encounter the actual difficulties of the path, this initial motivation curdles into laziness, greed, and hypocrisy. When this pilgrim visits the holy site, they do not see (*mthong*) the good qualities of the monks, but only see (*mthong*) the bad. They do not properly see (*mjal*) the images but rather look at them from afar (*rgyang bltas*). The verse deliberately draws a contrast between *mjal*, which connotes a respectful seeing/meeting with a high-status object, and *bltas*, which is a simple looking (root verb *lta ba*). Kathog Situ invokes the respectful *mjal* again to say that even when the bad pilgrim does see (*mjal*) a temple, it makes so little impression that they forget it as soon as it is no longer in front of their eyes. Even worse, the bad pilgrim changes their behavior when others are looking. When they are there, the bad pilgrim begs, but when they are not, the bad pilgrim outright steals. In each instance, the bad pilgrim's relation to perception is faulty—they fail to focus their attention on the proper objects, fail to look at what they see in the right way, and fail to act properly when not being watched.

The fact that Kathog Situ repeatedly uses words related to seeing indicates that he understands perception as a key place where pilgrimage can go wrong. Outwardly, this pilgrim may *appear* to be doing (most of) the right things—they are going to sites and behaving respectfully (at least when

[45] Kathog Situ is part of what has been termed the Nonsectarian (*ris med*) movement, which emphasized an openness to teachings from all sects. As such, we should read the repeated valorization of the pilgrim's lack of preference, partiality, bias, and sectarianism in that context.

[46] See Catherine Hartmann, "Against Pilgrimage: Materiality, Place, and Ambivalence in Tibetan Pilgrimage Literature," *Revue d'Etudes Tibétaines* 65 (October 2022): 127–158, for more on critics of pilgrimage in Tibetan history.

[47] This would seem to cut against pilgrimage practice. If all places are holy, why go on pilgrimage at all? This was indeed a criticism some Tibetan authors made against pilgrimage. See Hartmann, "Against Pilgrimage," 132–134.

others are present). But their external appearance does not match their inner devotion and motivation. The bad pilgrim looks at images at the holy site, but because they do so without respect, without ethical discipline, without remembering, without paying attention, and without pure motivation, they are not really *seeing* them, at least not in Kathog Situ's estimation. Thus, for Kathog Situ, what it means to *see* on pilgrimage requires more than simply looking at holy places.

We can appreciate what this means when we consider the middling pilgrim. This pilgrim, who sits between the purely selfless, ideal pilgrim and the lazy, covetous bad pilgrim, likely represents an achievable ideal Kathog Situ wants audiences to emulate. Most pilgrims are not going to reach the total equanimity of the best pilgrim, but they can at least avoid the degradation of the bad pilgrim. Kathog Situ describes the middling pilgrim as someone who registers the discomforts of pilgrimage, but nonetheless actively overcomes them. For example, Kathog Situ describes the pilgrim's devotion as "unshaken by fatigue."[48] Notably, this does not say that the pilgrim does not *feel* the fatigue that naturally comes from traveling long distances in extreme conditions—the middling pilgrim faces the same physical difficulties as the bad pilgrim—but rather that the middling pilgrim does not allow the physical tiredness (*ngal dub*) to cause them to lose heart and faith, or to cause them to fall into wrongdoing.

The middling pilgrim avoids sadness because of their faith or devotion (*dad pa*)[49] to the three supports—that is, to the physical representations of the Buddha's body, speech, and mind at the holy place. This notion of faith occurs frequently in pilgrimage literature, both in Tibet and in Buddhist pilgrimage more broadly. Recall from the previous chapter, for example, that the *Mahāparinibbāṇa Sutta* mentioned faith three times (P. *saddhā* and *passana*), saying that faithful visitors to sites associated with the Buddha will go to heavenly realms. In the same way, Tibetan pilgrimage literature often praises faith as one of the most important qualities pilgrims should cultivate.

Faith here goes beyond cognitive belief in the holiness of the pilgrimage place, although that is certainly involved to some degree.[50] Rather, it is useful

[48] *Rten gsum kin la dad pa ngal dub la mi skyo.*

[49] Closely allied with *dépa* is *möpa* (*mos pa*), a word with a closely allied set of meanings, and which might be translated as faith, devotion, inclination, or interest. Indeed, one frequently finds these two terms together as the binome *démö* (*dad mos*).

[50] For contemporary philosophical analysis of faith that undermines the notion that faith is simple belief, see Bradley Rettler, "Analysis of Faith," *Philosophy Compass* 13, no. 9 (2018): e12517; and Neil Van Leeuwen, "Religious Credence Is Not Factual Belief," *Cognition* 133, no. 3 (December 1, 2014): 698–715.

to think in terms of the Tibetan scheme of the three faiths (*dad pa gsum*). These include confident faith, a trust in the truth of the Buddha's teachings; longing faith, a desire to attain awakening like the Buddha; and sincere faith, a clear-minded awe of the Buddha.[51] Faith, therefore, involves a *trust* of unseen realities, an *aspiration* to reach a certain kind of state, and an *awe* at the power, glory, and good qualities of the object of faith. This means that faith is not a static state, but incorporates forward motion in that it involves the commitment, intent, or aspiration to certain kinds of action.[52] Faith, which incorporates each of these aspects, is said in the pilgrimage literature to powerfully shape the pilgrim's conduct, both in body and mind,[53] and to enhance the benefits that pilgrims will receive from visiting a holy site.[54] It also prevents the pilgrim from committing wrong actions by strengthening their resolve.

Kathog Situ further characterizes the middling pilgrim as gathering merit and pure perception (*dag snang tshogs gsog byed*). As discussed earlier, pure perception refers to a phenomenological state in which some object appears to the perceiver *as pure*. Ordinarily, *snang* is an involuntary verb and lacks an agent, indicating that it is something that *happens* rather than something one

[51] Confident faith (*yid ches pa'i dad pa*), longing faith (*'dod pa'i dad pa*), and sincere faith (*dang ba'i dad pa*). One also sees formulations of the "three faiths" which leave out longing faith and include irreversible faith (*phyir mi ldog pa'i dad pa*), or the phrase "four faiths," which includes all four. To see Gampopa's discussion of the three faiths, see Chos rje sgam po pa zla 'od gzhon nu, *Dam chos yid bzhin nor bu thar pa rin po che'i rgyan*, BDRC W1KG5451 (Kathmandu: Gam-po-pa Library, 2005), 26.

[52] Jamgön Kongtrül's *Treasury of Precious Instructions* contains this formulation as well. "If faith is lacking, there is no basis for the virtues. There are three kinds of faith. Sincere faith is faith drawn out by special objects. Longing faith is desiring to abandon samsara, achieve nirvana, and to act for beings' welfare. Confident faith is knowing that bad rebirths are because of non-virtue, high rebirths are because of virtue, and buddhahood results from putting into practice the secret mantra of the greater vehicle." *Dad pa med na yon tan gyi gzhi med pas / dad pa la gsum / dang ba'i dad pa yul khyad par can la drangs shing dad pa / 'dod pa'i dad pa 'khor ba spong zhing mya ngan las 'das pa sgrub pa ste 'gro ba'i don bya bar 'dod pa / yid ches pa'i dad pa mi dge bas ngan song / dge bas mtho ris / theg pa chen po gsang sngags nyams su blangs nas sangs rgyas par shes pa'o.* 'Jam mgon Kong sprul Blo gros mtha' yas, *Gdam ngag mdzod* (Delhi: Shechen Publications, 1999), 7:13, 482.

[53] Tibetan writers were certainly aware that misplaced faith could go badly. Drakpa Gyeltsen, for example, warns against blind faith in pilgrimage places by saying that "some people with faith are gullible (*col chung*), some people with faith are heedless (*tho co*), some people with faith are demons," and then proceeding to poke fun at what these types of people do. For the most part, however, discourses about pilgrimage praise faith and encourage pilgrims to develop it. *Dad pa la la col chung yin / dad pa la la tho co yin / dad pa la la 'dre gdon yin.* Grags pa rgyal mtshan, *Gnas bstod kyi nyams dbyangs*, 345.

[54] After describing the benefits of a particular holy place, for example, Jamgon Kongtrul tells potential pilgrims that they "will attain these benefits according to extent of your faith, devotion, and karmic destiny." *Phan yon de dag rang rang gi dad mos kyi nyer len / skal pa'i khyad par dang mtshungs ldan tu 'thob par 'gyur ba yin la.* 'Jam mgon kong sprul, *TsA 'dra rin chen brag gi rtog pa brjod pa yid kyi rgya mtsho'i rol mo*, 543.

does, but here *dag snang* is paired with an active transitive verb (*byed*). This is highly suggestive for what Kathog Situ thinks that our middling pilgrim should be doing—they should actively try to see the site as pure, in the way a being with purified perception would naturally see it. In comparison to the bad pilgrim, who focuses on the faults of the pilgrimage place, the middling pilgrim cultivates an attitude of seeing the pilgrimage place as pure even when there is reason not to do so. The middling pilgrim actively disciplines and controls their perceptual engagement with the world, using faith to cultivate a pure perception of the pilgrimage site that ultimately makes the exercise of pilgrimage beneficial. Even if the monks at the site truly do lack virtue, by seeing them as pure, the pilgrim benefits as though they did see a truly pure monk.

Kathog Situ's poem of advice underscores the centrality of seeing in Tibetan pilgrimage, and it also demonstrates how correct seeing requires certain mental and bodily qualities. These qualities of seeing are important because seeing exists on the boundary between the external world and the internal world of the pilgrim. For most pilgrims, they should try to see good external objects, but they should also cultivate the necessary mental qualities. Kathog Situ, in effect, is trying to shape the internal world of the pilgrim to ensure that the pilgrim sees correctly. Pilgrims will not necessarily be able to *will* themselves to see the pilgrimage place as a mandala, but they can actively cultivate these mental qualities that will—according to Kathog Situ—transform how they see on pilgrimage. Other writers expand on the mental qualities that enhance pilgrimage. Jigmé Lingpa, for example, tells pilgrims to cultivate mindfulness, bodhicitta, equanimity, and forbearance.[55] For each of these writers, pilgrimage is as much of a mental activity as a physical one, and one that requires sustained effort and attention.

[55] Jigme Lingpa writes, "Those of you circling the earth and on pilgrimage to holy sites, take care to have steady mindfulness! Master especially the two-fold *bodhicitta* and [know] the difference between a pious person and those [so-called] great meditators who go to the holy places. Be free of the preference for joy and sorrow—they are equal!" Elsewhere, he adds, "Withstand travel conditions with the armor of forbearance. Even if you get a hundred beatings in a single day, like a stick has pierced through the four elements [of your body], once you can transform that into the assured confidence of carefree yet disciplined action, that is what the tantric texts teach as traveling to the twenty-four holy places." *De bas gnas skor dang sa skor la / rgyu ba rnams bag yod kyis dran pa brtan / khyad par chos ldan gyi gang zag dang / sgom chen gnas skor la 'gro ba'i mtshams / byang chub sems gnyis la rang dbang thob / ro snyoms kyi skyid sdug la 'dam ga bral.* 'Jigs med gling pa, *Gnas bskor ba la spring ba'i gtam*, 577.6; and *Bzod pa'i go chas yul rkyen thub / nyin gcig la brdungs btags brgya byung yang / 'byung bzhi la dbyug pas bsnun pa ltar / ci mi snyam pa'i brtul zhugs kyi / spobs pa gdeng du gyur pa'i tshe / yul chen nyi shu rtsa bzhi ṣogs / bgrod par sngags kyi gzhung nas bshad.* Ibid., 578.1.

In terms of bodily qualities, Kathog Situ makes it clear that the pilgrim must maintain bodily discipline and ethical conduct. The pilgrim who steals or otherwise acts improperly compromises pilgrimage and renders the whole project worthless. Kathog Situ does not expand on this point, but other thinkers writing about pilgrimage do. Jamgon Kongtrul, for example, emphasizes that pilgrims must control the "three doors" of body, speech, and mind,[56] which underscores the connection between mind and body. And Pema Karpo writes that pilgrims "must go forth from home into homelessness and maintain ethical perfection by training in the footsteps of the foremost king of the Shakyas [i.e. the Buddha]."[57] In using the phrase "going forth into homelessness," a term which ordinarily describes entering monastic life, Pema Karpo likens the pilgrim to a monk who must maintain strict standards of bodily comportment. This type of bodily discipline both flows from mental qualities like faith, but it also supports them—by rigorously guarding bodily behavior, pilgrims can also transform their minds. This then shapes the way the pilgrim sees.

Practices of Seeing

The three areas just explored—Buddhist ideas about perception, Tibetan words for seeing, and advice texts to pilgrims—have shown that there are many dimensions to the apparently unified concept of seeing. "Seeing" sometimes indicates a direct sensory experience, and at other times it can indicate nonsensory, conceptual understanding. Accounts of seeing can highlight what appears to the perceiver, without any claims to the reality of what appears, or can highlight the reality of what appears while minimizing the role of the perceiver. The former highlights the subjective nature of perception, while the latter highlights the objective nature of perception. Next, the term "seeing" can highlight external, physical motions, or internal, mental states. For example, we can make sense of the statement, "He saw, but he did not *see*," by imagining a person who looks at an object but does not deeply register the object or its significance. Seeing can involve simply casting one's

[56] *'Dul ba dang mthun par sgo gsum sdom pa dang ldan pa.* 'Jam mgon kong sprul, *TsA 'dra rin chen brag gi rtog pa brjod pa yid kyi rgya mtsho'i rol mo*, 537.2.

[57] *Sngar gyi grub pa thob pa'i bshul snyeg pa dang / yid rtse gcig pas skor ba bskor ba ni khyim nas khyim med par rab tu byung dgos pa dang / de yang shAkya'i rgyal po gtso bo de'i rjes su slob pas tshul khrims phun sum tshogs par gnas te.* Ibid., 264.

eyes on an object, but it can also involve associated mental states or emotions. One can see an object with faith or as pure, which describes how one relates to the object. Finally, seeing can be either passive or active—people can simply open their eyes and have seeing just happen, or they can effortfully try to look at certain objects or to see in a certain way. Seeing stands at the boundary of sensory and conceptual, subject and object, physical and mental, and active and passive.

Because it bridges these different domains, seeing can take many forms. But it also means that vision is malleable. There are many points of intervention. Change the object seen, the conditions when it is seen, the mind of the seer, or any number of other factors and the *event* of seeing is transformed. By changing small things at these intervention points, people can change how they see and experience the world.

Much Buddhist thought and practice recognizes and builds on this understanding of vision. Buddhist traditions understand that vision can be changed, and they claim that it should be changed. Moreover, they offer a huge variety of practices to change perception, what I have termed *practices of seeing*. We have already seen some of these: monks may keep their eyes downcast to avoid seeing women, beautiful works of art may inspire faith and awe, or tantric practitioners visualize deities, all with the goal of transforming the way they see and therefore the way they experience reality. Even practices that outwardly have little to do with perception, such as performing meditation, taking ethical vows, giving money, or doing philosophy, can be understood as ways of impinging on the ordinary perceptual process and learning to see differently. In future chapters, we will turn to the specific practices of seeing that pilgrimage tradition encourages pilgrims to adopt.

Conclusion

However, before we move on to consider these practices of seeing, let us conclude by returning to the question that motivated this chapter: How should pilgrims see the holy place? Now that we have explored more deeply what it means to see in Buddhist, Tibetan, and pilgrimage contexts, we will be able to approach this question with a richer set of conceptual resources.

To begin, and at risk of stating the obvious, the pilgrim should physically see the holy place. We have explored how seeing can sometimes refer to a broad conceptual understanding in addition to its primary sensory meaning. However, in Buddhism's long-standing interest in powerful objects that transform those who see them, and in Kathog Situ's condemnation of pilgrims who only look from afar, we can recognize that pilgrimage is grounded in a material, sensory encounter with a holy place. While some Tibetan thinkers rejected pilgrimage,[58] and others explored the idea of entirely imagined, dreamed, or visualized pilgrimage journeys,[59] Tibetan tradition predominantly valued sensory encounters with physical places. Of course, pilgrims should also have a particular conceptual orientation to the pilgrimage place, and see it *as holy*, but we should not forget the sensory engagement on which the pilgrimage experience is grounded.

Second, pilgrims should recognize the gap that can sometimes exist between appearance and reality, especially when the perceiver has not developed the advanced perception of holy masters. As such, they should remember that their own perception is limited, and that their own failure to see the holy site as it truly exists is more a reflection of their own perceptual capabilities than a reflection of the site itself. This point will be developed further when we explore pilgrimage guides and the denaturalization of ordinary perception, but it is worth mentioning now.

Third, pilgrims should see with a certain kind of mental orientation, ideally one characterized with faith and ethical discipline. Pilgrims can physically visit the site and cast their eyes at the holy objects, but if they do so out of greed and without clear-hearted intention, they are not really *seeing* the object in the way the pilgrimage tradition intends. Those pilgrims who see the site without the proper mental attitude may still benefit from the site,[60] but they will not have the kind of experience the pilgrimage tradition seeks to cultivate.

Finally, pilgrims should make a deliberate effort to see correctly. While there are some accounts in the pilgrimage tradition of objects that transform people who see them, without any effort on the part of the perceiver, for the most part, pilgrimage texts such as Kathog Situ's emphasize that the pilgrim will need to deliberately cultivate the right kind of perception. Ideally, this effortful perception will eventually give way to an experience of spontaneously and effortlessly seeing the site as it is, but this type of perception must be

[58] Hartmann, "Against Pilgrimage."
[59] Huber, *The Holy Land Reborn*.
[60] Some Tibetan authors rejected the notion of automatic benefits for anyone who visits a holy place, but pilgrimage guides routinely make claims about the power of places to benefit even the most lax pilgrim. See Hartmann, "Against Pilgrimage," 127–131.

deliberately cultivated. In future chapters, we will dig deeper into the various deliberate practices of seeing that pilgrims can undertake, but for now it will suffice to say that pilgrims are expected to work to see the pilgrimage place in the right way.

If the pilgrim does these things correctly, the pilgrimage tradition promises transformative encounters with the pilgrimage place. For instance, the sixteenth-century author Pema Karpo describes how the ideal pilgrim will be able to fully transform their perception of the site. In his *Guidebook to Tsari*, he says that on the first circumambulation of Tsari, "Because it is merely the maturation of various causes, conditions, and empowerments, [the pilgrim] perceives (*mthong ba*) all kinds of mountains and lakes."[61] That is, the pilgrim sees the mountain as an ordinary physical object. On the second circumambulation, however, this perception is "matured because of devotion. [The pilgrim] comes to see everything as merely an illusion or a reflection."[62] In contrast to the first circumambulation, where the pilgrim sees ordinary physical objects, and takes them as self-existent, in the second circumambulation, the pilgrim still sees mountains and lakes, but knows that there is a gap between their own perception and reality. The pilgrim on the second circumambulation sees the same thing as the pilgrim on the first circumambulation, buthas come to regard it in a different way. Finally, on the third circumambulation, which Pema Karpo titles the "fully perfected view of all,"[63] the pilgrim develops the correct view of the site and "sees the divine faces manifested in [the mountain] just as they are . . . [The pilgrim] thus develops genuine maturation."[64] On this third circumambulation, the pilgrim fully transforms their perception and does not only have a shift in how they regard the site but also in how it appears to their senses. This final vision is both effortless—the faces just appear as they are—and effortful in that they are the result of the pilgrim's faith and devotion.

[61] *Dbang rgyu rkyen pa'i smin* [alternate reading: *dmigs*] *pa tsam du 'gyur bas / mthong ba yang ri mtsho sogs ci rigs par ro.* 'Brug chen Kun mkhyen Pad+ma dkar po, *Gnas chen tsa ri tra'i ngo mtshar snang ba pad dkar legs bshad*, 269.2. Alternate reading in 'Brug chen Kun mkhyen Pad+ma dkar po, *Gnas chen tsa ri tra'i ngo mtshar snang ba pad dkar legs bshad* in *Dpe rnying rtsa chen par ma'i skor phyogs bsdus*, Vol. 42, img. 465.2.

[62] *Bar ma bskor bas mos pas smin pa ste / thams cad kyang sgyu ma 'am gzugs brnyan tsam du mthong bar 'gyur ro.* Ibid., 465.

[63] *Mtha' ma thams cad lta ru yongs rdzogs pas.* Ibid. This "*lta ru*" is strange, and I am not entirely sure how to translate it. The general sense, however, is clearly that by this stage in the pilgrimage, the pilgrim has a perfected vision of the site.

[64] *Nang sprul pa'i lha zhal ji lta ba mthong zhing / des smin pa mtshan nyid par 'gyur te.* Ibid., 465.

Though Pema Karpo promises the experience of seeing gods in the mountains on the third circumambulation, it is likely that not all pilgrims will be able to bring about this total transformation of perception. The Tibetan pilgrimage tradition maintains that only a vanishingly small number of pilgrims will be able to see a physical mountain of rock and ice as a divine mandala. And indeed, as we will explore in future chapters, the failure to totally reshape perception can itself be productive. But the pilgrimage tradition exhorts them to try and reshape their malleable perception.

While answering the question of what it means to see on pilgrimage, this chapter has pointed to some of the techniques the Tibetan pilgrimage tradition advocates for transforming how people see. Future chapters will build on this account by introducing further techniques for transforming perception. These practices of seeing are active practices of looking at and interpreting the world and aim to cultivate a transformation in how they see the world.

Still, we might ask, what does it actually *look like* to see a mountain as a mandala? Readers may have gone through this chapter's analysis of *how* Tibetan pilgrims are supposed to see on pilgrimage and still wonder *what* they are supposed to see. Pilgrimage texts are ambiguous on this question. I do not take this as a flaw on their part. Instead, I read pilgrimage texts' challenge to pilgrims to see a mountain as a mandala as taking advantage of the fact that there are many ways to see. As such, there are many ways to see a mountain as a mandala, ranging from a general conceptual understanding that the mountain is a mandala, to a fleeting vision in which the pilgrim sees a mandala in front of their eyes, to a stable sensory transformation in which someone physically sees the mountain as a mandala. All of these are included in what I call co-seeing, in which the pilgrim sees the site both with their ordinary perception and with the mind's eye, and attempts to bring these two visions of reality together. Further, all involve an attempt to see that which is ordinarily invisible and inaccessible, and to make it real.

3

One Thing, Many Appearances

Perception and Reality in the Controversy over Kailash

Up until now, I have presented the goal of seeing the hidden wonders of the holy mountain as a fundamental element of Tibetan pilgrimage practice. However, Tibetan pilgrimage traditions were internally diverse, and so this central logic was not accepted by all. Some Tibetan writers rejected pilgrimage to certain mountains on the grounds that those mountains' ordinary appearance meant that they had no extraordinary hidden wonders, and so they were not worthy of the expense and effort of pilgrimage. Like the child who shouted that the emperor had no clothes, these objectors argued that the mountain's ordinary appearance indicated that the mountain was simply ordinary. In response, other Tibetan authors defended pilgrimage and argued that a mountain can appear ordinary while having an extraordinary form invisible to most people. For over five centuries, this debate raged over one mountain in particular: Kailash. By understanding the debate over Kailash's legitimacy, and the sometimes-surprising forms it takes, we will better understand how Tibetan thinkers understood the goal of transforming perception on pilgrimage.

Kailash, a mountain in far western Tibet, was believed by many to be a sacred mountain described in Buddhist scriptures known as Himavat, and sometimes called or associated with Kailāśa or Meru.[1] Kailash was famous for being the residence of the tantric buddha Cakrasaṃvara, as well as the site where advanced masters like Milarepa performed great deeds. However,

[1] Buddhist cosmology is very complicated, and there is no universal model on which Buddhist texts agree. Instead, there are many Buddhist texts that describe the geography of the world, more or less systematically, in different ways, and for different purposes. Each of the mountains named is at times treated as a single mountain, a mountain range, as the same as another mountain in this list, or distinct from the others. At present, Kailash—the mountain in western Tibet—is often associated with Meru, the cosmic mountain at the center of the world. However, scholars have debated how and when this identification emerged. For more on Buddhist cosmology and the history of Kailash in particular, see Eric Huntington, *Creating the Universe: Depictions of the Cosmos in Himalayan Buddhism* (Seattle: University of Washington Press, 2019), and Alex McKay, *Kailas Histories: Renunciate Traditions and the Construction of Himalayan Sacred Geography* (Leiden: Brill, 2015).

Making the Invisible Real. Catherine Hartmann, Oxford University Press. © Oxford University Press 2025.
DOI: 10.1093/9780197791585.003.0004

a scholar named Sakya Paṇḍita questioned its status as a sacred site in a text called the *Clear Differentiation of the Three Vows.* He claimed that Kailash was merely a mountain of rocks, devoid of any wonders or possible benefits to pilgrims. His condemnation of pilgrimage to Kailash launched a five-hundred-year-long debate in which dozens of commentators debated Sakya Paṇḍita's claims about the authenticity and the value of pilgrimage more generally.

This chapter will consider two interrelated questions that animated these debates: How can a mountain be considered sacred if it does not appear as such, and how can a person with ordinary perception determine its sanctity? These questions are essential to understanding this book's central question about how to see a mountain as a mandala, and answering them will shed light on Tibetan thinkers' understanding of pilgrimage, preparing us for further explorations in later chapters.

To address these questions, I will focus on a rebuttal to Sakya Paṇḍita's critique by Fourth Sharmapa of the Karma Kagyu, Shamar Chödrak Yeshe Pal Zangpo (1452–1524), titled *Settling the Issues around Himavat, Anavatapta, and the Four Rivers: The Scholar's Earring.* In it, he set out to defend Kailash's sacred status, as well as that of the lake and rivers surrounding the mountain.[2] While there are many texts written to defend Kailash from Sakya Paṇḍita's claims, Chödrak Yeshe's rebuttal specifically addresses the issue that Kailash does not look like scriptural descriptions of Himavat, making him a valuable contributor to our understanding of how to perceive and identify a holy mountain. Although Chödrak Yeshe's views do not represent the entire Tibetan pilgrimage tradition, he provides one of the most comprehensive philosophical accounts of how pilgrimage works, and so he is a useful figure to focus on.

Because this debate centers on the identity of a mountain that goes by multiple names in Sanskrit, Tibetan, and English, it is important to clarify terms. The mountain in western Tibet at the center of the debate is today most

[2] This chapter will focus on the issues associated with Kailash, but it should be said that there are also debates associated with the lakes and rivers around Kailash. There are two lakes associated with Kailash, known in Tibetan as Mapham (*mtsho ma pham*) and Lakngar (*lag ngar mtsho*). Mapham is associated with Sanskrit Anavatapta, which is described in Vasubandhu's *Abhidharmakośabhāṣya*, or Sanskrit Manasarovar, which is described in Hindu epics and Puranas. Four major rivers, described in the *Abhidharmakośabhāṣya* as the Ganga, Sindhu, Vaksu, and Sita, are said to flow from near Kailash. In modern times, these have been said to refer to the Brahmaputra, the Indus, the Sutlej, and the Karnali (an important tributary of the Ganga). However, premodern identifications of these rivers vary widely. For more on the four rivers and their various identifications over time, see McKay, *Kailas Histories*, 77–83.

commonly called Kailash. Tibetans, however, would call it Tise, Gangkar Tise, or Ribo Tise. Buddhist scriptures and treatises describe mountains named Meru, Sumeru, Kailāśa, Himavat, and Himālaya. In some texts, these mountains are clearly distinguished, and in others they are identified with one another. In some, each of these is treated like a single mountain, and in others, they are treated as mountain ranges. Each of these Sanskrit names, moreover, has its own Tibetan language equivalents. For clarity, in this chapter, I will refer to the mountain in Tibet as "Kailash" and the one mentioned in Buddhist scriptures as "Himavat." Sakya Paṇḍita asserts that the two are different, while Chödrak Yeshe claims that they are the same.

The controversy over Kailash revolves around the gap between fantastic scriptural descriptions of Himavat and the mundane appearance of Kailash. While Sakya Paṇḍita uses this as evidence that Kailash is not legitimate, Chödrak Yeshe argues that a single object can appear differently to different people, and that this explains the gap between description and appearance. He distinguishes between the extraordinary perception of buddhas, gods, and advanced masters and the ordinary perception most people use. Kailash appears extraordinary to those with extraordinary perception and ordinary to those with ordinary perception. Thus, there are multiple ways of seeing and knowing the world. Although Chödrak Yeshe values scriptural and testimonial accounts of extraordinary perception, he also recognizes the value of ordinary perception in understanding the material world and even providing clues to extraordinary ways of seeing. To perceive Kailash correctly requires both ways of seeing. Consequently, Chödrak Yeshe suggests how descriptions of extraordinary vision and ordinary perception can combine to produce co-seeing.

The Debate over Kailash

Let us begin by discussing the broader context for the texts to be examined: the debate over pilgrimage to Kailash. Throughout Tibetan history, Tibetan authors debated various aspects of the pilgrimage tradition, with some claiming that pilgrimage was a distraction from *real* practice, however that was defined.[3] The debate over Kailash initially emerged as a minor

[3] See Catherine Hartmann, "Against Pilgrimage: Materiality, Place, and Ambivalence in Tibetan Pilgrimage Literature," *Revue d'Etudes Tibétaines*, no. 65 (October 2022): 127–158.

subargument made in the context of broader debates about pilgrimage, but it eventually sparked dozens of texts and hundreds of pages worth of debate over five hundred years.[4]

Sakya Paṇḍita wrote the *Clear Differentiation of the Three Vows* around 1232 to clarify the practice of Buddhism in Tibet, which he believed had been distorted by inappropriate doctrinal innovations.[5] He wanted Tibetans to return to what he saw as more authentic and authoritative Indian Buddhist practices. As part of that overall goal, he criticized ordinary people who undertook tantric pilgrimage practices that—in his view—they were unqualified to perform. While making this point, almost incidentally, he also claimed that Kailash was not the correct mountain for tantric practitioners to visit, as it did not resemble the holy mountain its supporters claimed it was. But while this seemed a minor point to Sakya Paṇḍita, it ignited a fire that would burn for hundreds of years.[6]

In response to the *Clear Differentiation*, two main types of texts emerged: commentaries on the text by Sakya supporters and rebuttals from Kagyu objectors. It is unclear how widely these texts were read outside elite monastic settings, or the extent to which debates about the legitimacy of Kailash affected popular practice of pilgrimage, but there is at least some evidence that these debates became widely known.[7]

Within the Sakya tradition, the *Clear Differentiation* became a central pillar of monastic training, and many scholars wrote commentaries on

[4] The first scholar to document this controversy is Toni Huber, "Where Exactly Are Caritra, Devikota and Himavat? A Sacred Geography Controversy and the Development of Tantric Buddhist Pilgrimage Sites in Tibet," *Kailash: A Journal of Himalayan Studies* 16 (1990): 3–4, 121–164. It has also been discussed in an unpublished manuscript entitled "Two Early Reactions to Sa skya Paṇḍita's Rejection of the Ti se Ri bo" by Leonard van der Kuijp, which he kindly shared with me. Scholars disagree about the date this text was written, with some suggesting a date of 1230 (van der Kuijp, "Two Early Reactions," 2) and others a date of 1232 (Huber, "Where Exactly Are Caritra, Devikota and Himavat?" 126 and Jared Rhoton, trans., *A Clear Differentiation of the Three Codes: Essential Distinctions among the Individual Liberation, Great Vehicle, and Tantric Systems: The Sdom Gsum Rab Dbye and Six Letters* (Albany: State University of New York Press, 2002), 4.

[5] *Sdom pa gsum rab tu dbye ba.* Jared Rhoton has extensively studied this text, and for the most part I have followed his edition and translation choices, with some alterations made for clarity. See Rhoton, *A Clear Differentiation of the Three Codes.*

[6] Sakya Paṇḍita likely first expressed his rejection of Kailash's identification in his earlier *Gateway for Scholars* (*Mkhas pa la 'jug pa'i sgo*), written around 1220–1230 (van der Kuijp, "Two Early Reactions," 2; Rhoton, *A Clear Differentiation of the Three Codes*, 4). In this text, he takes issue with Tibetan translations of *Himālaya* and *Kailāsa*, but he does not expand on this point to criticize pilgrimage. See Sa skya Paṇḍita Kun dga' rgyal mtshan, *Rkhas pa rnams 'jug pa'i sgo zhes bya ba'i bstan bcos*, in *Sa pan kun dga' rgyal mtshan gyi gsung 'bum*, Vol. 1 (Lhasa: Bod ljongs bod yig dpe rnying dpe skrun khang, 1992), 367–501.

[7] In the 1940s, the lay pilgrim Khatag Zamyak references the debates and offers his own rebuttal to Sakya Paṇḍita. This will be discussed further in Chapter 6.

the text to help unpack its main claims.[8] Commentaries started appearing in the fourteenth century to expand on Sakya Paṇḍita's arguments about Kailash and buttress his claims.[9] However, not all Sakya commentary was universally approving, as Shakya Chokden (1428–1507) wrote several critical texts in the mid-fifteenth century which posed difficult questions about the *Clear Differentiation*. Gorampa, a contemporary of Shakya Chokden, wrote an extensive commentary on the *Clear Differentiation* and responded to Shakya Chokden's criticisms, including those about Kailash. To this day, the *Clear Differentiation* and its commentaries continue to be studied in the Sakya and Geluk traditions, meaning that Sakya Paṇḍita's criticisms of Kailash live on.

While the *Clear Differentiation* generated a great deal of favorable commentary from Sakyas, it also gave rise to myriad critical responses from the rival Kagyu school. In the first hundred years after it was written, scholars from traditions attacked in the *Clear Differentiation* mostly "chose dignified silence as the best reply,"[10] but written treatises began to appear in the mid-fifteenth century. The response by Chödrak Yeshe that forms the main subject of this chapter is one of the earliest texts that survive, although he references earlier texts by scholars that may have been written. Many more texts rebutting the *Clear Differentiation* followed by Gampo Jennga Trashi Namgyal (1513–1596?), Drukchen Pema Karpo (1527–1592), and Drikung Chungtsang Chökyi Drakpa (1595–1659). Some were independent treatises responding to the whole of the *Clear Differentiation*, but scholars also responded to the *Clear Differentiation* in passing while writing on other subjects.[11]

[8] The Sakya philosopher Gorampa (1429–1489), himself the author of a famous commentary on the *Clear Differentiation*, likened Sakya Paṇḍita's work to a "fourth pitaka." Rhoton, *A Clear Differentiation of the Three Codes*, 26.

[9] Authors included Lha btsun Bsam yas pa, Spos khang pa Rin chen rgyal mtshan, Dga' gdong pa Chos rgyal dpal bzang, and Las chen Gzhon nu seng ge. See David Jackson, "Commentaries on the Writings of Sa-skya Paṇḍita," *The Tibet Journal* 8, no. 3 (Autumn 1983): 14. Shakya Chokden also lists commentaries. See Shākya mchog ldan, *Sdom pa gsum gyi rab tu dbye ba'i bstan bcos kyi 'bel gtam rnam par nges pa legs bshad gser gyi thur ma*, in *The Works of Pen-chen Shakya mchog-lden*, BDRC W00EGS1016899, 7:7–244 (Kathmandu: Sachen International, 2006).

[10] Ibid., 27.

[11] For example, the *Flower Ornament of the Abhidharmasamuccaya* by Chomden Raltri. The latter contains what may be the very first response to Sakya Paṇḍita's rejection of pilgrimage to Kailash, one which was likely composed within seventy-five years of *The Clear Differentiation of the Three Vows* itself. See Bcom ldan ral gri, *Chos mngon pa kun las btus pa'i rgyan gyi me tog*, BDRC W24700 (No publisher, No date). Many responses to Sakya Paṇḍita also occur in commentaries to the *Single Intention* by Jigten Gompo.

Source and Approach

This chapter focuses on *Settling the Issues around Himavat, Anavatapta, and the Four Rivers: The Scholar's Earring*,[12] written by Chökyi Drakpa Yeshe Pal Zangpo (1453–1524), which defends pilgrimage to Kailash through scriptural citation and reasoning. Chödrak Yeshe was the fourth Sharmapa (*zhwa dmar pa*) of the Karma Kagyu and a prominent religious, scholarly, and political figure of his time. He composed *The Scholar's Earring* in 1504 at the request of Lowo Chodzé, the nephew of Lowo Khanchen,[13] who asked him to "clear away the doubts and expel the objections about Kailash and Mapham, about which there are various opinions and constant doubts."[14] Chödrak Yeshe takes up this challenge and uses the text to respond directly to Sakya Paṇḍita, even quoting verbatim the pilgrimage sections of Sakya Paṇḍita's text.[15]

In grappling with this text, and with the debates about Kailash, I follow Bruno Latour's methodological dictum to "follow the controversies."[16]

[12] T. *Ri bo gangs can dang mtsho ma dros pa chu bo bzhi dang bcas pa gtan la dbab pa mkhas pa'i rna rgyan.*

[13] The family trees reconstructed by Roger Jackson based on royal genealogies and histories of the Lo family show a figure named "rje blo gros rgyal mtshan" as the nephew of Glo bo mkhan chen. See David P. Jackson, *The Mollas of Mustang: Historical, Religious, and Oratorical Traditions of the Nepalese-Tibetan Borderland* (Dharamsala: Library of Tibetan Works and Archives, 1984), 120, 127, and 133. This figure is moreover said to be a monk and said to have "ascended the religious throne of his uncle" (149). This accords with Glo bo chos mdzad blo gros rgyal mtshan's name and period of activity. Jackson also apparently concurs with this identification; Jowita Kramer footnotes him as saying that this Blo gros rgyal mtshan figure is "known to have posed questions to the fourth Zhwa-dmar." See Jowita Kramer, *A Noble Abbot from Mustang: Life and Works of Glo-bo mKhan-chen (1456–1532)* (Wien: Universität Wien, 2008), 26, footnote 103.

[14] *Ti se ma pham la / sa dkar [B: bkar] grub mtha'i 'dod lugs mi gcig pa du ma zhig snga phyi bar gsum ru byung snang ba'i 'di la / dog sel rtsod spong mkhas pa rnams kyi rna ba'i rgyan du byed pa zhig bya bar rigs so zhes rgyang ring po nas bskul ba la brten te.* Chos grags ye shes, *Ri bo gangs can dang mtsho ma dros pa chu bo bzhi dang bcas pa gtan la dbab pa mkhas pa'i rna rgyan* (henceforth *Mkhas pa'i rna rgyan*), BDRC W1CZ886 (Mtshur phu dgon, No date), 19b.

[15] I consulted three editions of the *Scholar's Earring*. First was a block print comprising twenty-two folios from Tsurpu Monastery's printing house. Zhwa dmar 04 Chos grags ye shes, *Ri bo gangs can dang mtsho ma dros pa chu bo bzhi dang bcas pa gtan la dbab pa mkhas pa'i rna rgyan*, BDRC W1CZ886 (Mtshur phu, No date). Second was a later handwritten version that was put together and published in 1984 in Dharamsala. This may be based on the block print, but it contains several variant readings, some of which are helpful, particularly when the block print scan is blurred. Zhwa dmar 04 Chos grags ye shes, *Ri bo gangs can dang mtsho ma dros pa chu bo bzhi dang bcas pa gtan la dbab pa mkhas pa'i rna rgyan*, BDRC W00KG09824 (Dharamsala: Mnga' ris gzhung gces skyong khang, 1984). Third, a computer-input version that is contained in Chödrak Yeshe's *Collected Works (gsung 'bum)* was published in 2009 in Beijing. Zhwa dmar 04 Chos grags ye shes, *Ri bo gangs chen dang mtsho ma dros pa chu bo bzhi dang bcas pa gtan la dbab pa mkhas pa'i rna rgyan*, in *Collected Works of Chos grags ye shes*, BDRC W1KG4876, 6: 440–463 (Beijing: Krung go'i bod rig pa dpe skrun khang, 2009). The computer-input version differs from the other two in several minor readings, and because it leaves off an appendix that has been added to the first two texts.

[16] Bruno Latour, *Science in Action: How to Follow Scientists and Engineers through Society* (Cambridge, MA: Harvard University Press, 1987), 258.

Controversies expose rifts and force participants to say that which would ordinarily remain implicit. Many aspects of pilgrimage practice go without saying in Tibetan literature, and so it is rare to find texts that address contemporary scholars' questions directly. By tracing the specific points of contestation, I construct a philosophical account of how pilgrimage works. Although Chödrak Yeshe may be vague on certain topics—for him, much still goes without saying—the controversy provides an entry point for us to explore.

I approach this topic as an intellectual historian, and so I will focus on the arguments Chödrak Yeshe and others make, but it is also important to recognize the historical, social, and economic contexts in which these texts were written. The debates surrounding pilgrimage had significant economic and political implications, especially for the Kagyu school, which is associated with mountain pilgrimage by virtue of their connection with Milarepa. Many monasteries of the Drikung Kagyu and Drukpa Kagyu were located near mountain pilgrimage sites, and so they stood to benefit from the economic activity that accompanies pilgrimage.[17] During the course of my research, some colleagues joked that this was the real motivation behind the debates over Kailash. However, I want to take these authors' arguments seriously in their own right, rather than reducing them to window dressing for underlying power grabs.

Sakya Paṇḍita's Objections

I will start by fleshing out Sakya Paṇḍita's arguments in the *Clear Differentiation.* First, he argues that most Kailash pilgrims lack proper initiation and preparation for tantric pilgrimage. Acknowledging the tantric practice of visiting sacred sites (S. *pītha*, T. *gnas chen*), he accepts that tantric practitioners may wish to do so, but he insists that they must first have been training under a qualified master, obtained the requisite initiations, and then attained stability in their meditation practice at their own home.[18] According to Sakya Paṇḍita, tantric pilgrimage without these necessary preparations is a sham that is at best pointless and at worst actively harmful. Moreover, he

[17] For further analysis of the material and economic dimensions of pilgrimage, see Wim van Spengen, *Tibetan Border Worlds: A Geohistorical Analysis of Trade and Traders* (London: Routledge, 1999), as well as Lucia Galli, "Money, Politics, and Local Identity: An Inside Look at the 'Diary' of a Twentieth-Century Khampa Trader," in *Frontier Tibet: Patterns of Change in the Sino-Tibetan Borderlands* (Amsterdam: University of Amsterdam Press, 2019).

[18] For more on this subject, see Hartmann, "Against Pilgrimage," 137–138.

rejects nontantric pilgrimage entirely, arguing that the Buddha did not teach about pilgrimage in the sutras.[19]

However, the main objection to pilgrimage that will concern us in this chapter is his claim that Kailash is not Himavat,[20] because Kailash lacks the characteristics (*mtshan nyid*) that scriptures say Himavat has.[21] Therefore, *even if* pilgrims have the proper initiations for tantric pilgrimage, pilgrimage to Kailash is wrong because it is not the correct mountain. Sakya Paṇḍita cites descriptions found in Buddhist scriptures and important scholastic treatises, including the *Abhidharmakośabhāṣya*,[22] the *Lokaprajñapti*, the *Viśeṣastava*, the *Bhaiṣajyavastu*, the *Avataṃsaka*, and the *Kalacakra Tantra*.[23] These texts describe Himavat as having rose-apple trees, five hundred elephants and arhats dwelling there, as well as a golden canopy known as "Asura's Flank."[24] They often describe Lake Anavatapta as fifty *yojanas* wide with banks made of jewels. Four major rivers, including the Ganges, flow from animal mouths near the lake, carrying jeweled sands, and circling Himavat seven times. By contrast, Sakya Paṇḍita writes of Kailash, "not even elephants are found there—how much less a canopy of gold or rose-apple trees!"[25] It is a straightforward argument: Himavat is said to have rose-apple trees, Kailash lacks rose-apple trees, so Kailash is not Himavat. He also cites prophecies from the

[19] Ibid., 135–136.

[20] Sakya Paṇḍita also makes parallel arguments about Tsari/Caritra, which is another mountain mentioned in Buddhist scriptures and believed by many to correspond to a mountain in Tibet. However, he spends much more time on Kailash/Himavat, so I will mostly focus on that.

[21] It is not clear if Sakya Paṇḍita himself went to see these sites, or whether he is referring to general knowledge about how they look. I have not found any references to Sakya Paṇḍita visiting Kailash in any biographical writing.

[22] This work has been the primary influence on Tibetan cosmological thinking, even though other works present conflicting cosmologies. The passages about Himavat are in 3:48–57. For Sanskrit, consult Leo M. Pradhan, ed., *Abhidharmakośabhāṣyam of Vasubandhu* (Patna: K.P. Jayaswal Research Institute, 1975), 158–162. For Tibetan, consult *Chos mngon pa'i mdzod kyi bshad pa*, in Bstan 'gyur (dpe bsdur ma), BDRC MW1PD95844 (Beijing: Krung go'i bod rig pa'i dpe skrun khang, 1994–2008), Vol. 79, 356–361. For English, consult Leo M. Pruden, trans., *Abhidharmakosabhasyam* (Berkeley: Asian Humanities Press, 1988–1990), Vol. 2, 452–456. For more on the influence the *Abhidharmakośabhāṣya* has had on cosmological thinking, see Huntington, *Creating the Universe*, 30–46.

[23] The *Kalacakra Tantra* has been less influential in terms of cosmology, possibly because of its dizzying complexity and because of the difficulties integrating it with Abhidharma cosmology. See Huntington, *Creating the Universe*, 46–54. For the relevant passages about cosmology, including references to Meru, Kailash, and Himalaya (but not Himavat), see Khedrup Norsang Gyatso, *Ornament of Stainless Light: An Exposition of the Kalachakra Tantra*, trans. Gavin Kilty (Boston: Wisdom Publications, 2001), 80–84. Note that these passages treat Meru, Kailash, and Himalaya as separate places, and the latter two as regions or ranges rather than as a single mountain.

[24] S. *āsurapārśva*. See Siglinde Dietz, "A Brief Survey on the Sanskrit Fragments of the Lokaprajñaptiśāstra," *Annual Memoirs of the Otani University Shin Buddhist Comprehensive Research Institute* 7 (1989): 84.

[25] Rhoton, *A Clear Differentiation of the Three Codes*, 136–137.

Kalacakra Tantra and the *Abhidharmakośabhāṣya*[26] to argue that humans without magical powers cannot reach Himavat.[27] However, his main argument is visual: Kailash does not match the descriptions of Himavat found in Buddhist scriptures and scholastic treatises, and so it is not a legitimate pilgrimage place.

Sakya Paṇḍita preemptively addresses possible objections to his arguments that Kailash is not Himavat. For example, he considers the idea that these differences might be due to poetically exaggerated praises of Himavat in the scriptures that are not meant to be taken literally. He also considers the idea that the visual difference might be due to the passage of time. After all, if scriptures were written at the time of the Buddha, it may be the case that the Buddha's blessed presence made the site appear glorious, but that his absence has resulted in a decline in the mountain's beauty. Buddhists often claim that the world is at its best when a buddha is present, and then that the world deteriorates from there. However, he rejects both claims, arguing that the differences between the present Kailash and the scriptural Himavat are too large to attribute to poetic license or change over time.[28]

Chödrak Yeshe on Ordinary and Extraordinary Perception

Now we will turn to Chödrak Yeshe's response in the *Scholar's Earring*. He writes that his text will answer the following questions: "Are Himavat and Kailash the same or different? . . . Since there are all sorts of inconsistent

[26] Sakya Paṇḍita cites a Tibetan translation of the *Abhidharmakośabhāṣya* that reads: "Those without magical powers cannot travel there" (*der ni rdzu 'phrul mi ldan pas / bgrod par bya ba min*). However, some critics argue that the passage says, "It is difficult for people without magical abilities to go there" (*der ni rdzu 'phrul dang mi ldan pa'i mi 'gro bar dka'o*), and that *difficult* is different from *impossible*. The Sanskrit term *durgamanaṃ* literally means "difficult to go," but it can also be used contextually to mean "impassable, inaccessible, unattainable." Sakya Paṇḍita's interpretation is supported by several Tibetan translations of the *Abhidharmakośabhāṣya*, including the *Dpe bsdur ma* edition, as well as Xuenzang's Chinese translation (無由能至), and Zhendi's Chinese translation (非人所行處。若有通慧人乃可得行). Louis de la Vallée-Poussin's translation into French also has this reading. See Vasubandhu, *L'abhidharmakośa de Vasubandhu*, trans. Louis de La Vallée Poussin (Paris: Geuthner, 1923), 233. Other scriptural sources, such as the *Bhaiṣajyavastu*, also make it clear that nonmagical beings cannot go to Himavat. See *'Dul ba bzhi*, in *Bka' 'gyur (dpe bsdur ma)*, BDRC W1PD96682 (Beijing: Krung go'i bod rig pa'i dpe skrun khang, 2006–2009), 656–657.

[27] Sakya Paṇḍita does not discuss this, but we should note that the *Kalacakra Tantra* and the *Abhidharmakośabhāṣya* differ in how they describe the structure of the world. For more on these differences, see Huntington, *Creating the Universe*, 47–48.

[28] *Snyigs ma'i dus kyi shugs brtas pas / cung zad ngan par 'gro srid kyi / thams cad 'khrul par ga la srid.* Sakya Paṇḍita, *Clear Differentiation of the Three Vows*, ed. Jared Rhoton (Albany: State University of New York Press, 2002), 312, verse 340.

appearances (*snang ba*) of that holy place where there are said to be rose-apple trees, elephant border guards, and Siva's residence, what should be trusted?"[29] In other words, given that Kailash looks different from scriptural descriptions of Himavat, is Kailash Himavat or not?

Acknowledging that he is part of a lineage of Kagyu defenders of Kailash, he examines other arguments made in favor of Kailash. Some Kagyu commentators, including Jigten Gompo[30] and Chökyi Drakpa,[31] argued that Kailash's present appearance is different from its original state due to the passage of time, though Sakya Paṇḍita had already rejected this argument. They claimed that, although ordinary humans cannot see wondrous Himavat at present, if an ordinary human were somehow transported back to the time of the Buddha, they could look at Kailash and see Himavat. Other Kagyu authors attempted to reconcile the difference between scriptural description and present appearance of Kailash by arguing that there really is no difference between the two. They argued that the scriptural descriptions are both true at present. For instance, Chödrak Yeshe cites one unnamed "Rinpoche" as saying, "If one objects that the width of Anavatapta, which is said to be fifty *yojanas*, is not seen in this [Mapham], that is not a problem. Below the small lake which is visible, there is a larger one underneath."[32] In other words, this Rinpoche tries to reconcile what scriptures say with ordinary perception

[29] *Chu bo chen po bzhi gang las 'bab ces pa dang / gangs can dang ti se / ma dros pa dang ma bam [B: paM] gcig gam tha dad yin shes dang / phyogs de dag tu shing 'dzam bu dang / glang po che sa srung gi gnas dang / lha dbang phyug chen po sogs 'khod pa'i gnas la mi mthun pa ci rigs su snang ba las [B: /] yid rton du 'os pa ni gang yin.* Chos grags ye shes, *Mkhas pa'i rna rgyan*, 1b.

[30] Jigten Gompo is a significant figure in the history of pilgrimage to Kailash, as he was among the first to send disciples there. In a section where Chödrak Yeshe reviews various views on Kailash, he includes Jigten Gompo's writings on Kailash. These predate the *Clear Differentiation*, but they clearly anticipate Sakya Paṇḍita's concerns. Jigten Gompo's argument is a combination of change over time and different perceptual realms. According to him, a god and a human looking at the same mountain would see different things, and this difference is also due to the change over time. See Chos grags ye shes, *Mkhas pa'i rna rgyan*, 11a.

[31] Although Chökyi Drakpa writes his defense of Kailash after Chödrak Yeshe's, I draw special attention to it as the next chapter will focus on a text written by Chökyi Drakpa. His argument relies on decline over time, and he argues that if present-day lamas could replicate the Buddha's teachings and presence, the sacred places would regain their previous qualities. *De deng sang med la ri bo gangs can dang mtshos ma dros pa sogs kyi yon tan yang sngar yod pa de sangs rgyas kyi rdzu 'phrul gyis zhabs rjes bzhag pa sogs kyi tshe byin rlabs byung ba yin la / deng sang med pa'i phyir dang / yang sangs rgyas kyis chos gsung pa'i tshe yon tan gang byung ba de deng sang 'byung na / sangs rgyas kyis chos gsung pa'i tshe chos nyan pa po la lta dang lha min byang sems klu dang grul bum sogs 'gro ba mtha' dag 'byung bar bshad mod / deng sang bla ma rnams kyis chos gsung pa'i tshe'ang de nyid 'byung bar gyur na gangs can ti se dang mtsho ma pham pa sogs kyi yon tan yang sngar kho na ltar yod dgos la.* Chos kyi grags pa, *Gzhan gyi rgol ngal 'joms pa'i legs bshad lung rigs smra ba'i mgul rgyan*, 408.

[32] *Rje spyan snga rin po ches grub mtha' chen mor / ma dros pa'i rgyar dpag tshad lnga bcu mnyam par bshad pa 'di la mi snang ngo snyam na [B: /] skyon med de mtsho'i mthong rgya chung ba 'di'i 'og tu rgya che ba yod pa yin zhes gsungs pa ni.* Chos grags ye shes, *Mkhas pa'i rna rgyan*, 18b.

by saying that there is a larger fifty-*yojana* lake just underneath the smaller lake on the surface. This larger underground lake is at least in principle visible to ordinary perception but is blocked from vision by virtue of being underground.

These arguments—the decline over time argument and the underground lake argument—both agree with Sakya Paṇḍita's premise that scriptural descriptions can and should be observable in ordinary perception. Sakya Paṇḍita's argument assumes that Kailash's visual appearance (as agreed to by common knowledge) is sufficient grounds for deciding that Kailash is not Himavat, and so these responses by other Kagyu authors offer alternate explanations for the difference of appearance. However, Chödrak Yeshe takes a different approach and rejects Sakya Paṇḍita's premise that ordinary humans can see everything described in scripture. Instead, he argues that humans generally *cannot* see what scripture describes, and so Sakya Paṇḍita should not conclude that Kailash is not Himavat simply because ordinary beings do not see it as such.

To do so, Chödrak Yeshe distinguishes between two *ways* of seeing: ordinary perception and extraordinary perception. He defines the ordinary (*thun mong*) as that which is within the realm of direct perception (*mngon sum gyi yul du gyur pa*) for ordinary beings and the extraordinary (*thun mong ma yin pa*) as that which is beyond the realm of direct perception (*mngon sum gyi yul las 'das pa*) for ordinary beings. Most humans possess ordinary perception, while nonhuman beings like gods or *nagas* have extraordinary perception. Humans with advanced supernatural powers gained through meditation (S. *ṛddhi*, T. *rdzu 'phrul*) may also develop extraordinary perception. These powers, which have been discussed throughout the history of Buddhism, are said to involve higher perception (S. *abhijñā*, T. *mngon shes*), which includes the divine eye (*lha'i spyan*) and the divine ear, both of which perceive far more than their ordinary analogues. They also include magical powers, such as the ability to fly, the ability to walk through solid objects, and other such powers. Extraordinary perception may also include "pure perception" (*dag snang*), which as we have already discussed, involves seeing objects in totally pure and perfected forms. Chödrak Yeshe describes how those with the divine eye (*lha yi mig*) and purified people (*rnam dag mi*) routinely see aspects of reality that are invisible to ordinary people.[33]

[33] He writes: "On this point I say: if one does not see the noble beings, gods, asuras, and nagas who live in each individual area, how could one see the noble beings, gods, king of nagas, and great elephant of Himavat and Anavatapta? Wise people do not say that the things seen by purified people,

So humans mostly have ordinary perception, but a small number of advanced masters have extraordinary perception.

Chödrak Yeshe summarizes his view in the phrase "One thing [appears differently], because of different minds,"[34] which he reiterates throughout the *Scholar's Earring*. This means that beings with different minds, karma, and perceptual abilities perceive differently. As such, what someone sees is sometimes more of a function of their capacities than of the thing being seen. Ordinary human beings have ordinary perception, and so see things in an ordinary way, and special beings, such as gods or spiritual masters, have extraordinary perception, and so see things in an extraordinary way. The same object can thus appear differently to different kinds of beings.

Chödrak Yeshe uses the Ganga as an example to illustrate how ordinary and extraordinary perception lead to different ways of seeing. For instance, scriptures say that Ganga flows from the mouth of an elephant, while ordinary people see it as emerging from "mountain ridges that are some distance from [Kailash and] Anavatapta."[35] He argues that extraordinary beings see it the former way, and ordinary beings the latter.[36] This is like the classic Buddhist example of a god, a human, and a hungry ghost looking at a river. The god sees the river as full of ambrosia, the human sees it as full of water, and the hungry ghost sees it as full of blood and pus. Chödrak Yeshe maintains that although one material thing (*dngos po'i rdzas gcig*) underlies

the divine eye, or beings of the same class are lies because they themselves do not see the wealthy homes and possessions of yaksas, gods, nagas, and asuras, but only [see] the trees, springs, cliffs, and mountains which are labelled as the dwellings of non-humans. Intelligent people on the side of honesty, take note of this!" *'Dir smras pa / so so'i yul du bzhugs pa'i 'phags pa dang / lha dang lha min klu rnams ma mthong na / gangs can ma dros gnas kyi 'phags pa dang / lha dang klu rgyal glang chen ji ltar mthong / mi ma yin pa'i gnas su gdags pa yi / shing dang chu mig brag dang ri rnams las / gnod sbyin lha klu lha min longs spyod dang / khyim gyi 'byor pa ci yang ma mthong bas / de rnams ris mthun tshogs dang lha yi mig / rnam dag mi yis mthong ba brdzun pa zhes / 'di na shes dang ldan pas mi smra ltar / gzu bo'i blo can rnams kyis mkhyen par mdzod.* Ibid., 18b–19a.

[34] Chödrak Yeshe's statement, literally, "One thing, because of many minds" (*dngos gcig yid ni tha dad phyir*), may seem elliptical, but its meaning becomes clear as he develops his account of perceptual difference. The Tibetan phrase "one thing, because of many minds" includes the separative particle *ni* after the word for mind (*yid*), emphasizing the fact that individual mental difference is the key factor for differing perceptions.

[35] Ibid., 15b.

[36] *Chu bo de rnams kyang rdzu 'phrul med pa'i mis mngon sum gyi yul las 'das par brjod na / lung sman gyi gzhir ganga gang las 'bab pa'i mtsho de nyid ma dros pa yin par gsungs pa'i gleng gzhi dang mthun pa'i chu bo de'i sgur bcwa brgyad yod pa'i 'gram du yul dbus dang / sindhu 'bab pas de'i yul dang / si ta'i byang du sham bha la yod ces mdo sngags las bshad pa thams cad rdzu 'phrul med pa'i mis mngon sum du mthong ba dang shes par mi rung ngo.* Ibid., 14a. He also gives the example of Shambala, which he says is described in scriptures and yet entirely invisible to ordinary people.

these different perceptions, it can appear different due to the different types of minds observing it.

How Scripture Challenges Ordinary Perception

Buddhist scriptures, Chödrak Yeshe argues, provide reliable accounts of the world, but they do so according to a particular point of view. Different scriptures, moreover, may convey different points of view, so it is important for people to interpret scripture correctly by being mindful of that point of view. He organizes the *Scholar's Earring* by first analyzing "trustworthy sources" (*yid ches pa'i khungs*), by which he means scriptures and scholarly treatises, then turning to the analysis of other scholars, and finally his own position.[37] He quotes from at least eighteen Buddhist texts and treatises about Himavat and Anavatapta.[38] Although these accounts sometimes conflict with one another, Chödrak Yeshe attributes these differences to the varying perspectives of the beings who wrote them. For example, he writes that:

> The distinguishing features of the Lake Anavatapta and the four rivers are [that they are] huge and have sands of jewels, foundations of precious gems, are adorned with lots of flowers of divine trees, and so forth. However, [such features] are not seen by different kinds of human beings. Rather [they] are pronounced in the *Avataṃsaka* according to what appears in the realm of direct perception of the Lord of *nagas*, his retinue, and those with equal merit.[39]

[37] *Yid ches pa'i khungs rnam par dgong pa / mkhas grub rnams kyi bzhed pa la dpyad pa / rang gi 'dod pa brjod pa ste / gsum gyis shes par bya'o.* Ibid., 1b.

[38] Chödrak Yeshe cites numerous Indic texts from a variety of genres, including sutra, vinaya, abhidharma, Mahayana sutras, tantric texts, *stotra* poetry, commentaries, and treatises. These texts include the *Bhaiṣajyavastu*, Vinaya (he does not specify which text within the larger category of Vinaya), *Smṛtyupasthāna*, *Mahāmāyūrī*, *Cakrasaṃvara Tantra*, *Hevajra Tantra*, a commentary on the *Mahāmāyūrī*, the *Avataṃsaka*, *Prajñāpāramitā*, *Sutra of the Questions of King Anavatapta*, *Aryasanghata*, *Abhisamayalamkara*, *Lokaprajñapti*, *Karamaprajñapti*, *Yogācārabhūmi*, *Abhidharmakośabhāsya*, *Viśeṣastava* and its commentary, *Sutra of Maitreya's Prophecies*, and *Kalacakra Tantra*.

[39] *Mtsho ma dros pa dang chu bo bzhi tshad rgya che ba rin po che'i bye ma la gnas pa dang / rin po che'i sa gzhi dang shing ljon pa lha rdzas kyi me tog du mas mdzes pa la sogs pa'i khyad par gyi chos rnams / mi'i 'gro ba ris mi mthun gyis mthong bar ma gyur mod / klu'i bdag po 'khor bcas dang skal ba mtshungs pas mngon sum gyi yul du snang ba de ltar phal po che las bka' stsal te.* Chos grags ye shes, *Mkhas pa'i rna rgyan*, 17a.

On this interpretation, scriptural descriptions of Himavat and other places are accurate, but they describe the world from a godly perspective rather than from a human perspective. He writes that the *Avataṃsaka Sutra*, for example, describes Himavat and Anavatapta as it appears to the king of the *nagas*, the *Lokaprajñapti* describes them as it appears to the king of elephants Supratistha, and the *Abhidharmakośa* describes them as they appear to gods or humans with magical powers.[40] All of these are accurate accounts of reality, but because they are from a nonhuman and extraordinary point of view, most humans cannot see them. Only highly realized humans who have merit equal to that of the gods, and thus have those gods' extraordinary perception, can see Himavat as the scriptures describe it.

Chödrak Yeshe thus maintains that scriptures are important sources of knowledge about holy places. They provide access to perspectives beyond the direct perception of most humans, revealing wonders that would otherwise remain hidden. Such knowledge, he also suggests, can be provided by the testimony of advanced masters who possess extraordinary perception. These figures, such as Milarepa or Padmasambhava, can see the wonders hidden to most people. Were humans to rely merely on their own perception and knowledge, they would be limited by their own delusion. Scripture is thus necessary to break humans from their habitual and deluded patterns of seeing the world.

By providing these accounts of wonders beyond ordinary perception, Chödrak Yeshe suggests that scriptures can aid in transforming one's perception by enabling people to see wonders beyond their direct perception. For example, Chödrak Yeshe suggests that some people will learn these teachings (*thos pa*, literally meaning "hearing," but in this context meaning learned or having received oral instructions on the teachings) and so be able to see the pure lands of the Buddha's enjoyment body and supreme emanation body directly (*mngon sum du mthong*).[41] He does not elaborate, but he clearly links hearing teachings or scriptural descriptions and then being able to see these extraordinary wonders for oneself. He thereby suggests that scriptures aim at transforming perception.

In that same vein, different scriptures are written for different kinds of people. This reflects the different capacities of the target audiences, and it helps the target audience move toward a more advanced way of seeing.

[40] See Chos grags ye shes, *Mkhas pa'i rna rgyan*, 17a and 17b.

[41] *Rgyal ba longs spyod rdzogs pa dang mchog gi sprul pa'i sku'i zhing khams mngon sum du mthong zhing thos par gyur pa na'ang.* Ibid., 16a.

Chödrak Yeshe writes that the *Avatamsaka Sutra* is written for learned people, and so it describes "inconceivable numbers of manifold worlds that are fundamentally and in essence adorned with flowers."[42] By contrast, scriptures such as the Abidharma, sutras, and vinaya are written for those with minimal wisdom (*shes pa sla ba*), and they describe Kailash in terms of how gods and *nagas* see it.[43] Both scriptures provide an extraordinary account that pushes the visual capacities of the target audience and denaturalizes their ordinary perception, but the specific extraordinary vision described differs. That is because scriptures are in accordance with the type of person they are trying to transform. Chödrak Yeshe argues that this understanding helps resolve potential contradictions between scriptural texts, and it helps us to understand *why* these texts describe the extraordinary nature of Kailash.[44] We might say that these scriptural descriptions help educate the imagination, encouraging people to think beyond the ordinary experience of their everyday lives.

That different scriptures are aimed at different kinds of people and provide different perspectives on Kailash explains the apparent contradiction between the ordinary appearance of Kailash and the wondrous descriptions of Himavat. Once one realizes that they appear differently to different perceivers, there is no contradiction. Chödrak Yeshe writes, "The four rivers and their surroundings, which are [both] ordinary and extraordinary, are actually one substantial, physical thing (*dngos po'i rdzas gcig*). However, because individuals with magical powers have a superior way of seeing, and beings without magical powers have an inferior way of seeing, [the extraordinary appearance of Himavat] is either said to be in the realm of direct perception or outside the realm of direct perception."[45] With this understanding, readers can understand how scripture functions to provide knowledge inaccessible to ordinary perception, and to properly interpret what might seem like contradictions.

[42] *Phal chen la sogs par / gzhi dang snying po me tog gis brgyan pa'i 'jig rten gyi khams rab 'byams bsam gyis mi khyab pa'i rnam par gzhag pa bstan to.* 16a.

[43] *Gang dag mchog gi sprul pa'i sku'i zhing stong gsum mi mjed kyi 'jig rten tsam yin par mthong zhing shes par sla ba rnams la / theg pa thun mong ba'i 'dul ba dang mdo sde dang / mngon pa gsungs pa las / bye brag tu ri rab kyi tshad dbyibs mdog mi 'dra ba ni lha dang lha ma yin sogs mthong ba tha dad pa'i ngor mdzad nas bshad la.* Ibid., 16a–b.

[44] *Mdo rgyud las byung ba rnams sangs rgyas kyi zhing sbyong tshul dang / gdul bya'i snang ba mthun par byung ba yin pa'i dbye ba shes na 'gal ba med par rtogs nus pa yin te.* Ibid., 16b.

[45] *De 'dra'i thun mong dang thun mong ma yin pa'i chu bo bzhi po 'khor bcas rnams dngos po'i rdzas gcig la / mthong tshul mchog dman gyis / rdzu 'phrul ldan mi ldan so sos mngon sum gyi yul las 'das pa dang / mngon sum gyi yul du gyur pa'i tha snyad 'jog pa yin.* Ibid., 14a.

How Ordinary Perception Can Support Scripture

Even as Chödrak Yeshe distinguishes between ordinary and extraordinary perception, he also suggests that they are not entirely separate. Humans with ordinary perception can find evidence that points to and confirms the extraordinary vision of Kailash. The *Scholar's Earring*, then, is not an argument that ordinary people with ordinary perception cannot know anything about the world and should thus listen to their religious superiors. Rather, it shows how ordinary perception can be *combined* with the testimony of advanced perceivers to gain knowledge about the world.

As such, he bases much of his argument that Kailash is Himavat on ordinary perception of material reality. For example, as defense of the claim that the Ganga flows from Lake Manasarovar near Kailash, he cites that the people who have gone there have seen it.[46] Sakya Paṇḍita had claimed that Kailash is not Himavat because Kailash does not have the qualities Himavat is said to have. However, one of those qualities is that the Ganga flows from the lake near Himavat. As such, Chödrak Yeshe repeatedly returns to the fact that the Ganga is said to flow from Kailash, a fact that all observers agree to, to argue that Kailash is Himavat. If ordinary beings' perception is utterly flawed and unreliable, such testimony would be completely irrelevant, but Chödrak Yeshe treats it as a key point of evidence in Kailash's favor. At various points in the text, he refutes Sakya Paṇḍita by citing the direct perception (*mngon sum*) of ordinary perceivers.[47] Elsewhere, he writes that Kailash is proven (*grub pa*) to be Himavat, "because of the proof (*tshad ma*) of people who have gone there together along the north-south route, and because of the proof (*tshad ma*) of people who have gone to where the Ganga flows from Mapham."[48] In using the technical term "means of knowledge" or "proof" (T. *tshad ma*, S. *pramāna*) to characterize this eyewitness testimony, Chödrak Yeshe draws on the long-standing Buddhist position that direct perception is, along with inference, one of only two valid means of knowledge.

[46] *Gangā yang ma pham las 'bab par der phyin pa'i mis tshad mas grub pa'i phyir.* Ibid., 13a. Here, he is approvingly quoting the thirteenth-century writer Chomden Raltri. However, he does not entirely agree with Chomden Raltri. Chomden Raltri seems to think that the Himavat of the *Abhidharma* is not the same as the Himavat of the *Kalacakra*, and that they have been wrongly conflated, a position which leads Chödrak Yeshe to refer to Chomden Raltri as "perpetuating the problem." *Bcom ldan ral gris . . . skyon gzung zhing.* Ibid., 13a.

[47] *Mngon sum dang 'gal ba'i tshul.* Ibid., 15b.

[48] *Mnyan yod dang ti se ni lho byang thad mnyam du phyin pa* [B: omits *phyin pa*] *der phyin pa'i mi'i tshad mas grub pa dang / gangA yang ma pham las 'bab par der phyin pa'i mis tshad mas grub pa'i phyir.* Ibid., 13a. See also Bcom ldan Ral 'gri, *Chos mngon pa kun las btus pa'i rgyan gyi me tog.*

He relies not only on his own perception of the mountain but also on common knowledge based on many people's perception of it. For instance, he refers to that which is known in the world (*'jig rten du grags pa*), that which is established in common perception (*mthun snang du grub pa*), and that which is ordinary (*thun mong*) and exists in the direct perception of people in the world. These phrases refer to the common ordinary perception that humans have. Each of these perceivers has their own flaws and limitations, but together, their consensus view of reality is reliable. Chödrak Yeshe also writes that "the *Bhaiṣajyavastu* explains how the other three rivers flow from [Anavatapta], and that is a common perception (*mthun snang*) for most worldly beings (*'dzam gling pa phal cher la*),"[49] indicating that the three rivers besides the Ganga which flow from Anavatapta do not appear totally differently to each being based on their individual karma, but rather, *for the most part*, human beings are similar enough that the rivers appear to them collectively in roughly the same way. In another passage, he refers to the Ganga as it is generally perceived as "this one which is known to ordinary and worldly people."[50] He takes this general knowledge, built on ordinary perception, as a valid way of knowing about Kailash.

At another point, Chödrak Yeshe concedes a point for the sake of argument to his imaginary opponent, saying, "Let us allow that people without magical abilities cannot travel the seven hundred *yojanas* [to Himavat] and so do not see the rivers circling the lake clockwise seven times and so forth."[51] Even then, he writes, "Since we are certain that the four rivers flow through Jambudvipa from there, and at a time when it is universally known to people these days and [Kailash and Himavat] are recognized as a single [mountain], all of this debate is entirely pointless. That's it!"[52] Again, he is pointing not to the visual perception of a highly realized person, but rather a kind of common reality about which most people agree. In this case, that is the fact that the four rivers flow from the area around Kailash.[53] This consensus of

[49] *Lung sman gyi gzhi las / chu bo gzhan gsum de las 'bab par bshad cing / 'dzam gling pa phal cher la mthun snang du gyur pas so.* Ibid., 14a.

[50] *'Jig rten pa dang thun mong du grags pa 'di.* Ibid., 17b.

[51] *Ji ltar zhe na / gangs mtsho dang chu bo bzhis mtsho la g.yas su lan bdun bskor ba sogs kyi gnas dpag tshad brgya phrag bdun lhag pa de / rdzu 'phrul dang mi ldan pas mi bgrod cing mi mthong du chug.* Chos grags ye shes, *Mkhas pa'i rna rgyan*, 13b–14a.

[52] *De las chu bo bzhi gling 'di'i phyogs so sor 'bab par ni nges na / ding sang gi skye bo rnams yongs su grags pa dang ngos 'dzin gcig par byas pa'i tshe / rtsod pa thams cad don med pa 'ba' zhig tu zad do.* Ibid., 14a.

[53] Definitively identifying the four rivers described in premodern sources with contemporary rivers, and then assessing whether Chödrak Yeshe is right or wrong on these identifications, is a task that is beyond the scope of this book. There are several rivers that flow from the area around Kailash, and many of them eventually feed into the major rivers of Asia, including the Ganges. However, each

ordinary perception yields real knowledge about the world, even if it cannot see the extraordinary nature of the mountain directly.

Chödrak Yeshe thus understands scriptural descriptions about the extraordinary nature of pilgrimage sites *and* ordinary perception to both be valid ways of knowing about Kailash. Scriptural accounts expand the limited capacities of ordinary humans, and ordinary human perception can confirm aspects of extraordinary descriptions. Combined, they provide a formidable defense of Kailash. As Chödrak Yeshe writes, "It is necessary to make great effort [to combat] that which is contradictory to both scripture and what is known in the world."[54] When scripture and ordinary perception support each other, it is very difficult to overturn them.

Pilgrimage as Conventional

Chödrak Yeshe's defense of Kailash received praise but also raised the hackles of at least one reader, who wondered if Chödrak Yeshe had inadvertently undermined the entire basis of pilgrimage practice.[55] Lowo Chodzé, a member of a powerful family from Mustang,[56] responded to Chödrak Yeshe's defense of Kailash with follow-up questions about the doctrinal and philosophical foundations of pilgrimage practice. These questions prompted Chödrak Yeshe to write an additional text that he appended to the initial text to comprise the *Scholar's Earring*.[57]

of these major rivers has many tributaries and sources. For more on the identification of the four rivers in both premodern and modern sources, see McKay, *Kailas Histories*, 77–83. My own interest is on the way Chödrak Yeshe draws on consensus perception to make his arguments.

[54] *Zhes lung dang 'jig rten du grags pa gnyis ka dang 'gal ba lhur len dgos par 'gyur ro.* Ibid., 14a.

[55] Lowo Chodzé opens his response to Chödrak Yeshe's initial text with effusive praise, writing, "If anyone hears this *Scholar's Earring*, which is your good explanation, their mind will be charmed as if by the song of a celestial musician. If anyone experiences the meaning, it is like tasting ambrosia. So it is an amazing object (*gnas*) which delights scholars!" *Shes brjod nas / 'on kyang de nyid la zhib tu dpyad pas / bstan bcos sdom pa gsum dang / deng sang gi phal mo che sgrogs pa'i 'dogs pa'i* [B: *dogs pa'i*] *gnas rnams ni legs par sel* [B: *sol*]. Ibid.

[56] Lowo Chodzé is the nephew of the more well-known Lowo Khanchen (Glo bo mkhan chen, 1456–1532). See David P. Jackson, *The Mollas of Mustang*, 120, 127, and 133. This figure is moreover said to be a monk and said to have "ascended the religious throne of his uncle" (149). This accords with Glo bo chos mdzad blo gros rgyal mtshan's name and period of activity. Jackson also apparently concurs with this identification; Jowita Kramer footnotes him as saying that this Blo gros rgyal mtshan figure is "known to have posed questions to the fourth Zhwa-dmar." See Kramer, *A Noble Abbot from Mustang*, 26, footnote 103.

[57] Note that Beijing edition of the *Scholar's Earring* omits Chödrak Yeshe's response to Lowo Chodze.

The central question that Lowo Chodzé raised was whether Kailash is actually real or not.[58] When Chödrak Yeshe defended Kailash, he claimed that one thing was perceived in different ways because of different minds. But Lowo Chodzé worried that the idea of one thing (*dngos gcig*) being perceived differently by different beings implies that there is some external object that is causing each of these perceptions. This may seem like a strange objection, but both Lowo Chodzé and Chödrak Yeshe are committed to an understanding of Buddhism that asserts that people experience the world as if they are in a dream. According to that understanding, people see objects and think that those objects are real, but like the dreamer who dreams of a forest, what they see is a product of their own mind, rather than the direct result of seeing some externally real thing. Lowo Chodzé is asking whether Chödrak Yeshe thinks that pilgrimage mountains are externally real.[59] If Chödrak Yeshe claims that they are externally real, then that contradicts his Buddhist philosophical positions. But if Chödrak Yeshe claims that they are not externally real, then what is the point of pilgrimage? Why should pilgrims go through the time and expense of pilgrimage if the mountains they are visiting are not even real?[60]

[58] Lowo Chodzé also questioned why Chödrak Yeshe used both Mahayana and non-Mahayana texts in defending Kailash, as it raised questions about his account of reality. He writes, "Furthermore, if you explain [the nature of Kailash/Himavat] having posited the nature of things in the way of the small vehicle [i.e., as actually existent], it is difficult to consider a scripture such as the *Mahāyānasaṃgraha* as authoritative (*tshad ma*). In that case, if one establishes [the nature of things] based on the Abhidharmakośa along with the commentary [because you do not consider Mahayana scriptures authoritative], it seems to me that the classification of Himavat and the lakes is a topic which is still difficult to explain." *Yang theg pa chung ngu'i tshul la dngos po'i gnas lugs sor gzhag nas 'chad pa'i tshe / theg bsdus kyi lung de lta bu tshad mar 'gyur ba dka' zhing / de ltar na / mdzod rtsa 'grel gzhir gzhag na / gangs ri mtsho gsum gyi rnam gzhag da dung 'chad pa dkar ba'i gnas su bdag gis dgo bas* [B: *go bas*]. Ibid. In response, Chödrak Yeshe affirms that Mahayana texts such at the Mahāyānasaṃgraha are held to be superior to non-Mahayana texts such as the *Abhidharmakośa*, but he argues that the so-called Hinayana works are not necessarily wrong, but rather simply need more interpretation. Therefore, he argues that he is justified in taking the *Abhidharmakośa* as a basis for knowing about the layout of Himavat, Anavatapta, and the rivers.

[59] Lowo Chodzé cites the *Mahāyānasaṃgraha* and other Yogacara texts to support the idea that differing perceptions of the same "thing" demonstrate that there is no "thing," or object (T. *don*, S. *artha*) at all. Instead, what humans take to be external objects are representations (*ākāra*) produced by one's own karma and mind.

[60] Are you asserting or not asserting that the snow mountain does not exist, as is taught in the context [of the *Mahāyānasaṃgraha*]? If you are asserting [that the mountain does not really exist], then there are no sacred sites which can be used [to train] in the system of the best inner secret tantra. If you are asserting [that the mountain does exist], what is the meaning of that scripture [i.e., the *Mahāyānasaṃgraha*]? *Zhes pa'i skabs gnas* [B: *nas*] *bstan pa'i don la ma grub pa'i gangs ri bzhed dam mi bzhed / bzhed na gsang sngags nang gi dam pa dang sbyor rgyu'i / gangs ri'i rnam bzhag med par 'gyur / mi bzhed na lung gi don du gang du btsal.* Chos grags ye shes, *Mkhas pa'i rna rgyan*, 20a. He makes this argument with specific reference to the *Mahāyānasaṃgraha*, a fourth-century Yogacara text by Asanga, the elder brother of Vasubandhu. This is unexpected because the *Mahāyānasaṃgraha* has received very little attention in Tibetan writing. It may speak to the text's relative popularity in the time and place where Lowo Chodzé was writing, but this is still quite

Chödrak Yeshe responds to Lowo Chodzé's question by asserting that "there is no contradiction between there being no truly existent external objects and there being holy places (*gnas*) which are unsurpassed purifiers."[61] In other words, he maintains that pilgrimage places are not—in a permanent and external sense—*real*, but that pilgrimage is still worthwhile in that pilgrimage to places like Kailash purifies and benefits pilgrims.

To argue his point, Chödrak Yeshe first explains the two truths doctrine in Buddhism, which distinguishes between conventional and ultimate truth. First, there is conventional truth, which is the truth people perceive through ordinary everyday experience. It is the level of reality that humans normally interact with, and it includes the physical world, human identities, social institutions, and philosophical concepts. Conventional truth, however, often conceals or obscures deeper realities. For instance, a person might see a tree and think of it as a solid, independent object, but under deeper analysis, the person would recognize that the tree is made up of constantly changing particles and is inextricable from the air, sunlight, water, soil, and microorganisms that sustain it. In everyday conversation, it is useful to refer to trees, cars, and other objects as real, but people should remember that these objects are *conventionally* real and would look very different under deeper analysis. Ultimate truth, however, is the ultimate nature of reality beyond ordinary perceptions and concepts. It is beyond explanation in words, but Tibetan Buddhists may sometimes characterize it as emptiness (meaning that all things are impermanent, interdependent, and empty of inherent existence) or as luminous, blissful awareness. These two truths, moreover, are inseparably united, two sides of the same coin. This understanding, Chödrak Yeshe asserts, will clarify any confusion that people have about pilgrimage.

He asserts that pilgrimage places do not exist ultimately (*don dam*).[62] Special beings who give accounts of the mountain's extraordinary appearance are not describing how the mountain *really exists* in ultimate reality. Chödrak Yeshe argues that there is no such thing. He cites a well-known commentary on the *Kālacakra Tantra* to say that "Ultimately, the world lacks

mysterious. The *Mahāyānasaṃgraha* itself does not discuss pilgrimage or holy places, nor do any of the major commentaries I have consulted reference these topics. The issue for Lowo Chodzé, at any rate, seems to be the *Mahāyānasaṃgraha*'s position on whether objects exist externally and whether there is any common basis for different beings' perceptions.

[61] *Bla med dag sbyor gyi / gnas dang phyi don bden grub dag / 'gal ba med par 'chad nus tshe.* Ibid., 20a.

[62] Ibid., 21a.

measured size" and instead, even conventional reality changes "according to the merit and sin of beings."[63] Instead, these beings have a different perspective on conventional reality. Correspondingly, for Chödrak Yeshe,[64] pilgrimage mountains do not exist external to human minds. He revisits example of the god, human, and hungry ghost looking at the river, and each seeing it in a different way.[65] He acknowledges that this example might lead someone to assume that there is one "thing" (T. *dmigs pa, don*)[66] underlying these three different perceptual experiences, but he advises caution, noting that Buddhist philosophical texts resist that conclusion. Instead, this example proves that "consciousness has no objective support."[67] What people see and what they experience is a function of their karma, expectations, and concepts, rather than indicative of externally existing objects.

As such, the entire practice of pilgrimage takes place within the conventional realm. He writes, "if you know the intention, the *Scholar's Earring* does not repudiate the fact that external objects (*phyi don*) are not truly established and [the idea that] external objects (*phyi don*) exist merely in conventional terms."[68] Kailash, like everything else humans interact with daily, is conventionally real. This may be surprising to readers who, remembering how conventional truth is said to conceal or obscure ultimate truth, interpret conventional truth to be illusory or merely false. However, we should remember that a conventional truth is nonetheless *true*. People can get it

[63] *Don dam par ni 'jig rten gyi khams la tshad gzhal du med de sems can rnams kyi bsod nams dang sdig pa'i dbang gis so.* Ibid., 17a. Original in John Ronald Newman, "The Outer Wheel of Time: Vajrayāna Buddhist Cosmology in the Kālacakra Tantra," PhD Diss., University of Wisconsin, 1987, 472.

[64] He writes, "Therefore, one should not take as separate the understanding that the object doesn't exist out in the world and that it doesn't exist really or ultimately and so forth." *Des na don la ma grub pa'i zhes don gnas la'am don dam la sogs go ba gzhan du gzung bar mi bya'o.* Ibid., 21a. That these two positions are connected reflects Chodrak Yeshe's Yogacara tendencies.

[65] *Chu klung gi dngos po lar rang gi las kyi rnam par smin pa'i dbang gis / yi dwags kyis rnag khrag la sogs pas gang bar mthong ba dang / de nyid la dud 'gro nya la sogs pas gnas kyi blos gnas par byed pa dang / mi rnams kyis ni mngar ba dang ba dang bsil ba'i chur rtog cing khrus byed do / 'thung ngo / der 'jug go / nam mkha' mtha' yas skye mched la snyoms par zhugs pa'i lha rnams kyis ni nam mkhar mthong ste gzugs kyi 'du shes rnam par gshig go.* Ibid., 21a–b.

[66] These are technical terms that correspond to the Sanskrit terms *ālambana* and *artha* respectively. The term *ālambana*, which literally means support but is often translated as percept in the context of philosophy of perception, indicates that which is the cause of perceptual cognition. The term *artha* also has many meanings, but in the context of philosophy of perception, it generally means the intentional object of perception, the (external) object that we take ourselves to be perceiving. In denying the existence of both an *ālambana* and an *artha* as the support of consciousness, Chödrak Yeshe is affirming the general Yogacara point that what we consciously experience is produced by our own mind and not necessarily externally existing objects.

[67] *Des na rnam par shes pa dmigs pa med pa nyid du 'gyur ba yin no.* Ibid., 21a.

[68] *De ltar shes na mkhas pa'i rna rgyan gyi tshigs su bcad pas phyi don bden par ma grub pa dang / tha snyad tsam du phyi don mi 'gog pa dang.* Ibid., 22a.

wrong about conventional reality, as when someone claims that fish drive cars, but they can also get it right, as when they say that fish live in water. Chödrak Yeshe continues that "the entire presentation of the holy places, such as the twenty-four [holy places] in the impure human body, is in terms of conventional truth."[69] The tantric traditions of sacred geography that identify locations on earth as holy, as well as those that identify locations in the human body as holy, are conventionally true. As such, their claims that these holy places function to purify those who visit them are conventionally true as well.

If pilgrimage is all about conventional reality, then what do we do with the claims that humans see the mountain in an ordinary way and gods see it in an extraordinary way? In this case, we must not confuse the divine perception of Kailash as ultimate reality. Gods' extraordinary perception of the mountain is also conventional truth. If we recall that conventional truths describe the everyday appearance of the material world, divine perception of Kailash as extraordinary is still an everyday conventional reality. It is a different conventional reality than most humans perceive, but that is because different social groups have different sorts of conventions. There are thus multiple conventionally true ways to see and describe reality, depending on what set of conventions are relevant. Some may be better or more helpful than others—when a hungry ghost sees a river as full of pus, they suffer, and it would be better if they saw it like a god sees it, as full of ambrosia—but both ways of seeing yield conventional truth—that all things are impermanent and interdependent. Chödrak Yeshe's account, then, is that there are multiple conventionally true ways to see the mountain. One way is ordinary in that it is visible to ordinary humans. Another way is extraordinary in that it is usually invisible to ordinary humans.

Even as Chödrak Yeshe emphasizes that pilgrimage mountains are totally conventional, he also asserts that conventional truth and ultimate truth are both separate *and* fundamentally indivisible.[70] As such, the ultimate reality that is self-arisen gnosis (*rang byung ye shes*)[71] pervades conventionally real objects such as the holy places. It "is inborn, blissful, endowed with supreme qualities and emptiness, and takes on the form of the animate and

[69] *Gnas kyi rnam gzhag kun tshang ba / kun rdzob bden pa'i dbang du mdzad.* Ibid., 20b.

[70] *Bden gnyis so so dang dbyer med.* Ibid., 20b.

[71] Note that here Chodrak Yeshe is offering a positive account of ultimate reality. Many Madhyamaka thinkers would usually present negative accounts of ultimate reality as being empty of inherent essence, but Chodrak Yeshe is showing his Yogacara leanings here.

inanimate [in] the three realms."[72] The essence of the holy places, he argues, is a division (*dbye ba*) of this self-arisen gnosis, and the holy places themselves "are taught as the embodiment of the four bodies, ten grounds, and five paths."[73] The holy places are thus conventionally real in terms of their appearance, but they also partake in the nature of ultimate reality (albeit no more than anywhere else does). Moreover, they are *taught* (*bstan*) as the embodiment of the Buddha's teachings. People who visit the mountain understand it to represent something that points to ultimate truth. As such, while pilgrimage is conventional, he declares that this understanding of pilgrimage "unites the two truths—it is spoken of as the holy places such as Himavat."[74]

Chödrak Yeshe concludes by repeating a statement from the original text of *The Scholar's Earring* about the relationship between appearance and emptiness, and then elaborates on how the appearance of pilgrimage places affects the mind which experiences them. He writes:

> Having contemplated these intentions, [it is clear that] although phenomena (*chos*) have no essential nature and are of one essence (*ro*), just like illusion-like misleading conventions, they are experienced as inseparable appearance and emptiness. The holy places (*gnas*) are wonders that teach the dharma (*dam chos ston par mdzad rnams ya mtshan gnas*).[75]

In other words, Chödrak Yeshe is suggesting that even though everything humans see and perceive is empty of essential nature, the fact of emptiness does not mean that nothing appears. Instead, the appearance of the world with all its trees, lakes, and mountains is inseparable from emptiness. Yes, appearances are empty, but they still *appear*. And some appearances, like that of Kailash and other pilgrimage places, have beneficial functions like teaching the dharma. Chödrak Yeshe thus lays out his case for why pilgrimage

[72] *De yi rang bzhin dri ma med / lhan skyes 'gyur med bde chen dang / stong nyid rnam kun mchog ldan pa / khams gsum brtan g.yo'i rnam pa can*. Ibid., 20b.

[73] *De nyid sa bcu lam lnga dang / sku bzhi'i bdag nyid can du bstan*. Ibid.

[74] *'Di ni bden gnyis zug 'jug don / gangs can la sogs gnas su gsungs*. Ibid., 20b.

[75] *Dgongs pa 'di rnams la bsams nas / chos rnams rang bzhin med par ro mnyam yang / kun rdzob 'khrul pa sgyu ma ji bzhin du / snang stong dbyer med legs par thugs chud nas / dam chos ston par mdzad rnams ya mtshan gnas*. Ibid., 21b. This translation is somewhat hesitant, because it is unclear what function *gnas* is playing in the sentence. I have taken it to refer to holy places, but *ya mtshan gnas* might also indicate a nominal phrase meaning "a topic to be wondered at" or as a verb indicating "exists as wondrous." In any of these cases, the subject is clearly the holy mountain, so the difference does not amount to much.

places like Kailash can benefit pilgrims even though they do not exist in any ultimate way.

According to Chödrak Yeshe, these benefits are multiple. He describes holy places as "unsurpassed purifiers" (*bla med dag sbyor kyi gnas*)[76] that can remove defilements and impurities. In addition, pilgrimage is accessible to all, even to those who do not understand abstract philosophy. He writes that pilgrimage to holy places is "free of the conceptual elaborations of the causal path and fruit, regardless of the type of individuals—low, middling, and supreme."[77] Holy places do not require the conceptual complexities of the causal path and are therefore easier to understand. Thus, unlike Sakya Paṇḍita's view of holy places as elite sites for highly trained initiates, or of certain tantric commentators' suggestion that pilgrimage is *only* for childish or inferior beings,[78] Chödrak Yeshe claims that the holy places are for people at any level of realization, including those who are low, middling, or supreme.

Another benefit is that pilgrimage promotes the cultivation of faith (*dad pa*). We have already seen how pilgrimage is repeatedly associated with faith. Chödrak Yeshe does not discuss this very much, but he does suggest that seeing Kailash—even if it is an illusory conventional appearance—promotes faith in the dharma. He writes:

> Here's how it should be put: from the very moment something appears, it is empty of truly established essence. One experiences the dawning of an appearance, but it is illusory, in accordance with emptiness. [When, for instance, one sees Kailash,] the mind becomes faithful with regard to the teaching of the true dharma of conjoined emptiness and interdependent arising.[79]

The text does not even say explicitly what causes the mind to become faithful. However, given the context, it is reasonable to think that he is talking about the appearance of Kailash. We have also seen pilgrimage tied to faith in the *Mahāparinibbāṇa sutta* and will see how faith recurs in many Tibetan

[76] Ibid., 20a.

[77] *Rgyu lam 'bras bu'i spros dang bral / de tshul gang zag dman pa 'bring / mchog gi dbye bas gnas rnams kyang.* Chos grags ye shes, *Mkhas pa'i rna rgyan*, 20b.

[78] Some Tibetan objectors to pilgrimage did argue that pilgrimage was only for childish beings. See Hartmann, "Against Pilgrimage," 134–138.

[79] *Snang dus nyid nas rang bzhin bden grub pas stong la / stong bzhin du sgyu ma lta bu'i snang ba shar ba thugs su chud de / stong dang rten 'byung zung 'jug gi dam chos ston pa la sems dad par gyur zhes smros so.* Ibid., 21b.

writings about pilgrimage. All of them suggest that there is something about seeing physical places, layered as they are with narrative and meaning, that promotes faith in a way that abstract concepts cannot.

Conclusion

This exploration of Chödrak Yeshe's response to the controversy over Kailash has provided a rare glimpse into how philosophers like Chödrak Yeshe thought pilgrimage worked. His separation between ordinary and extraordinary perception, and reliance on both as providing knowledge about Kailash, inspired the idea of co-seeing that runs throughout this book. Further, it helps us recognize the theory of mind, landscape, and perception that facilitates the transformation of perception. This theory of mind and landscape may or may not have been explicitly conscious to ordinary pilgrims, but it likely shaped their expectations—and therefore their experiences—nonetheless.

This chapter has shown that the debate over Kailash centered on issues of perception and appearance. Sakya Paṇḍita and Chödrak Yeshe are both clearly working with the problem of perceptual difference. Why do scriptures describe Himavat one way, but our ordinary senses tell us something else? Sakya Paṇḍita uses the difference between scriptural Himavat and ordinary perceptions of Kailash to argue that Kailash is not Himavat, but Chödrak Yeshe develops a different argument. Faced with objections about Kailash's appearance, Chödrak Yeshe leans into the fact that Kailash does not look like how scriptures describe it. Far from being a reason to discredit Kailash, for him, this discrepancy between ordinary perception and scriptural description is to be expected. He believes the mountain's extraordinary nature is concealed from ordinary perception, making it hidden from most pilgrims.

In defending Kailash, Chödrak Yeshe draws on both ordinary perception and testimonies of others' extraordinary perception. Many scholarly accounts of Tibetan pilgrimage suggest that sacred geography schema overlay the landscape, such that the physical landscape, and ordinary perception of it, is totally overruled. However, Chödrak Yeshe does not consider ordinary perception totally flawed, or to be abandoned. It yields a particular point of view that can be limited in certain arenas but is useful in others. In other words, Chödrak Yeshe both maintains that ordinary human perception is deeply flawed, and that ordinary human perception tells us true things about the empirical world. He suggests that both divine perception—which humans can access though scripture and potentially develop themselves—*and* ordinary perception are important if the goal is to see Kailash/Himavat correctly. These two ways of seeing the mountain are as different as a heap of jewels and a pile of rocks, but both ways of seeing can and must work together to construct correct understanding of the world. Pilgrimage, as a practice that engages ordinary perception of the physical world, is crucial to this process.

Chödrak Yeshe upholds the goal of learning to see the mountain's extraordinary nature, although he is vague about what that means. At different points, he references learned people who can see an extraordinary vision of the mountain directly[80] and people with merit equal to that of the gods being able to see the mountain as extraordinary,[81] but it is not entirely clear what these beings see. He describes some of them as seeing the mountain as the Buddha's enjoyment body, as a pure land, or as the various wondrous descriptions provided in scriptures. (Only once does he describe it as a mandala.)[82] Despite the ambiguity, Chödrak Yeshe endorses the transformation of perception and acknowledges the diverse ways this might occur. There is not one way to see the extraordinary nature of a mountain like Kailash, but instead multiple ways to break through ordinary perception and learn to see the world differently. All these fall into the idea of co-seeing—seeing it in multiple ways at once.

Most pilgrims—Chödrak Yeshe implies—will not be able to see the extraordinary nature of the mountain and will instead have the experience of trying and failing to see it. For these pilgrims, they may see the mountain with ordinary perception and imagine the extraordinary vision—described in scripture and pilgrimage guides—that they cannot see themselves. This case counts as co-seeing as well, in that the pilgrim "sees" the landscape in one way with their ordinary eyes and in another in their mind's eye. And while this is a kind of failure, it is nonetheless a productive one. It denaturalizes ordinary perception as the single way to see the world, and it suggests that there is something that lies beyond. In future chapters, we will explore practices of seeing that engage pilgrims' perception and build up their experience of those wonders as real, but the initial step is the recognition of the failure to see it as spiritually advanced beings do.

80 Ibid., 16a.
81 Ibid., 17a.
82 Ibid., 18b.

Chödrak Yeshe's account also sheds light on our overall question of how pilgrims come to experience the extraordinary nature of the pilgrimage site as real and present. In Chödrak Yeshe, we see two important features that Tanya Luhrmann and others have identified as facilitating real-making. First, he presents an account of how the mind, landscape, and perception are deeply entangled. When pilgrims look at the world around them, what they see reflects both the external landscape and their own mind, blurring the boundary between external and internal. Second, he presents an account of an extraordinary world that lies outside the direct perception of pilgrims and must instead be imagined. The extraordinary world described in scriptures is, in important ways, both internal to and external to the pilgrim, in that pilgrims must imagine it, and that it is asserted to be just outside the pilgrim's perceptual capacity. The extraordinary world is thus *in-between*. These qualities create the conditions within which pilgrims can come to interpret this extraordinary in-between landscape as physically present. How do they do so? This process requires deliberate practice—and so in the second half of this book, we will turn our attention to the practices of seeing that facilitate these kinds of experiences.

4

Opening Doors to Sacred Realms

Chökyi Drakpa's Visionary Transformation

Even though Tibetan pilgrimage traditions center the goal of transforming perception, vanishingly few people in the historical record claim to have personally achieved the ability to look at a mountain and see it as a mandala. In 1618, however, Rigdzin Chökyi Drakpa (1595–1659), an important leader in the Drikung Kagyu, claimed to have obtained a direct perception of a mountain as the sixty-two-deity mandala of Cakrasaṃvara. By doing so, moreover, he claimed to have opened the doors (*sgo phye*) of this mountain, called Gyangme, and thus to have effectively founded a new site for pilgrimage. This chapter will explore Chökyi Drakpa's account of his visionary transformation—as contained in a work he wrote called *Guidebook to Gyangme: Vajradhāra's Feast*[1]—to understand how this text imagines the transformation of Chökyi Drakpa's perception, the transformation of Gyangme into a pilgrimage place, and how accounts like Chökyi Drakpa's make the ordinarily invisible landscape of sacred places real and present for future pilgrims.

The chapter will make three main claims. First, *Vajradhāra's Feast* models an idealized transformation of perception on the part of Chökyi Drakpa. It shows the practices of seeing he uses to skillfully shift between ways of seeing, look past surface appearances, and ultimately cultivate co-seeing so that he can see the mountain as a mandala. Second, *Vajradhāra's Feast* models an idealized transformation of Gyangme into a holy mountain. It shows how Chökyi Drakpa's actions forge a lasting interpenetration between the extraordinary nature of the site as Cakrasaṃvara's mandala and the ordinary nature of the site as it appears to everyday perception. This makes the extraordinary, numinous power of the site available to

[1] Chos kyi grags pa, *Rgyang me'i gnas yig rdo rje 'dzin pa'i dga' ston*, in *Collected Works of Chos kyi grags pa*, BDRC W22082, 2: 457–477 (Kulkhan: Drikung Kagyu Institute, 1999).

Making the Invisible Real. Catherine Hartmann, Oxford University Press. © Oxford University Press 2025.
DOI: 10.1093/9780197791585.003.0005

pilgrims, even if they cannot see the mountain as a mandala themselves. Third, taking a step back from the internal logic of the text, narratives like *Vajradhāra's Feast* are part of what makes the sacred power of pilgrimage sites like Gyangme real for people. Pilgrims visiting these sites hear these stories, and they experience the landscape as full of meaning even if they themselves cannot see it as a mandala. In this way, *Vajradhāra's Feast* and texts like it are part of the construction of sacred space. In brief, this chapter will show how *Vajradhāra's Feast* tells a story about how perception can transform, tells a story about how a place can transform, and tells a story that transforms a place.

I read *Vajradhāra's Feast* not as a transparent account of what actually happened, but rather as an idealized narrative that participates in the broader *imaginaire* of Tibetan mountain pilgrimage. That is, *Vajradhāra's Feast* tells a story that shapes cultural imagination about what is possible on pilgrimage. Later pilgrims will rarely be able to transform their perception in the way Chökyi Drakpa does, but their experience of pilgrimage will be shaped by the model he lays out nonetheless. As such, it is important for an intellectual history of pilgrimage to understand the internal logic of texts such as *Vajradhāra's Feast*, without getting sidetracked trying to assess the truth or falsehood of Chökyi Drakpa's claims. Once we understand this internal logic, and how it shapes the *imaginaire* of pilgrimage, then we can try to understand how it affects the external world.[2]

This chapter will proceed first by providing background on the person, place, and text that forms the basis of our analysis, as well as on the broader phenomenon of "opening doors" in Tibetan pilgrimage. It will then give a brief summary of *Vajradhāra's Feast* (a full translation can be found in the Appendix). Next it will analyze the practices of seeing that Chökyi Drakpa undertakes to transform his perception and then theorize how these actions make Gyangme into a sacred place. The chapter concludes by considering how virtuosos like Chökyi Drakpa envision new worlds and tell stories that make the invisible real for future pilgrims.

[2] *Vajradhāra's Feast* is also a *claim* by Chökyi Drakpa. He is claiming to be the kind of person who can open a holy place and who is thus worthy of high status and authority.

Background

Textual Source

This chapter focuses on Chökyi Drakpa's *Guidebook to Gyangme: Vajradhāra's Feast*, a text of twenty folio sides included in Chökyi Drakpa's *Collected Works*.[3] The work narrates Chökyi Drakpa's pilgrimage to the holy mountain of Gyangme in the first person and tells the story of how he becomes able to see it directly as the mandala of Cakrasaṃvara and thus "opens the door" of the mountain for later pilgrims. He gives the text the title of *Vajradhāra's Feast*, indicating that the text is meant for tantric practitioners.[4] He tells this story, he says, to exhort pilgrims to visit the site and to describe the benefits of going there.[5]

This work is notable because it is one of a relatively small set of purportedly first-person descriptions of opening the doors of a holy place by a historical figure. Most descriptions of how the doors of holy places were opened are contained in pilgrimage guides (*gnas yig*) or different historical texts (*lo rgyus*), but these are most often third-person accounts held to be written by others long after the time the opening occurred. Chökyi Drakpa's work is the earliest example I have found of a first-person account written by someone who claimed to have personally opened the doors of a holy mountain.

I have consulted the only version that seems to be available. The text is computer-input, and it was published by the Drikung Kagyu Institute in India in 1999. It seems likely that this version is based on a block print or manuscript version of the text, but I have thus far been unable to acquire a copy of the original text.

[3] 'Bri gung chung tsang Rig 'dzin Chos kyi grags pa, *Rgyang me'i gnas yig rdo rje 'dzin pa'i dga' ston*.

[4] *Vajradhāra* literally means "one who holds a *vajra*" and generally refers to a tantric buddha named Vajradhāra. Vajradhāra, also called Mahāvajradhāra, is considered by many Tibetan Buddhist schools, including the Kagyu school to which Chökyi Drakpa belongs, to be the supreme primordial Buddha. Vajradhāra is an important figure in the *Cakrasaṃvara Tantra*, which is significant insofar as Chökyi Drakpa will ultimately achieve a direct perception of Gyangme as the mandala of Cakrasaṃvara. See David Gray, *The Cakrasaṃvara Tantra* (New York: American Institute of Buddhist Studies, 2007). Vajradhāra can also be a respectful term for tantric practitioners, and so the title may refer to the text being a feast for the tantric practitioners who read it. It is unclear which meaning of Vajradhāra is intended.

[5] Chökyi Drakpa titles his work a *gnas yig*, indicating that it is a guide for pilgrims. This genre will be discussed further in Chapter 5. He also mentions that he intentionally wrote it to be easy to understand, indicating a general audience, and describes the benefits for future pilgrims in detail. See *Rdo rje 'dzin pa'i dga' ston*, 469. Chökyi Drakpa's text is somewhat unusual in that it relies on first-person narration of his experience there. For the most part, *gnas yig* are written in a third-person voice.

Chökyi Drakpa likely wrote *Vajradhāra's Feast* in the earth-horse year of 1618. The text's colophon does not include a date of composition, but in the text, he mentions the horse year and clearing away the upcoming obstacles of his twenty-fifth year, which suggests that his travel to Gyangme likely happened when Chökyi Drakpa was twenty-four.[6] Chökyi Drakpa's autobiography's supports this date—the autobiography describes him "seeing many wondrous signs" at Gyangme, and it refers readers to the *Guidebook to Gyangme: Vajradhāra's Oral Instructions.*[7] This passage in the autobiography lacks an explicit date but occurs not too long after a mention of the fire-snake year of 1617, supporting a dating of 1618 for *Vajradhāra's Feast.*[8]

About Chökyi Drakpa

Chökyi Drakpa (1595–1659), also known as Kunkhyen Rigdzin Chödrak, is an important figure in the history of the Drikung Kagyu, a lineage founded by Jigten Sumgön (1143–1217) and based around Drikung Thil Monastery north of Lhasa. His father, Chogyal Rinchen Phuntsok (1547–1602), was the lineage holder of Drikung, but when he passed away, the single line of lineage holders branched into two lines. Chökyi Drakpa became the first Chungtsang of the Drikung Kagyu, and his elder brother Gyalwang Konchog Rinchen (1590–1654) became the first Chetsang.[9] To this day, Drikung Chungtsangs remember Chökyi Drakpa as the founder of their lineage.

Chökyi Drakpa wrote voluminously on a variety of subjects, including philosophy, medicine, ritual, hagiography, and a long autobiography. One recurring theme, however, is place and pilgrimage. The Drikung Kagyu school maintains long-standing associations with mountain pilgrimage because of its founder Jigten Sumgön's affinity for the practice. Tibetan tradition remembers Jigten Sumgön as one of the first masters to send his disciples to practice in the mountains of Kailash and Tsari. Chökyi Drakpa embraces

[6] The thirteenth, twenty-fifth, and thirty-seventh years are all often considered "obstacle years," which are unlucky for Tibetans. Note that Tibetans consider themselves one year old on the day of their birth.

[7] *Rgyang me'i gnas yig rdo rje 'dzin pa'i zhal lung.* Ibid., 147.

[8] Ibid., 139.

[9] *Che* and *chung* mean "large" and "small," respectively.

this affinity for pilgrimage, went on many pilgrimages himself, and wrote several texts on the subject.[10]

About Gyangme

Chökyi Drakpa's work is a pilgrimage guide to Gyangme and of the site Sarma Yangdzö located within Gyangme. Perhaps surprisingly, not much is known about this site beyond what Chökyi Drakpa writes about it. It is located, he says, in eastern Tibet, in upper Dokham, in the valley of Ngö (*rngod*). There is a valley by this name about midway between Kongpo and Chamdo in Kham, and a mountain called Tashi that is said to contain many holy places, including a cave, so this seems like a likely site.[11] Ngö is also cited in some works as the location of a village called A la rong that is the birthplace of the Fourth Karmapa Rolpé Dorje, but it is not well known as a contemporary place of pilgrimage. In Kathog Situ's *Pilgrimage Guide to Central Tibet*, written in late 1918 to 1920, Kathog Situ describes visiting Ngö. He mentions a lake island (*rngod rgya mtsho gling*) and a monastery named A re Monastery (*rngod a re dgon*) but does not describe them in detail and does not mention a place named Gyangme or Sarma Yangdzö.[12] I have not found other written sources on Gyangme or Sarma Yangdzö.[13]

It is possible, then, that although Chökyi Drakpa promoted Gyangme, and claimed it as a holy site, it did not become an important pilgrimage center. We can only speculate about why this is so, but one guess might be that only a generation after Chökyi Drakpa opened the doors of Gyangme, the Gelukpa sect headed by the Fifth Dalai Lama became ascendant, leading to the conversions of many monasteries in the area and possibly overshadowing a Kagyu-affiliated site like Gyangme.

[10] These include a polemical response to Sakya Paṇḍita's attack on Kailash's legitimacy, and he also wrote works about the visions he has at various holy places, praises to specific holy places, and guidebooks to holy places.

[11] Kelsang Lhamo, personal communication, March 2023.

[12] KaH thog si tu Chos kyi rgya mtsho, *Gangs ljongs dbus gtsang gnas bskor lam yig nor bu zla shel gyi se mo do*, BDRC W27524 (Chengdu: Si khron mi rigs dpe skrun khang, 2001), 40.

[13] There are works about a site named Sarma Yangdzö that is at Tsari, but these seem to be entirely unrelated to the place discussed in this text.

Opening the Doors of the Holy Place

Chökyi Drakpa's account is an instance of the important trope of "opening the doors" (*sgo phye*) of a holy mountain.[14] Chökyi Drakpa never explains this term—for him, it goes without saying because he can assume that readers have the relevant cultural knowledge[15]—but we should pause to unpack what it means so that we have the necessary context to interpret this text. My account of the standard model for opening holy mountains by necessity generalizes a complex and internally diverse tradition, and not all mountains follow this model.[16] Nevertheless, it provides a context for reading *Vajradhāra's Feast.*

Accounts of opening the doors of a holy mountain begin with the association of a particular mountain with a primordial tantric deity, who is said to dwell (*gnas*) in the mountain. For example, the three major pilgrimage mountains of Tsari, Kailash, and Lapchi are often said to be the body, speech, and mind of Cakrasaṃvara. Such identifications draw on practices and narratives found in Indian Buddhist tantras, especially the *Cakrasaṃvara Tantra*, which describe certain places being the sites of epic battles between tantric deities and evil demons. Cakrasaṃvara's triumphs in these battles and consequent residence at the site imbue it with great potency.

[14] Note that this discussion focuses on holy mountains. Holy places such as Lhasa that are part of the built environment generally do not have to be opened. However, much of this discussion about opening the doors is largely coextensive with the logic of opening the doors of hidden lands (*sbas yul*).

[15] Chökyi Drakpa is not alone in using the notion of a holy place having doors without explaining what that means—for most Tibetan accounts, it simply goes without saying. I have yet been unable to locate any source that analyzes or explains this concept in an abstract or theoretical way. The following, then, is my own understanding of what it means to open the doors of the holy place. It is based on my experience reading many works that have made use of the concept. Other scholarly descriptions of opening the doors can be found in Toni Huber, *The Cult of Pure Crystal Mountain: Popular Pilgrimage and Visionary Landscape in Southeast Tibet* (Oxford: Oxford University Press, 1999), 25–26; Katia Buffetrille, "The Pilgrimage to Mount Kha Ba Dkar Po: A Metaphor for Bardo?" in *Searching for the Dharma, Finding Salvation: Buddhist Pilgrimage in Time and Space: Proceedings of the Workshop "Buddhist Pilgrimage in History and Present Times" at the Lumbini International Research Institute (LIRI), Lumbini, 11–13 January 2010*, ed. Christoph Cueppers and Max Deeg, 197–220 (Lumbini: Lumbini International Research Institute, 2014), 198; and Katia Buffetrille, "The Great Pilgrimage of A Myes RMa-Chen: Written Traditions, Living Realities," in *Mandala and Landscape*, ed. A. W. Macdonald, 75–132 (New Delhi: D.K. Printworld, 1997), 89.

[16] For example, we find mountains that do not record one specific door-opener, such as in Buffetrille, "The Great Pilgrimage of A Myes rMa-Chen," 89, or mountains such as Tsari, where there are multiple doors associated with different cardinal directions and opened at different times.

Next, a mythologized holy master like Padmasambhava or Milarepa practiced there in the legendary past. Their practice confirms and reinforces the sacred nature of the mountain and gives it the additional power of these legendary masters' presence. However, the identification of the site with a tantric Buddha and the presence of legendary masters do not on their own make the mountain a pilgrimage place. At this point, the potency of the site is too intense—it attracts fierce demons who are hostile to outside visitors and who block those visitors from accessing the site's sacred power. It is only when a spiritually advanced master—like Chökyi Drakpa claims to be—opens the doors that ordinary pilgrims can access the blessings there. To do so, the aspiring master must have advanced tantric ritual training to overpower the demons currently living at the mountain. He (it is always a he) must also have the right karmic lot (*skal*) or karmic connections (*rten 'brel*), the proper motivation, and often must have been foretold by prophecy.

To open the doors, the tantric master must perform two tasks. First, he must ritually gain control over the mountain by taming (*'dul ba*) the fierce local spirits, place protectors, demons, and *dakinis* and converting them into dharma protectors. Such beings would ordinarily pose a threat to pilgrims seeking to visit the holy place, but the ritual master tames them, thus allowing ordinary pilgrims into the site.[17] Second, the tantric master must recognize the physical landscape of the holy place as the divine mandala of the presiding tantric deity. Using skillful perception and ritual aids, the tantric master can see past the outer appearance of the mountain and see that inwardly it is actually the palace of Cakrasaṃvara.[18] This act opens the doors of the site, allowing pilgrims to visit and benefit from the blessings there.[19]

[17] Narratives of opening the sacred place may also involve the tantric master establishing dominance over representatives from rival sects or religions.

[18] It is not entirely clear how these two aspects of opening the doors of the holy place are related. Some accounts of opening the holy place, especially those by Lelung Shepé Dorje, focus mostly on taming the local spirits, while others, like that of Chökyi Drakpa, focus more on obtaining a direct perception of the mountain as mandala. Others, like the legends of opening the doors of Tsari studied by Toni Huber, have both elements. See Huber, *The Cult of Pure Crystal Mountain*, 26.

[19] Why, we might ask, is this activity characterized as the opening of doors? Sometimes, when asking Tibetan informants what "opening the doors" means, they would gloss it as starting or founding the pilgrimage site. Pushing further, I would ask people: What were the doors, exactly? What were they made of? And what exactly opened them? They would invariably laugh, with some commenting on my foreigner's way of thinking (*phyi rgyal pa'i bsam blo*). Lobsang Shastri, personal conversation, March 12, 2019.

Summary of *Guidebook to Gyangme: Vajradhāra's Feast*

A full translation of *Guidebook to Gyangme: Vajradhāra's Feast* can be found in the Appendix. A brief summary, however, will help to frame my analysis of the work.

Chökyi Drakpa begins *Vajradhāra's Feast* by praising Gyangme's good qualities and describing how he decided to go there. Upon his arrival, he extensively describes the physical features of the site, along with their geomantic significance. Gyangme is a liminal space that both bristles with hostile demons—Chökyi Drakpa writes that those without the correct karma will be instantly killed there[20]—and contains signs of the dharma, including images of deities, auspicious syllables, and hidden treasures (*gter ma*).[21] At one point, Chökyi Drakpa and his companions see rainbows swirl around Chökyi Drakpa, and he vanishes for a few moments, temporarily becoming part of the site itself, rather than a mere visitor to it.[22] The group travels past various lakes and caves and eventually arrives at a lake at the base of the mountain.

There, the local spirits signal their discontent at this foreign presence and trigger an earthquake. This terrifies the group, but Chökyi Drakpa withdraws from the chaos into a meditative state. He has a vision of a monk who identifies himself as the master Padmasambhava and tells Chökyi Drakpa that he is destined to open the doors of Gyangme. Chökyi Drakpa demurs, fearing that he is too weak to succeed where others have failed. But Padmasambhava assures him that if he recognizes that external difficulties are merely projections of his own mind, he will succeed. Chökyi Drakpa accepts and resolves to open the doors of the holy place. This delights Padmasambhava, who gives Chökyi Drakpa directions for how to reach the top of the mountain.

The next morning, Chökyi Drakpa and his companions begin their ascent. Throughout, the rocks and cliff faces are covered in images of gods and auspicious symbols, which Chökyi Drakpa takes to be a good sign. Chökyi Drakpa performs rituals and reveals hidden treasures. They continue traveling upward, finding more caves and images. Some of the group have a vision

[20] He writes that "those without the appropriate karmic destiny have incorrect views, and so will have their life-veins cut instantly by wisdom *dakinis* and karma protectors just for going there." *Skal med rnams log lta skyes pa'i mthus der phyin pa tsam gyis ye shes kyi mkha' 'gro dang las kyi mgon po nas srog rtsa skad cig nyid la gcod par byed pa.* Ibid., 454.

[21] These are objects or texts hidden by a previous master to be revealed when the time is right.

[22] *Bdag gar song bar 'ja' tshon gyis bskor ba sogs kun gyis mthong bar gyur to.* Ibid., 453.

of Padmasambhava, but Chökyi Drakpa notes that those among them who still had impurities were unable to see the vision. They continue searching for another cave Padmasambhava described, but darkness is falling and they cannot find it, and so return to their campsite in disappointment.

Chökyi Drakpa performs several rituals, however, and the group sees two white boulders—which he takes to represent Cakrasaṃvara and his tantric consort—moving to and fro atop the lake. He declares that this makes their campsite into a holy place called Sarma Yangdzö, and he predicts that the site will benefit future pilgrims. Chökyi Drakpa then dreams that Manjusri and Padmasambhava initiate him into a secret tantric lineage. Chökyi Drakpa's companions recite mantras and have a vision of Padmasambhava themselves.

Right then, Chökyi Drakpa has a direct perception of Gyangme as the sixty-two-deity mandala of Cakrasaṃvara. He writes that his careful examination and analysis sustains this vision,[23] and he asserts that each stone at Gyangme possesses divine essence.

As the group leaves Gyangme, Chökyi Drakpa reports that the landscape also celebrates his achievement. He claims that his opening of Gyangme means that those who travel there will benefit—he says that those who practice there will quickly achieve their goals, and that those with the correct karmic connections may obtain their own direct perception of the mountain as Cakrasaṃvara's palace.

Vajradhāra's Feast ends with a colophon that contains a short summation of the text—Chökyi Drakpa describes it as the story of "previously unseen mountain faces" at the holy place[24]—and hints at even more profound experiences he did not record "for fear of writing them in words."[25] He hopes that the text is clear and easy to understand, and he ends with a blessing of good fortune.

Chökyi Drakpa's Skillful Seeing

Chökyi Drakpa is one of the few people in the Tibetan literary record to have claimed to transform their perception enough to see a mountain as a

[23] *Bdag gis legs par brtags shing dpyad pas ri de nyid 'khor lo sdom pa lha drug cu rtsa gnyis kyi dkyil 'khor du mjal.* Chos kyi grags pa, *Rgyang me'i gnas yig*, 466.

[24] *Sngar ma mjal ba'i ri zhal.* Ibid., 468.

[25] *De'i 'phros don tsam du mkha' 'gro 'bum gter gyi dag pa'i snang ba rnams ha cang zhib mo dag kyang yi ger 'jigs pa sogs na 'bri ma nus.* Ibid., 468.

mandala, and *Vajradhāra's Feast* is one of even fewer first-person accounts of how such a transformation occurred. So what makes this happen? The text depicts Chökyi Drakpa as a special person to start—he is a religious virtuoso who is already connected to Gyangme by prophecy and karmic destiny, and therefore someone who differs from most ordinary pilgrims. He already possesses skills of perception and interpretation. However, he also undertakes deliberate practices of seeing in order to see Gyangme as the mandala of Cakrasaṃvara. In this section, we will examine *Vajradhāra's Feast* to understand how it charts Chökyi Drakpa's transformation, and we will take note of the practices he undertakes to bring it about. We will see these same practices of seeing in future chapters, but whereas in those chapters they will be pitched to or performed by ordinary pilgrims, in Chökyi Drakpa, we can see them as performed by a religious virtuoso.

Reading and Interpreting the Landscape

Throughout *Vajradhāra's Feast*, Chökyi Drakpa points to publicly available features of Gyangme and describes how these visible features point to ordinarily invisible meanings. For example, upon seeing Gyangme for the first time, he writes that Gyangme is "no different" (*khyad par med pa*) from the holy land of India and "indistinguishable" (*dbyer med*) from the holy mountains of Tsari and Kailash.[26] Later, he describes a mountain near Gyangme as having the form of Tanaduk, king of mountains (*ri rgyal blta na sdug gi tshul*) in the Tibetan medical tradition.[27] In claiming these associations, Chökyi Drakpa locates Gyangme in terms of a familiar and meaning-laden sacred geography and claims some of their potency for Gyangme.

Throughout *Vajradhāra's Feast*, Chökyi Drakpa also reads the landscape in terms of geomantic analysis (*sa dpyad*).[28] For example, in one passage, he writes:

[26] We should note that this identification of Gyangme with Kailash is significant, as Kailash is said to be the earthly abode of Cakrasaṃvara, whose mandala Chökyi Drakpa will go on to directly perceive at Gyangme.

[27] Todd Fenner, "The Origin of the rGyud bzhi: A Tibetan Medical Tantra," in *Tibetan Literature: Studies in Genre*, ed. José Ignacio Cabezón and Roger R. Jackson, 458–469 (Ithaca, NY: Snow Lion, 1996), 462.

[28] Tibetan geomancy takes as its basis the idea that features of the landscape can be analyzed to understand the nature of a place, and about whether that place is conducive for certain activities, including building a home or performing ritual. The full complexity of Tibetan geomantic analysis is beyond the scope of the present work, which focuses instead on a broad range of practices of seeing, rather than this one highly technical system. However, those interested in traditions of

> To our east, the unending chain of rivers and snow-capped mountains were like a great rocky tiger bridge. To our south, the central river looked like a turquoise thunder dragon. To our west, the red cliffs looked like a red she-bird. To our north, there was a great rocky edge at the peak of a forested mountain which looked like a dark turtle flipped on its back. What is more, all the mountains, forests, and rivers in the plain seemed to be prostrating and praying.[29]

He follows this description by writing, "The geomancy of the site was very auspicious, and had many wonderfully auspicious signs."[30] Elsewhere, he notes a mottled rock shaped like a helmet, "a far-off mountain that looked like a stack of books,"[31] or "the mountain crags in front of us [that] looked like wish-fulfilling jewels."[32] These descriptions suggest close examination of the landscape for visual clues and resemblances. Further, this analysis reveals Gyangme to be particularly conducive for dharma practice.

In addition to these geomantic resemblances, Chökyi Drakpa frequently interprets landscape features as signs (*rtags*). For example, at one point he sees deep pits and interprets them as symbolizing (*mtshon du phyir*) the six realms of rebirth.[33] Chökyi Drakpa also writes:

geomancy, and how they affect building practices, should consult the work of Patra Maurer, such as "Sa dpyad and the concept of bla ri," in *This World and the Next: Contributions on Tibetan Religion, Science and Society*, ed. Charles Ramble and Jill Sudbury, 67–79 (Andiast: International Institute for Tibetan and Buddhist Studies GmbH, 2012), or "Landscaping Time, Timing Landscapes: The Role of Time in the sa dpyad Tradition," in *Glimpses of Tibetan Divination: Past and Present*, ed. Petra Maurer, Donatella Rossi, and Rold Scheuermann, 89–117 (Leiden: Brill, 2019), in addition to the book-length *Die Grundlagen der tibetischen Geomantie dargestellt anhand des 32. Kapitels des Vaiḍūrya dkar po von sde srid Sangs rgyas rgya mtsho (1653–1705): Ein Beitrag zum VerstAndnis der Kultur-und Wissenschaftsgeschichte Tibets zur Zeit des 5. Dalai Lama Ngag dbang blo bzang rgya mtsho (1617–1682)* (Halle: International Institute for Tibetan and Buddhist Studies, 2009). For those interested in how geomancy intersects with ideas about sacred landscape, see Martin A. Mills, "Re-Assessing the Supine Demoness: Royal Buddhist Geomancy in the Srong btsan sgam po Mythology," *Journal of the International Association of Tibetan Studies* 3 (2007): 1–47, and the article to which it responds, namely Janet Gyatso, "Down with the Demoness," and Elizabeth Stutchbury, "Perceptions of Landscape in Karzha: 'Sacred' Geography and the Tibetan System of 'Geomancy,'" in *Sacred Spaces and Powerful Places: A Collection of Essays*, ed. Toni Huber (Dharamsala: Library of Tibetan Works and Archives, 2007).

[29] *Chu dang gangs rgyud rgyun mi chad pa shar du brag zam stag rgya bo'i tshul lta bu / lhor gzhung chu g.yu 'brug sngon mo'i tshul can / nub kyi gad pa dmar po bya dmar mo'i tshul can / byang du nags ri de'i rtse mor brag mchu c hen po gab nyug byed pa 'dra ba rus sbal rgya bo'i tshul can dang / gzhan yang thang de la ri dang nags dang chu thams cad kyang 'dud cing bstod pa ltar yod pa.* Ibid., 467.

[30] *Sa'i dpyad kyang shin tu bkra shis shing ya mtshan gyi dge ltas du ma dang ldan pa.* Ibid., 467.

[31] *Pha ri brag po ti brtsegs pa 'dra ba.* Ibid., 460.

[32] *Mdun ri brag nor bu dgos 'dod stsol ba'i tshul can.* Ibid., 467.

[33] These are as follows: god, *asura*, human, animal, hungry ghost, hell being.

> This holy place has a round shape that is encircled by snow-capped mountains—that is a sign of the blessing of pacifying.[34] There are many streams of vermillion that have a square shape—this is a sign of increasing. There are many red crags shaped like half-moons—this is a sign of magnetizing. All the rocks are rough and triangular—this is a sign of subjugating.[35]

On this account, Gyangme is not merely the backdrop to advanced tantric practice, but itself actively points to the dharma.

In each of these three examples, Chökyi Drakpa *reads* the landscape and does not merely look at its surface appearance. This skillful reading of the landscape allows Chökyi Drakpa to access what is hidden to others. For example, at one point he recognizes a particular lake as being the spirit-lake of a protector deity and decides to perform a tantric feast ritual there. This leads to him uncovering treasures that had been hidden nearby. Later, he identifies seals and the sacred syllable "HUM" marked on a box. He opens the box to reveal treasure texts to his companions. In both cases, Chökyi Drakpa looks at the landscape that his companions can see, but sees the deeper, extraordinary meaning.

These passages depict Chökyi Drakpa as someone who is already skilled in perception, in that he can read meanings in the landscape that are hidden to others, but also as someone who is actively searching the visual landscape at Gyangme to find these hidden meanings. He pays careful attention to the ordinary material landscape of Gyangme, even noting the shapes and textures of the rocks along the way. It is here, in the material landscape, that he can begin to see the extraordinary nature of the site.

Engaging with Others' Perception

Chökyi Drakpa also repeatedly calls attention to what others in his party can or cannot see. Calling attention to these multiple perspectives does several things. It underscores Chökyi Drakpa's skill in perception by showing that he can see what others cannot, demonstrates his ability to move

[34] Notice that he reads four types of tantric ritual activities into the landscape: pacifying, increasing, magnetizing, and subjugating. These are the four functions of an enlightened being's activities, and they correspond to the four types of goals pursued in tantric rituals.

[35] Chos kyi grags pa, *Rgyang me'i gnas yig*, 452.

between different ways of seeing, and denaturalizes ordinary perception by highlighting its deficiencies.

For example, *Vajradhāra's Feast* notes multiple occurrences when Chökyi Drakpa's companions fail to see what he sees. At one point during their travels, Chökyi Drakpa describes how one rock face shows an image of Padmasambhava surrounded by eight of his different manifestations. "Although this vision was shown to all," he writes, "because of the darkness, some were unable to see it." He continues describing how "one or two of those who didn't see it stopped their minds, and the vision occurred, so it was clear their karma was pure."[36] This episode highlights that not everyone sees the world in the same way. While Chökyi Drakpa can easily see the mark of Padmasambhava, many of his companions cannot, whether due to darkness or karmic obscurations. The one or two who are eventually able to see it must exert great effort to do so.

These companions who cannot see the image are stuck in their ordinary, deluded perception and cannot see the mountain as Chökyi Drakpa can. *Vajradhāra's Feast* thus repeatedly denaturalizes ordinary perception. Against commonsense assumptions, *Vajradhāra's Feast* and Chökyi Drakpa insist that naïve ordinary perception is not a reliable guide to reality.

However, even as *Vajradhāra's Feast* highlights the deficiencies of ordinary perception, he also enlists his companions' ordinary perception as a witness to the extraordinary nature of Gyangme. For instance, at one point Chökyi Drakpa notes that "everyone saw" him being engulfed in rainbows.[37] Elsewhere, when Chökyi Drakpa and his companions are returning down the mountain to the camp alongside Turquoise Lake, Chökyi Drakpa and his companions have another visionary experience.[38] In front of their eyes, two white boulders begin moving back and forth across the water. Only Chökyi Drakpa understands that they symbolize Cakrasaṃvara and his consort, but

[36] *Mjal ba yang kun la bstan kyang mun pa nag pas mi mthong bar 'dug pas ma bstan zhing gcig gnyis gis rang gi blos bcad nas mjal song bas yang las dag par mngon no.* Ibid., 460. I am not entirely sure how to take *blos bcad*, which is not a common phrase. The term literally means "cut by mind." Michael Aris translates it as "to decide" in *Sources for the History of Bhutan* (Delhi: Motilal Banarsidass, 2009), 144–145. It might also be possible to read it as a copy error for *blos dpyad*, which would sound the same and is written similarly, which would indicate "to analyze." This reading would be supported by the fact that Chökyi Drakpa later describes how analyzing something he sees helps him see it more clearly a few pages later (466). In either case, his companions do something with their minds and are then able to see the image of Padmasambhava.

[37] *Kun gyis mthong bar gyur.* Ibid., 453.

[38] It is possible that this passage is merely redescribing the earlier assertion that the Lake is the *yabyum* form of Cakrasaṃvara or whether this is an entirely new visionary experience. I am inclined to think the latter.

the entire group can see the rocks floating above the water, indicating that he is not alone in this otherwise incredible vision. He refers to it as a "shared vision" (*mthong bar mthun snang byung*) and writes that it made the lake a site (*gnas*, literally holy place) of wonder and amazement.[39] Such statements serve to illustrate that Chökyi Drakpa's engagement with the place is not a delusional fantasy on the part of Chökyi Drakpa. Rather, the site's power—and Chökyi Drakpa's special ability to navigate it—is entirely real, with effects that are visible to ordinary perception. For if even his companions can see these things, Gyangme must be very powerful indeed.

In the examples above, Chökyi Drakpa reports what his companions can see, and he plays with ordinary perception. Sometimes, his companions cannot see the special things he sees, which he uses to highlight the deficiencies of ordinary perception. At other times, his companions can see the special things he sees, which he uses as evidence of the great power of Gyangme. In the first case, ordinary perception is no guide to reality, while in the second case, it is. Chökyi Drakpa neither unquestioningly trusts ordinary perception nor does he entirely dismiss it as delusory. Rather, as we saw with Chökyi Drakpa carefully examining the rocks of Gyangme, he pays careful attention to ordinary perception and to who can see what, but he demonstrates skill in discerning *when* to trust ordinary perception and when to look beyond.

Shifting Between Ordinary and Extraordinary

One moment where Chökyi Drakpa looks beyond is when he deliberately cultivates a visionary encounter upon arriving at Turquoise Lake at the base of the mountain. They hope to ascend the mountain so that Chökyi Drakpa can perform the rituals necessary to open the doors at Gyangme, but the local demons and place spirits resent this incursion. They incite a massive earthquake, which makes the lake waters rise up and the rocks shake back and forth. Chökyi Drakpa seems to be on the verge of terror but stops himself. Instead, he reports, "I made a resolution in my own mind, and thereby calmed myself."[40] Rather than responding to the frightening external events

[39] *Mthong bar mthun snang byung bas shin tu ya mtshan zhing ngo mtshar che ba'i gnas su gyur to.* Ibid., 462.
[40] *Rang sems kho nar thag chod pa'i mthus rang zhir song ba.* Ibid., 455.

around him—as most people in his situation would—Chökyi Drakpa instead turns inward.

This act of withdrawing from the world of his ordinary senses catapults him into a visionary state in which he seems to be in a place he calls Trolung (*spro lung*)[41] and meets a monk who identifies himself as Padmasambhava. Chökyi Drakpa confesses that he doubts whether he can fulfill this destiny, saying, "It seems like I cannot get through to the peak of this [mountain]. The path is difficult, there is so much snow, and I am weak and inadequate."[42] In other words, though he has spent much of the guidebook implicitly or explicitly highlighting his own good qualities, here he tells Padmasambhava that he fears he cannot complete the task assigned to him.

Padmasambhava, however, reassures Chökyi Drakpa that he is indeed destined to open the doors of this pilgrimage place. Padmasambhava grants Chökyi Drakpa's weakness, and acknowledges Chökyi Drakpa's concerns about the heavy snows and other difficulties of the path, but tells Chökyi Drakpa that such obstacles only *appear* to be blocking the way. He says, "Although the path *seems* difficult and full of snow, in reality, [the difficulty] depends on the ease or dis-ease of your own mind. So don't concern yourself with external stones and earth!"[43] The real blockage, according to Padmasambhava, is not rocks and snow, but Chökyi Drakpa's own mind. As such, Padmasambhava tells Chökyi Drakpa not to be concerned with the external stones and rocks that appear in his ordinary perception and to recognize the world of ordinary perception as a function of his mind.

Once he can master his mind, he can shift between ways of seeing and recognize that ordinary external obstacles are no obstacle at all. After some further conversation with Padmasambhava, Chökyi Drakpa accepts his destiny to open Gyangme and asks Padmasambhava for instructions to navigate the mountain. This episode demonstrates both that Chökyi Drakpa already has skill in shifting between ways of seeing—he can enter into a visionary realm when the earthquake strikes—and that he has more to learn in order to complete his mission.

[41] It is not clear what Chökyi Drakpa means by this term. There is a monastery called 'Bri gung spro lung, there is a Spro lung village near 'Bri gung yang re sgar monastery, and there is a hidden land (*sbas yul*) called Spro lung that Sle lung bzhad pa'i rdo rje (1697–1740) opens in the late 1720s. The term can also be translated to mean "emanated valley," so it is possible that he is not referring to a specific physical location, but instead to the fact that this is a visionary place.

[42] *Bdag gis nga ni 'di'i phur mi thar ba 'dra / lam sdug cing kha che ba dang rang 'khos ka zhan pa.* Ibid., 455.

[43] *Lam sdug cing kha ba che ba ltar 'dug kyang don du rang sems bde mi bde la rag las pa yin pas phyi rol gyi sa rdo la mi ltos.* Ibid., 456.

Ultimately, Chökyi Drakpa's success will derive from his understanding that there are multiple *ways of seeing* reality at Gyangme and in his skill in developing ways of seeing each of them. Like his companions, he can see the everyday, ordinary reality of Gyangme. Unlike his companions, he can skillfully read and interpret this ordinary landscape to see that there is more there. Moving beyond this ordinary perception, Chökyi Drakpa can also see Gyangme as the site of Padmasambhava's activities in the mythic past and enter into visionary states where he can speak with this otherwise inaccessible master. Finally, he can understand that the primordial Buddha Cakrasaṃvara dwells in Gyangme, and so by the end of his trip he will be able to see Cakrasaṃvara directly. Chökyi Drakpa is thus able to see Gyangme in multiple ways. He does not treat any of these ways of seeing as false (although he acknowledges that ordinary perception can be deceptive), but instead can skillfully engage with all of them. Chökyi Drakpa, like most humans, has easiest access to ordinary reality because that is what his ordinary perception most readily engages with, but he also demonstrates an ability to interact with the extraordinary reality present at Gyangme. This skill will be crucial to his ultimately obtaining a direct perception into the reality of Cakrasaṃvara's mandala.

The Spontaneity and Effort of Direct Perception

Toward the end of *Vajradhāra's Feast*, Chökyi Drakpa and his companions have successfully climbed to many of the caves of Gyangme, but they must turn back before finding one final cave. Disappointed, Chökyi Drakpa worries that they will have to leave with the mission uncompleted. However, as they are leaving, Chökyi Drakpa has a dream in which *dakinis* provide blessings and Vaishravana is mounted on a lion atop a cliff named "Treasure of the Hundred Thousand *Dakinis*." Following the dream, he decides to lead his companions to the top of this cliff, where they have one final visionary experience.[44]

[44] Much in this section is obscure. To start, the cliff "Treasure of the Hundred Thousand *Dakinis*" has not been mentioned thus far, and it is not clear what it is, where it is, or why it has that name. Chökyi Drakpa does not introduce it. It seems to be an elevated place from which Chökyi Drakpa can see the mountain of Gyangme, for Chökyi Drakpa will go on to describe seeing the mountain from atop the cliff. Second, it is also not entirely clear when (or if) Chökyi Drakpa's dream ends and yields to waking reality, for the end of the dream is not clearly marked. Indeed, it might well be argued that this section is deliberately ambiguous on the point of whether it is a dream or waking reality. I have taken the dream portion to end when Chökyi Drakpa uses the verb "to see/encounter"

Chökyi Drakpa and his companions hold a tantric feast ritual and begin to see apparitions appearing in the sky. First, they see Manjusri, who reveals himself twice, each time surrounded by a host of attendant gods. Then Padmasambhava appears at the peak of Gyangme and grants them empowerment and initiation into the tantric practice of *The Summary of the Guru's Intention*, which sends forth rays of multicolored light. The group, amazed, recites mantras and Padmasambhava reappears, this time dissolving into Chökyi Drakpa's heart. Chökyi Drakpa suddenly remembers Padmasambhava giving him teachings in past lives, indicating that the connection between the two spans across lifetimes, and that Chökyi Drakpa's experience at Gyangme was indeed foretold.

Having received this empowerment, Chökyi Drakpa looks at the holy mountain of Gyangme and sees it anew. He writes, "I saw that mountain [i.e., Gyangme], which is Cakrasaṃvara's palace, as the palace of Glorious Cakrasaṃvara in actuality."[45] Notice the contrast between his first, general identification of the mountain as Cakrasaṃvara's palace and the claim that he can suddenly see it that way in actuality (*dngos su*).[46] The first identification conveys a general understanding of the relationship between the mountain and the mandala, while the second speaks to his direct personal experience of seeing them as identified. The word Chökyi Drakpa uses for this secondary witnessing is *mjal*, which can translate both as "to see" and "to meet." To see Cakrasaṃvara in this way is also to meaningfully *encounter* the deity. The text underscores the importance of this visionary encounter by describing how rainbow lights flash as Chökyi Drakpa sees Cakrasaṃvara, and how he sees a dazzling, almost psychedelic, array of bodily forms, including the eight different manifestations of Cakrasaṃvara.

Chökyi Drakpa describes this experience both as spontaneous—the visual display simply occurred (*bstan byung*)—and as requiring conscious effort on his part. That is, in describing this experience, Chökyi Drakpa writes, "I

(*mjal*) followed by the terminating particle *lo*, and for the following section to describe nondreaming events.

[45] *Bde mchog pho brang gi ri de yang dpal 'khor lo sdom pa'i pho brang dngos su mjal zhing.* Ibid., 466.

[46] Gyatso notes that in Treasure traditions, the term *dngos*, although it directly translates as "reality," often describes visual signs experienced in waking reality, as opposed to meditative experience (*nyams*) or dreaming (*rmi lam*). See Janet Gyatso, "The Logic of Legitimation in the Tibetan Treasure Tradition," *History of Religions* 33, no. 2 (1993): 109, especially note 27.

was carefully examining and analyzing (*rtags shing dpyad pas*), and so I saw (*mjal*) the mountain as the sixty-two-deity mandala of Cakrasaṃvara."[47] He uses an instrumental particle (*pas*) to link the first half of the sentence to the second half, suggesting that "carefully examining and analyzing" *causes* the vision of the mountain as the mandala of Cakrasaṃvara. Chökyi Drakpa can have this vision of the mountain *by means of* his examining and analyzing. The mandala does not simply present itself to him, but rather he must work to fully see it. In other words, even this direct connection Chökyi Drakpa establishes between his own ordinary world and the extraordinary realm of Cakrasaṃvara is not stable and self-perpetuating. Rather, it must be maintained through Chökyi Drakpa's active efforts.

We might assume that these two aspects of seeing are mutually exclusive, but Chökyi Drakpa does not treat them in that way. Instead, he sees them as coexisting in this climactic moment. It is a moment of what I have been calling *co-seeing*, in which he sees the mountain in multiple ways at once and brings them together in his experience.

Here, once again, Chökyi Drakpa demonstrates the qualities, practices, and skills necessary to reach the rarely accomplished goal of transforming perception. Chökyi Drakpa claims certain qualities that mark him as special from the outset, including his noble birth, karmic connections with Gyangme and Padmasambhava, and advanced ritual training. But he also undertakes practices of seeing that we will see again and develop further in future chapters. These practices include seeking out visual encounters with holy images and special places, closely examining the landscape for signs, directing his attention, inducing visionary states, performing rituals, and analyzing visual phenomena. These qualities and practices combine to give him great skill in moving between different ways of seeing, and in engaging with both the ordinary and extraordinary nature of Gyangme. He is thus exceptionally well situated to break through the various levels of reality present at Gyangme.

However, even with all these advantages, it is not easy for Chökyi Drakpa to accomplish this transformation—he must work hard, and he experiences hardship and doubt. Though the goal of seeing a mountain as a mandala structures Tibetan mountain pilgrimage, this difficulty helps us understand why vanishingly few claim a complete transformation of perception. Even

[47] *Bdag gis legs par rtags shing dpyad pas ri de nyid dpal 'khor lo sdom pa lha drug bcu rtsa gnyis kyi dkyil 'khor du mjal zhing.* Chos kyi grags pa, *Rgyang me'i gnas yig*, 466.

in narratives where a transformation of vision successfully occurs, then, it is still very difficult, fragile, and easy to miss.

Gyangme's Transformation

Chökyi Drakpa claims that his climactic moment of direct perception changes the world. He himself emerges with new blessings and removed karmic obstacles,[48] but Gyangme transforms as well. Its doors newly opened, it is now a holy mountain that pilgrims can visit to gain blessings and merit. In this section, we will ask how such a transformation occurred.

According to the logic of *Vajradhāra's Feast*, Gyangme was already sacred when Chökyi Drakpa arrived. Because it was a place where Cakrasaṃvara dwelled and Padmasambhava practiced, it was already overflowing with sacred potency. Gyangme *gathers* the potent traces of their holy presence and retains their memory. Nonetheless, prior to Chökyi Drakpa's activities there, that potency was not yet accessible to a broader public—it was too raw and only attracted fierce spirits and demons. This raw power of the place—and of the spirits dwelling there—needed to be tamed by a tantric master.

How did Chökyi Drakpa accomplish this, and what exactly was accomplished? The text does not spell this out—from its perspective, it goes without saying. However, I suggest that we can read this act of founding a pilgrimage place, following Janet Gyatso's analysis of the logic of the Tibetan Treasure tradition,[49] as creating an enduring connection between levels of reality. Or, to use the language of "opening the doors," Chökyi Drakpa's activities at Gyangme, and ability to see Gyangme both in its ordinary aspect

[48] Tibetans, who use a twelve-year calendrical cycle, commonly treat the ages of thirteen, twenty-five, thirty-seven, and so on as "obstacle" years, and as Chökyi Drakpa approaches the age of twenty-five, he wants to clear away potential obstacles and threats to his lifespan. See Chos kyi grags pa, *Rgyang me'i gnas yig*, 462.

[49] Janet Gyatso describes Treasure narratives as constructing *bridges* between the primordial origin of the Treasure and the historical present where the Treasure is being revealed. See Gyatso, "The Logic of Legitimation," 132. Chökyi Drakpa, too, is attempting to build a bridge between the realm of Cakrasaṃvara and his own temporal present. The way in which he constructs a bridge between these two realms differs from Treasure narratives in that—the incidents of him finding Treasure texts aside—Chökyi Drakpa does not recover some item or text that originates in the atemporal buddha realm. In the case of the Treasure tradition, the Treasure revealer produces a textual or material object that in some sense materializes the bridge between the Treasure revealer's present and the primordial buddha realm, providing a means for later practitioners to participate in the heirophany between realms. In Chökyi Drakpa's case, however, his direct perception of the holy mountain as Cakrasaṃvara's mandala does not produce an object, per se, but rather makes the place itself into a door between realms.

and its extraordinary aspect, open a door between them. This does not collapse the realm of Cakrasaṃvara and the realm of everyday material reality into one another; however, it does allow the power of Cakrasaṃvara to flow into that everyday material reality. As *Vajradhāra's Feast* puts it, after Chökyi Drakpa's activities at Gyangme, "all the rocks and stones of this holy place of Gyangme have the essence of gods and goddesses. All the waters there resound with the recitation of profound secret mantras."[50] Chökyi Drakpa's visionary activities have broken the boundaries between these two realms and opened the doors between them, allowing Gyangme's inherent sacred potency to become available to a broader group of future pilgrims.

In opening the doors of Gyangme, Chökyi Drakpa opens new potential realities for future pilgrims. For those with the proper karma and dedicated practice, he promises that they, too, will directly perceive (*mngon sum du mthong*) the mountain as Cakrasaṃvara's palace,[51] thus reenacting Chökyi Drakpa's founding vision of the site. That is, because Chökyi Drakpa saw the mountain as a mandala palace, later pilgrims will be able to follow in his footsteps and achieve this direct perception more easily. That said, not all pilgrims will be able to see the mountain as mandala for themselves. Even if the extraordinary nature of the mountain remains invisible to them, however, the fact that Chökyi Drakpa opened the doors of the mountain means that they will gain blessings and benefits from the mountain. Chökyi Drakpa claims that "If you practice at another place, things will seem to go slowly, but if you practice there [at Gyangme], you will quickly attain [your aims]—the place has many such wonders."[52] Elsewhere, he writes that a particular site on the mountain will "introduce even ordinary people to one-pointed mind,"[53] enabling those people to achieve a focused mental state that ordinarily takes a great deal of advanced training. In other words, future pilgrims do not need to obtain a direct perception of the mountain to benefit from its extraordinary blessings. By opening the doors, he has opened new possibilities for interacting with the mountain and made its power real for those who otherwise could not attain them.

[50] *Rgyang me'i gnas 'di'i ri brag thams cad lha dang lha mo'i rang bzhin dang / chu thams cad kyang gsang sngags zab mo'i 'dzab kho na'i sgrar yod pa dag.* Chos kyi grags pa, *Rgyang me'i gnas yig*, 466.

[51] *'Phags pa 'jig rten dbang phyug thugs rje chen po'i pho brang du mngon sum du mthong bar gyur to.* Ibid., 468.

[52] *Gnas gzhan du bsgrubs na bul 'dra yang gnas der bsgrubs na myur du 'grub par 'gyur pa sogs ya mtshan du ma dang ldan zhing.* Ibid., 468.

[53] *De nyid la skye bo phal pa dag kyang sems rtse gcig tu ngo 'phrod par 'gyur.* Ibid., 463.

Conclusion: Modeling Visionary Transformation

This chapter is about two visionary transformations—the transformation of Chökyi Drakpa's vision so that he can see Gyangme as a mandala and the transformation of Gyangme into a pilgrimage place as a result of that vision. *Vajradhāra's Feast* is a rare text in that it depicts these transformations in a first-person account of someone who claims to have opened the doors of a holy mountain. However, it also draws on and contributes to the broader *imaginaire* of Tibetan mountain pilgrimage—the collective imagination of what can happen on pilgrimage. *Vajradhāra's Feast* models idealized visionary transformations, and so it helps us understand how those transformations were imagined and understood. Understanding how Chökyi Drakpa was able to accomplish these transformations also gives us insight into the imaginative possibilities of other, less-well-known pilgrims. Such pilgrims may have seen themselves as unlikely to match the accomplishments of someone like Chökyi Drakpa, but their experiences of pilgrimage were shaped by his idealized model nonetheless. As such, it is worth reflecting on how *Vajradhāra's Feast* depicts these two visionary transformations.

First, Chökyi Drakpa's success at learning to see Gyangme as a mandala illustrates what this visual transformation may look like and how it is achieved. Chökyi Drakpa's moment of success is a visionary experience in which he directly perceives the sixty-two-deity mandala of Cakrasaṃvara. It is a relatively short experience, and it is both spontaneous in that it seems to happen *to* him and effortful in that he must "analyze" his perception in order to see it. Before the visionary experience, he knew in a general sense that the mountain was a mandala, and after the visionary experience, he knows that it is a mandala, but in a new, direct way based on his personal experience. He accomplishes this, moreover, as result of his preexisting special qualities—he has the right karmic connections and tantric realizations—and effortful practices of looking at Gyangme. In particular, Chökyi Drakpa constantly reads the landscape and moves between the surface appearances of the place to the unseen deeper meaning. We will encounter these same techniques fleshed out in more detail in future chapters.

We might further characterize Chökyi Drakpa's seeing as that of a visionary or seer. The terms "seer" and "visionary" have a rich range of meanings and associations, but for the moment I will take those terms to mean someone who has a unique ability to see what most people in the present cannot ordinarily see. This may be a vision of the future but also includes visions of figures from the past or other sorts of trans-spatial, trans-temporal, or trans-dimensional experiences. This vision then opens up new possibilities in the present. I follow Ann Taves here in placing the seer or visionary "alongside the artist as the creator of things that, in Martin Heidegger's sense (1971: 43–44), open up new worlds."[54] The artist sees something no one else can and then makes it real in a way that opens new possibilities for how to live in the present or how to imagine the future. In that sense, Chökyi Drakpa is a visionary because he sees something no one else can, and makes it real in the world.

Second, *Vajradhāra's Feast* illustrates how visionary practices like those of Chökyi Drakpa transform and create sacred space. The story Chökyi Drakpa tells about Gyangme fits the general lore surrounding Tibetan holy mountains. There is a mountain that is identified with other, more famous mountains and said to be the residence of a tantric Buddha. That same mountain is said to have been the site of legendary activities by Padmasambhava, Milarepa, or some other holy master. Then, a tantric master uses ritual mastery and advanced perception to recognize the mountain as the mandala it truly is and to defeat the demons living there. After that, the mountain is "open" for general pilgrims, who can benefit from the blessings there. *Vajradhāra's Feast* is more detailed than most accounts, allowing us to see these dynamics at work, but it does not fundamentally shift the general logic. Some accounts of opening the doors focus more heavily on taming the local demons, while Chökyi Drakpa's focuses more on obtaining a direct perception of mountain as mandala. For Chökyi Drakpa, we can say that his co-seeing—his ability to see Gyangme both in its ordinary and extraordinary aspects—forges a lasting interpenetration between the extraordinary aspect of the mountain as Cakrasaṃvara's palace and the ordinary aspect of the mountain as being made of rocks and stones. In other words, his act of seeing permanently changes the world. This interpenetration allows future pilgrims, even those who cannot themselves see the mountain as the mandala or sacred abode of the tantric deity Cakrasaṃvara, to benefit from the connection between the worlds, and allows some fortunate pilgrims to reenact Chökyi Drakpa's vision of the mountain as Cakrasaṃvara's mandala.

[54] Anne Taves, "History and the Claims of Revelation: Joseph Smith and the Materialization of the Golden Plates," *Numen* 61, no. 2–3 (2014): 182–207, 186.

One question readers might have at this point is what role Gyangme itself played in its transformation. My analysis has focused on Chökyi Drakpa's actions and how these actions opened the doors of the mountain, making it into a sacred place, but this focus runs the risk of rendering the mountain itself into an inert and passive ground for human actions. This is certainly not how Chökyi Drakpa understands the situation.[55] *Vajradhāra's Feast* pays a great deal of attention to the material and physical nature of Gyangme, and it contains extensive descriptions of the place's particular features. In addition, *Vajradhāra's Feast* portrays Gyangme as active—it shows Gyangme reaching out to Chökyi Drakpa to send signs in the form of self-arisen images, geomantic signs, or rocks that float above the water. The spirits that live there also communicate their pleasure or displeasure in the forms of avalanches and earthquakes. As much as Chökyi Drakpa has to work to maintain the direct perception of Cakrasaṃvara he obtains, we might also say that the mountain makes the vision happen *to* him. All of Chökyi Drakpa's experiences at Gyangme emerge from complex interactions with the mountain, as well as the material *stuff* that Chökyi Drakpa encounters and interacts with there. Chökyi Drakpa thus does not reject the external material world as fundamentally delusory, but rather skillfully interacts with it. And the material world, in turn, facilitates Chökyi Drakpa's vision.

As such, while the main focus of this book is the practices of seeing people undertake to create and maintain sacred worlds that feel real, another book might well reconsider all the evidence assembled to tell a story about the agency of the material world in a way that de-centers human agency. This book is not that book, but it is still important to note the moments where the material world itself seems to be the agent opening up new possibilities.

Stepping back from how *Vajradhāra's Feast* tells the story of how perception can transform and how a place can transform, I also want to make the claim that stories like *Vajradhāra's Feast* are themselves part of what constructs sacred space. *Vajradhāra's Feast* tells a richly detailed story about Gyangme, including its associations with sacred landscapes, holy masters, and wondrous events. Those who hear this story, whether from the text itself, from a caretaker who leads pilgrims through the site and relates the story, or from general oral traditions, will encounter a place rich with meaning and populated by all the beings who had been there before. As has been suggested

[55] Chökyi Drakpa in this way anticipates the points made by New Materialists Bruno Latour and Jane Bennett, who argue against the scholarly tendency to see humans as agents and the material world as inactive patients.

by scholars of space and place, places are not mute backdrops to human intentions and experiences. Rather, places gather histories, narratives, actions, and culture, embedding them in the landscape itself. When people encounter a physical place, then, they also encounter the rich meaning and set of associations that make up that place. On this logic, Chökyi Drakpa's actions, and the text which tells the story of those actions, inscribe them into the landscape, changing the place itself and shaping the way later pilgrims encounter it. Particularly given Chökyi Drakpa's written account of his pilgrimage to the place, later pilgrims to the place will bear his descriptions in mind, imagining what Chökyi Drakpa saw even as they try to see it for themselves. Such pilgrims will still have to do the work of focusing their attention and searching for signs of its ordinarily invisible wonders, but they will visit a place that is primed to facilitate transformative visual experiences.

5

How Pilgrimage Guides Use Language and Landscape to Cultivate Co-Seeing

Scratch a rock
and a legend springs
—Arun Kolatkar, *Jejuri*[1]

In the last chapter, we examined an account of an advanced master successfully seeing a mountain as a mandala, and that laid the traces—in landscape and writing—for later pilgrims to visit the mountain. Later pilgrims probably lacked the rare combination of talent and training that allowed Chödrak Yeshe to fully transform his perception, but they may still have had meaningful visual encounters on pilgrimage. In this chapter, we will turn to part of the pilgrimage tradition that structures pilgrims' encounter with holy places and ultimately facilitates those meaningful encounters: pilgrimage guide texts. These are texts written for pilgrims that explain important features of the site and lead pilgrims through them. Our focus will be on the literary strategies these texts use to describe sites for pilgrims, with the goal of considering how texts reshape pilgrims' experience of the holy mountain. Specifically, I will ask how the literary features of these texts facilitate co-seeing, the experience of perceiving the mundane and extraordinary simultaneously.

My aim will be to explore how these guide texts engage—and seek to transform—pilgrims' perception of the holy mountain. My questions are as follows: What sort of audience do they anticipate, and how do they go about describing the pilgrimage place to that audience? How do texts guide pilgrims' eyes, and are there specific patterns in terms of how they do so? How might we understand how these textual descriptions work on the text's anticipated audience?[2]

[1] Arun Kolatkar, *Jejuri* (New York: New York Review Books Classics, 2005), 22.
[2] Some readers may object that these questions treat the text as an independent agent that undertakes various actions. It is not my intention to suggest that texts operate independently of their authors. In saying "the text does xyz . . . ," this is merely a simpler way to say "the narrative strategies encoded into the text by the author do xyz . . ."

Making the Invisible Real. Catherine Hartmann, Oxford University Press. © Oxford University Press 2025.
DOI: 10.1093/9780197791585.003.0006

To answer these questions, I will first introduce the genre of pilgrimage guides and discuss their typical features, attending carefully to the theoretical and methodological issues involved in reading pilgrimage guides to investigate questions of perceptual experience. I will then examine examples from a variety of pilgrimage guides and show how these guides use a variety of literary strategies to direct pilgrims' attention and ultimately shape how the pilgrim sees the site. Specifically, I argue that they (1) denaturalize pilgrims' ordinary perception, (2) recontextualize that perception in terms of the site's wonders, (3) invite the pilgrim to reflect upon their own perception, and then (4) use highly poetic metaphorical language to redescribe the pilgrimage place. Using these literary strategies, they direct pilgrims' attention both to how the site appears in ordinary perception and to the extraordinary vision of the site that the pilgrim cannot yet see but will come to see with practice. Guides thus facilitate co-seeing, which brings the extraordinary aspect of the site into the direct experience of the pilgrim. This then makes it feel real and vital, as though legendary figures could spring forth from every rock.

The Genre of Pilgrimage Guides

Before beginning, an introduction to the genre of pilgrimage guides is in order. These texts praise a particular holy place (*gnas*), often a holy mountain or temple complex, and encourage audiences to embark on pilgrimage to that place. Often written in the voice of a human tour guide,[3] guides lead the potential pilgrim through the site and describe individual objects so that the pilgrim will fully appreciate them.

Pilgrimage guide texts can be found under multiple genre labels, as often occurs in Tibetan literature. The most general term is *néyik* (*gnas yig*), which combines the honorific for place, *né* (*gnas*),[4] which refers to holy places, with *yik* (*yig*), a word meaning writing. Other genre labels used for texts related to

[3] As we will see, there is evidence that written guides are derived from the oral traditions of human pilgrimage guides. Dkon chog bstan 'dzin Chos kyi blo gros, for example, mentions consulting caretakers at pilgrimage sites when he is compiling his written pilgrimage guide. Elena de Rossi Fillibeck, *Two Tibetan Guide Books to Ti se and La phyi* (Bonn: VGH Wissenschaftsverlag, 1988), 84.

[4] For more on the Tibetan notion of the *gnas*, see Toni Huber, "Putting the Gnas Back into Gnas-Skor: Rethinking Tibetan Pilgrimage Practice," in *Sacred Spaces and Powerful Places in Tibetan Culture: A Collection of Essays*, ed. Toni Huber (Dharamsala, H.P.: The Library of Tibetan Works and Archives, 1999), 77–104.

pilgrimage and place include néshé (*gnas bshad*, explanation of a holy place), nétö (*gnas bstod*, holy place praise, also sometimes *sa bstod*, praise of the place), *lamyik* (*lam yig*, itinerary),[5] *karchak* (*dkar chag*, inventory),[6] or *logyü* (*lo rgyus*, history). These labels are not distinct, and two texts with the same label may differ greatly. Similarly, two similar texts may have different labels, and a text may refer to itself using a different label from its title. This chapter focuses on texts that praise specific holy places and invite people to make a pilgrimage there, using any of these genre terms.[7]

Guides tend to follow a strikingly similar pattern. They narrate some of the history of the site, emphasizing the activities of highly realized masters who visited the site. They also point out important features for pilgrims to see, including "self-arisen" phenomena at the site, the natural beauty of flora and fauna, handprints or other marks associated with spiritual masters, and various other signs that indicate the site's power. Guides may also tell pilgrims about the inner, secret, or hidden reality of the site, which ordinary pilgrims will be unable to see. This inner appearance describes how the site looks to advanced beings like buddhas, gods, or spiritual masters, in contrast to the outer appearance of how it appears to ordinary people. Guides end by describing the benefits of visiting the holy place, such as merit, blessings, or a good rebirth. While the specific details in each of these domains vary depending on the site, this general pattern remains constant across the genre.

Perhaps unexpectedly, pilgrimage guides do not offer practical information on getting to the pilgrimage place, or on the necessities of lodging, food, or directions. Even when one arrives at the site, the descriptions of particular places are light on physical detail, such that it would be difficult to navigate a site based solely on the written guide. Tibetan guides thus differ from modern-day travel guides such as *Lonely Planet*, which aim to contain

[5] This term literally means path text or path writing, although it can be used to refer to an itinerary for pilgrims to follow, a text in which someone writes an account of their travels, or a passport-type document signed by a local official that allows the holder to pass through a particular area.

[6] These texts are often called tables of contents or inventories, which can be used to list the texts in a particular collected works (*gsung 'bum*), the items held in a library, or in the case of famous places, the texts, images, and other features found at the site. These inventories can range from simple lists of items without any commentary to detailed accounts that relate the history and significance of the items.

[7] Some readers may ask what grounds I have to say that these texts are about *pilgrimage* rather than simply being about the place, without expectation that people will travel there. For example, there are *sthalapurāṇa* (narratives of places) in the South Asian context or *difangzhi* (地方誌, local gazetteers) in the Chinese context. Unlike those genres, *gnas yig* often describe benefits for pilgrims and use the optative voice saying that pilgrims should go there. In addition, anthropological evidence suggests these texts are used by pilgrims.

everything a traveler might need to know. Instead, pilgrims likely relied on trade routes and person-to-person knowledge about where to go and how to survive.

Some scholars have described guides as "formulaic"[8] because they tend to repeat similar tropes across different holy places. Others have characterized guides as obscuring the physical landscape. For instance, one scholar writes that "in the description of the guide the environment sometimes disappears completely. It becomes entirely subsumed and explained by religion, which superimposes its structures on it, thereby leaving only a glimpse of the actual physical scenery."[9] In other words, scholars have sometimes seen pilgrimage guides as repetitive and as writing over local landscapes, without concern for the actual landscape itself. Both scholars make these observations in the context of deep knowledge of and respect for the genre, but one unintended consequence of such characterizations of guides is that they can be seen as theoretically uninteresting. Instead, I propose that these features can actually provide insights into the sophisticated literary techniques guides use to influence their audiences. Further, I contend that the recurring and repetitive features of these texts demonstrate extensive engagement with, rather than disregard for, the actual physical landscape.

While hundreds of pilgrimage guides are extant in manuscripts, block prints, or modern reprinted editions, the history of their composition and use remains obscure. A large proportion of guides are unsigned and undated, making it difficult to say with any degree of certainty when and where they were written, or indeed how and whether particular guides were used.

Some textual evidence sheds light on how pilgrims used guides. For example, the pilgrim diary of Khatag Zamyak, written from 1944 to 1956 and discussed in the next chapter, mentions him consulting pilgrimage guides for the sites he visited no fewer than sixteen times.[10] He describes purchasing pilgrimage guides for particular places, reading guides with travel companions while at holy places, and also cites guides when relating the history of places. We have very few pilgrim diaries, so it is difficult to know if this is common,

[8] Charles Ramble, for example, in his article "The Complexity of Tibetan Pilgrimage" writes that pilgrimage guides (*gnas bshad*) are "largely formulaic, and differ from one another mainly in matters of local detail." That is, the structure of these texts is often very similar, with only the specific place names seeming to change. See Charles Ramble, "The Complexity of Tibetan Pilgrimage," in *Searching for the Dharma, Finding Salvation*, ed. Christoph Cueppers and Max Deeg (Lumbini: Lumbini International Research Institute, 2014), 179–196, 194.

[9] Frederica Venturi, "A *Gnas Yig* to the Holy Place of Pretapurī," *Revue d'Etudes Tibétaines* 51 (2019): 415–447, 423.

[10] Kha stag 'dzam yag, *Nyin deb*, 15, 36, 43, 76, 83, 84, 87, 91, 93, 95, 99, 110, 126, 156, 168, 171.

but it is not unreasonable to assume that Khatag Zamyak's use of pilgrimage guides is representative of others.

In addition, anthropologists attest to the continued use and importance of pilgrimage guides. They describe pilgrims as carrying written guides or encountering oral versions.[11] Toni Huber, for example, notes that many of the laypeople that he interviewed about pilgrimage to Tsari could recite, even years later, verse sections from a particularly famous pilgrim guidebook to Tsari. Though these pilgrims had not necessarily come into contact with a written or printed form of a guide, the prevalence of these guides was such that they were commonly passed around, heard, recited, and memorized.[12]

These same anthropologists disagree on the extent to which guides influence actual pilgrimage experiences. Toni Huber, for example, speaks of pilgrimage guides as acting as a "narrative map" that allows pilgrims to understand and navigate the site,[13] and as "popular vehicles for the creation and maintenance of a specific magical view of reality."[14] But he also warns that textual study of pilgrimage guides should be "combined with the results of field investigations at pilgrimage sites,"[15] lest scholars assume that pilgrimage guides describe actual pilgrim practices. Katia Buffetrille expresses even more skepticism of the value of studying pilgrimage guide texts. She agrees with Huber that pilgrimage guides do *try* to change the way pilgrims experience the pilgrimage site, specifically by giving them a Buddhicized mental model of the site that changes how they conceptualize it.[16] However, she questions how effective guides are at changing pilgrims' experiences and influencing their behavior and explores examples of sites at which the

[11] See especially Toni Huber, *The Cult of Pure Crystal Mountain: Popular Pilgrimage and Visionary Landscape in Southeast Tibet* (Oxford: Oxford University Press, 1999), and Katia Buffetrille, *Pèlerins, Lamas et Visionnaires: Sources Orales et Écrites sur les Pèlerinages Tibétains* (Wien: Arbeitskreis für Buddhistische Studien Universität Wien, 2000).

[12] "In pre-1959 Tibet, many people such as laypersons with no written literacy could hear, memorize, and recite these types of texts accurately without ever having contact with a written or printed version." Huber, *The Cult of Pure Crystal Mountain*, 60.

[13] Huber, *The Cult of Pure Crystal Mountain*, 61.

[14] Toni Huber, "Guide to La-Phyi Mandala: History, Landscape, and Ritual in Western Tibet," in *Mandala and Landscape*, ed. A. W. Macdonald, 233–286 (New Delhi: D.K. Printworld, 1997), 235.

[15] Ibid., 235.

[16] In "Reflections on Pilgrimages to Sacred Mountains, Lakes and Caves," Katia Buffetrille argues that pilgrimage guides embody a typically "Buddhist" understanding of the world and "lead the ordinary pilgrim from simple perception of the physical landscape to conception of the place as sacred [Buddhist] landscape" (21). Katia Buffetrille, "Reflections on Pilgrimages to Sacred Mountains, Lakes and Caves," in *Pilgrimage in Tibet*, ed. Alex McKay (London: Curzon Press, 1998), 18–34.

pilgrimage guides seem to have little to nothing to do with pilgrims' behavior at that site.[17]

We should remember these cautions. There is a gap between what guides say pilgrims *should* do and what they *actually* do. Nevertheless, it is still worth asking how pilgrimage guides influence pilgrims, which both Huber and Buffetrille agree is a major goal of pilgrimage guides. This chapter aims to address this question by using literary analysis to examine these texts. When we do so, we can see patterns in the ways that they describe holy places, and we can begin to understand how they shape pilgrims' experience of the holy site.

Theoretical Approach: Metaphor and Attention

I have made several references to the idea that pilgrimage guide texts "shape" audiences and the way they see and experience the pilgrimage place. But how does this happen? It is not enough, I would suggest, to say that pilgrims view certain places as special or as sacred simply because some text tells them to do so. Humans do not work that way. Rather, we should try to understand the mechanisms by which texts influence how people see. As such, I will try to reconstruct the experience of the audience encountering a text and ask how the text elicits a certain kind of participation and response from the audience.[18] In that respect, I focus on the literary features of the text, and I draw on literary theory, particularly that of Paul Ricoeur, to think about how metaphors and literature more broadly shape, or "figure," the way people see the world by leading them to attend to two different visions of reality.

Ricoeur outlines a theory of metaphor to argue that poetic language trains readers in "seeing-as" and ultimately cultivates readers' ability to see the world differently.[19] When readers encounter a metaphor such as "Achilles

[17] See Katia Buffetrille, "The Blue Lake of A-Mdo and Its Island: Legends and Pilgrimage Guide," *The Tibet Journal* 19, no. 4 (Winter 1994): 2–22; Katia Buffetrille, "The Great Pilgrimage of A Myes rMa-Chen: Written Traditions, Living Realities," in *Mandala and Landscape*, ed. A. W. Macdonald, 75–132 (Delhi: D.K. Printworld, 1997); and Katia Buffetrille, "The Pilgrimage to Mount Kha ba dkar po: A Metaphor for Bardo?" in *Searching for the Dharma, Finding Salvation: Buddhist Pilgrimage in Time and Space*, ed. Christoph Cueppers and Max Deeg, 197–220 (Lumbini: Lumbini International Research Institute, 2014).

[18] Such changes are possible because—as both theorists of place and space and Buddhist philosophers argue—humans do not have access to the bare physical particulars of a place. Instead, what they experience is a complex mixture of ideologies, cultures, habits, and constructed physical spaces. Pilgrimage guides, insofar as they contribute to this ideological-cultural mode of place, shape how pilgrims experience that place.

[19] This idea of "seeing as" is drawn from Gestalt psychology via the works of Paul Ricoeur. The concept highlights the fact that humans do not perceive the world in terms of isolated sense

is a lion," Ricoeur suggests, the reader first tries to make sense of it in literal terms and fails. However, she continues to try to make sense of the statement and searches for the ways in which Achilles might be like a lion. In so doing, she sees Achilles both as the same as a lion, which may involve seeing Achilles's courage, pride, tawniness, or ferocity, and as *not* the same as a lion. That is, the reader does not think that Achilles really is a lion. Rather, Ricoeur argues that the power of metaphorical truth is that, during this phenomenological experience of seeing-as brought on by the metaphor, Achilles both is and is not a lion. The metaphor plays with the tension between those statements and thus preserves the "is not" within the "is."[20] The reader thus learns to see Achilles in a new way. Again, this does not mean that she no longer sees Achilles as a man, but rather that her vision has been enriched such that she can see Achilles both as a lion and as a man, even though those two statements seem to be opposed to one another. The text can be said to *figure* Achilles and shape the way the reader sees him. The text does not make Achilles into a lion, per se, but through engagement with a text in which this metaphor occurs and new attention to Achilles, a reader may find a new world that opens up before her in which she sees Achilles in this new way.

In an essay entitled "Naming God," Ricoeur expands this analysis of individual metaphors to religious texts, suggesting that they draw on the same figurative capacity of language but in the scope of entire texts rather than a single phrase.[21] Instead of saying "Achilles is a lion," biblical texts say, "God is . . . XYZ." This is true even when there are no identifiable individual metaphors. Rather, the text as a whole makes a predication about the nature of God ("naming" God, in Ricoeur's terms). In so doing, the text breaks with everyday understandings, discloses a new world to the reader, and invites the reader to imagine that kind of world.

Inspired by Ricoeur's analysis, I argue that pilgrimage texts figure the pilgrimage place in a similar way to how these biblical texts figure or "name" God. That is, in describing the pilgrimage site in a particular way, pilgrimage guides make a predication about the site that breaks with ordinary ways of seeing, discloses a way of seeing, and invites the pilgrim to imagine seeing the site in

particulars, and then later interpret these sense particulars in terms of objects. Rather, people perceive the world all at once *as* particular objects and wholes. Seeing as, in this view, is not merely passive seeing, but rather "it is an experience and an act at one and the same time." Paul Ricoeur, *The Rule of Metaphor: The Creation of Meaning in Language* (London: Routledge, 2003), 213.

[20] Ricoeur, *The Rule of Metaphor*, 213.

[21] Paul Ricoeur, "Naming God," in *Figuring the Sacred: Religion, Narrative, and Imagination* (Minneapolis: Fortress Press, 1995), 217–235.

that way. In other words, it leads them to pay attention to the site in a new way. This does not necessarily mean that the pilgrim sees the site exactly in the way that the pilgrimage guide describes it. In the same way, readers who encounter the metaphor that Achilles is a lion will each have their own way of resolving the tension inherent in the metaphor and their own understanding of the meaning. In each case, figuration meaningfully transforms their perception of the place, which allows them to see the site in two ways at once: as it is in ordinary perception and as it is according to the text. This is the idea that I have sought to capture in the term "co-seeing." Pilgrimage guides, on this interpretation, use language in such a way as to direct pilgrims' attention, cultivate this kind of co-seeing, and ultimately shape the way pilgrims experience the site.[22]

How Pilgrimage Guides Draw the Eye

> And then, [we arrived at] that mansion palace of Cakrasaṃvara called Gangkar Tise [Kailash], praised by siddhas, the dwelling place of 500 arhats. There was no obscuring cover of clouds or darkness. I worshipped and recited the guru *sādhanā* for Jetsun Milarepa and so saw his face. I thought, "what good karmic connections!" and immediately prostrated three times in a state of joy. I stayed at the edge of the lake that night.[23]
>
> —Tsongpon Khatag Zamyak, *A Pilgrim's Diary: Tibet, Nepal, and India, 1944–1956*

[22] One anonymous reviewer raised the interesting question of whether my argument about co-seeing suggests that the attainment of pure vision on the part of advanced practitioners is merely metaphorical. Would an advanced practitioner see only the mandala and not the mountain? How would such a position square with different interpretations of Mādhyamaka? While it is beyond the scope of this chapter to delve into the complex question of how advanced practitioners see the world, they are worthy of further consideration. It is rare that pilgrimage texts delve into these explicitly philosophical discussions, but one source that does so is Chos grags ye shes, *Ri bo gangs can dang mtsho ma dros pa chu bo bzhi dang bcas pa gtan la dbab pa mkhas pa'i rna rgyan*, BDRC W1CZ886 (Mtshur phu dgon, No date). In it, Chos grags ye shes responds to objections about whether pilgrimage traditions either posit the external existence of pilgrimage mountains or, if they deny such existence, what the point of pilgrimage is. Chos grags ye shes responds with an extended description of how pilgrimage is in line with Mādhyamaka philosophy. For more on this text, see Catherine Hartmann, *To See a Mountain: Writing, Place, and Vision in Tibetan Pilgrimage Literature* (PhD Diss., Harvard University, 2020), 158–225. In this chapter, my theory of co-seeing is more aimed at understanding how pilgrimage guide texts work on ordinary practitioners without pure perception.

[23] *Gnyis pa thub pas bsngags pa'i gangs dkar ti se zhes 'khor lo bde mchog gi pho brang gzhal yas khang / dgra bcom pa lnga brgya yi bzhugs gnas / sprin dang nag sogs kyis sgrib g.yog med pa de / rje btsun mi la'i bla sgrub kha 'don bya skyabs mchod pa'i 'go nas zhal mjal bas / rten 'brel legs snyam de ma thag phyag gsum btsal yid spro ba'i ngang de dgong mtsho 'gram der zhag 'dug byas.* Tsongpon Khatag Zamyak, *A Pilgrim's Diary*, 166.

The rest of this chapter will use examples drawn from pilgrimage guides to demonstrate the repeated features that guides use to cultivate experiences such as the one above. Throughout, I will ask how these features change the way pilgrims might experience the pilgrimage place. I suggest that they do so via four related modes: denaturalizing ordinary perception, recontextualizing the site in terms of its wondrous features, inviting pilgrims' participation, and using metaphor to figure the pilgrimage place.

Denaturalizing Ordinary Perception

To begin, as pilgrimage guides describe a particular holy site, they emphasize the ways that its true nature differs from how it appears in ordinary perception. That is, pilgrimage guides reject the commonsense assumption most of us have that our perception allows us to see the world more or less the way it is. This is why the guide is necessary in the first place—to reeducate the deluded perceptions of ordinary people. For example, one pilgrimage guide to a mountain in modern-day Bhutan states that ordinary pilgrims "see the sky as completely empty of the dharma body; they do not clearly see that the intermediate space is the enjoyment body; and they don't pay respect, even though the earth is filled with the emanation body. Even if the Buddha were to come to their door, they would see a dirty beggar. But if they are not fooled by fabrications, wonders will arise."[24] By dharma body, enjoyment body, and emanation body, the guide refers to the three ways the Buddha manifests in the world. So the guide says that the earth and sky around the mountain are actually the very body of the Buddha. The problem is that, even though the Buddha and his teachings pervade the landscape, ordinary people fail to see it that way. The text's goal, then, is to remove pilgrims' delusions, so people can see the true nature of the holy mountain.

Similarly, a guide to Tsari writes that the mountain appears differently to different sorts of beings. Ordinary humans will see it one way, hungry ghosts will see it another, and gods will see it still another way. It states, however,

[24] *Chos skus nam mkha' gang yang stong par mthong / longs skus bar snang gang yang gsal mi mthong / sprul skus sa gzhi khyab kyang bab ma bcol / sangs rgyas sgo rtsar byon na yeng po mthong / chas mos mi mgo bskor na ya mtshan skyes.* "Brag dkar po'i gnas yig dkod pa rgya mtsho'i sprin phung," in *Bod kyi gnas yig bdams bsgrigs*, ed. Tshe ring dpal 'byor (Lhasa: bod ljongs bod yig dpe rnying dpe skrun khang, 2012), 373.

"Although it appears as many different phenomena, the way things really are is never changing. That is proven by the vision of buddhas."[25] This account places human perception alongside other ways of seeing, which downgrades the centrality of human vision and frames ordinary human perception is one—not very good—way of seeing the mountain. The way the mountain *actually is* is the way buddhas see it.[26]

Another pervasive way guides highlight that there are multiple ways to see the mountain is by describing the site in terms of its outer, inner, and secret appearance. For instance, a guide to Drak Karpo in Bhutan states:

> Emaho! Wondrous pure holy place (*gnas*)!
> Outwardly it looks like an octagonal mound.[27]
> Inwardly, it is Padmasambhava's realm of lotus light.[28]
> Secretly, it is the pure land, Abhirati, where the lords of the three Buddha families dwell.[29]

In other words, those who only see the surface appearance of the mountain miss the deeper wondrous reality of the holy place. The hermeneutic of "outer, inner, and secret" is fairly common to Tibetan religion, and it is common to see descriptions of outer, inner, and secret teachings; outer, inner, and secret offerings; and so on. In these cases, the category of "outer" is used to describe things that are for the general public, whereas that which is "secret" is the more essential or true version that is reserved for the select few. In the pilgrimage context, however, insofar as the outer, inner, and secret aspects of the pilgrimage place describe how it exists in relation to various types of perception.

[25] *Chos can gyi ngo nas du mar snang yang / chos nyid kyi tshul nam yang 'gyur ba med pa sangs rgyas rnams kyi gzigs pas grub pa'i phyir ro.* Pad + ma dkar po, *Gnas chen tsa ri tra'i ngo mtshar snang ba pad dkar legs bshad*, 209.

[26] As discussed in the previous chapter, the way the mountain *really is* in an ultimate sense, according to the complex Mādhyamaka philosophy endorsed by most Tibetan Buddhist philosopher, would be emptiness (*stong pa nyid*). Here I use "actually" to draw a contrast between outer appearance and inner reality, both of which Buddhist philosophers would suggest are ways of talking about conventional reality.

[27] Tsitta, the Tibetan transliteration of the Sanskrit *citta*, is imagined as an octahedronal palace. See Herbert V. Guenther, *Meditation Differently: Phenomenological-psychological Aspects of Tibetan Buddhist (Mahāmudrā and Snying-thig) Practices from Original Tibetan Sources* (Delhi: Motilal Benarsidass Publishers, 1992), 84.

[28] This is a hidden land (*sbas yul*) that is considered a place of refuge in turbulent times.

[29] *E ma ho / gnas dam pa ngo mtshar can / phyi ltar tsitta'i dbyings dang 'dra / nang ltar padma 'od kyi zhing / gsang ba ltar na mngon dga'i zhing.* "Brag dkar po'i gnas yig dkod pa rgya mtsho'i sprin phung," 375.

Those with coarse perception will see the outer, ordinary aspect, those with more refined perception will see the inner, extraordinary aspect, and those with perfected perception will see the secret aspect of the pilgrimage site. The ordinary perception is not wrong, exactly, but it is still not as good as the perfected, extraordinary perception of advanced beings. In ranking the different ways the mountain can be seen according to the scale of outward, inward, and secret, the text suggests that the goal is to move past the external and perhaps somewhat superficial appearance and get to the deeper reality. As such, though most pilgrims will only be able to perceive the outward dimension of the pilgrimage place, they are nonetheless made aware that it will appear differently to someone with the capacities to see the deeper, and by implication better or more-than-real, existence of the pilgrimage place.

Guides thereby lead pilgrims to place their own visual experience of the site in terms of a broader context of varying levels of perception and to question whether the way they see the mountain is the right way. This denaturalizes ordinary human perception and perhaps motivates pilgrims to try to transform their own visual perception.[30]

Recontextualization

Having thus rejected the idea that ordinary perception sees the mountain the way it is, pilgrimage guides then proceed to reframe pilgrims' perception of the holy place. For example, guides interpret the landscape in the context of a broader Buddhist cosmology.

For example, one guide to Wutai Shan contains a passage that reads:

> Rising high a hundred-fold above,
> The mandala of lands around its base,
> A sign leading on to untainted freedom,
> Those who wander throughout their lives.
>
> A mountain of five lovely, jeweled peaks,
> Blazing with splendor that chases the midnight sky,

[30] Pilgrimage guides seldom explicitly theorize how they work to effect transformations of perception.

A sign that the work of five wisdoms,
Is protecting beings without end.[31]

Another pilgrimage guide to Sekhar Guthog states:

When I, an aimless wandering beggar,
arrived here at this holy place of *Nya*,
This sort of wondrous vision appeared in my mind,
and I understood this as a holy place which teaches the dharma of signs. . . .[32]

The mountain in front which is like a heap of treasure
is a sign of the complete provision of necessities.
These grasses adorned with forests
are a sign of spontaneously arising experiences.
The mountain behind with a great cave shelter
is a sign of the lama's blessings.[33]

These passages pick out features of the natural landscape and interpret them as signs (*brda*) or symbols (*mtshon*) of some deeper message about how dharma works through the site. In both cases, the guide directs the pilgrim's attention to certain aspects of the visible landscape. It then connects this feature that pilgrims can see with something that they *cannot* initially see. Mountains and grasses, which might otherwise seem like pretty but otherwise neutral features of the landscape, are revealed to be full of hidden meaning. They suggest a broader system of signs in which the pilgrimage site reaches out to pilgrims in order to teach them about the dharma.

[31] *Phyi gnas kyi 'og gzhi dkyil 'khor kun / phyogs gzhan las rgyar phrag du mas mtho / de srid par 'khyams pa'i skye bo'i tshogs / zag med kyi thar par 'dren pa'i brda / ri rin chen mtshar sdug lhun po lnga / dgung mkha' la bsnyegs 'dra gzi byin 'bar / de ye shes lnga yi 'phrin las kyis / mtha' yas pa'i 'gro ba skyob pa'i brda.* Translation by Kurtis Schaeffer, "Tibetan Poetry on Wutai Shan," 215–242.

[32] This term *brda chos* is not particularly common, but reading them together is supported by the fact that the meter is 1 + 2+2 + 2+1 throughout the verse.

[33] *Nga brya bral sprang po rgyal khams pa / gnya' gnya'i gnas su 'dir slebs pa'i tshe / yid ngo mtshar snang ba 'di ltar shar / 'di brda chos ston pa'i gnas su go /. . . mdun na rin chen spungs 'dra'i ri / dgos rgyu rang la tshang ba'i brda / rtsi shing nags kyis brgyan pa 'di / nyams myong shugs kyis 'byung ba'i brda / rgyab ri brag skyibs che ba ni / bla ma byin gyis rlob pa'i brda.* "Sras mkhar dgu thog gtsug lag khang sogs kyi gnas yig," 49. Note that the author seems to be quoting/paraphrasing Dpa' bo gtsug lag 'phreng ba's song about the site here.

Other guides contain geomantic analyses (*sa dpyad*) that examine shapes in the landscape and what these shapes reveal about the natural forces thought to reside in the land.[34] For example, one guide to Gyangme reads:

> To the east, the water and the unending chain of snowy mountains were like a rocky bearded tiger. To the south, the central river looks like a turquoise thunder dragon. The red cliffs of the west. . . . Furthermore, all the mountains and forests and water in that plain seem to be bowing and praising. The geomancy is very auspicious, and it has many miraculous good omens.[35]

Here again, the guide analyzes and interprets the landscape in terms of underlying hidden forces. Such geomantic analyses, which often focus on how certain mountains or rock formations look from the perspective of someone at the site (for instance, a scorpion, or a half moon, or other animal or geometric shapes), reveal the potent forces already present in the landscape and, as such, give insight into whether the site is conducive to Buddhist practice or whether it is besieged by autochthonous demonic forces that would hinder such practice. Underlying this analysis is a logic of visual resemblance in which outer forms are scrutinized on the assumption that they correspond to the underlying qualities of the area. Again, the guide builds up the idea of the site as holy by describing the land as full of meaning that can be interpreted by the qualified viewer. The sheer abundance of features identified and interpreted as signs suggests that the whole landscape is full of hidden meaning, if only the pilgrim learns to look for it.

Guides also praise their subjects as places of natural beauty where animals wander carefree and birds sing melodiously. Such descriptions often consist of multisensory descriptions of babbling brooks, sweet-tasting spring waters, and fragrant flowers blooming, as demonstrated in another guide to Tsari:

> The trees with their abundant leaves dance when stirred by the wind, and some bloom with all kinds of flowers—utterly beautiful! The rivers burble

[34] See footnote 288 for more on the Tibetan tradition of geomancy.

[35] *Chu dang gangs rgyud rgyun mi chad pa shar du brag zam stag rgya bo'i tshul lta bu / lhor gzhung chu g.yu 'brug sngon mo'i tshul can / nub kyi gad pa dmar po . . . gzhan yang thang de la ri dang nags dang chu thams cad kyang 'dud cing bstod pa ltar yod pa / sa'i dpyad kyang shin tu bkra shis shing ya mtshan gyi dge ltas du ma dang ldan pa.* Chos kyi grags pa, *Rgyang me'i gnas yig rdo rje 'dzin pa'i dga' ston*, 467–468.

> sweetly and there are lakes and pools. Animals move about lazily in groups or sit about, and there is the resounding music from the flapping of birds' wings.[36]

This natural effervescence signifies the good qualities of the holy place. In the passage above, for example, the author highlights the lovely flowers and contented wildlife at Tsari to praise Tsari. Tsari's beauty is not incidental to its greatness as a pilgrimage mountain. Rather, the site's beauty and the site's spiritual potency are intimately connected, whereby the surface beauty of the site signifies that the place itself is ripe for spiritual practice. It might even be taken to suggest that the holiness of the site gives rise to this kind of abundant beauty.

Another recurring feature that plays on the idea of the pilgrimage place as potent and blessed is the description of "self-arisen" (*rang byon*) images. For example, a guide to Drak Karpo writes:

> There are many images of the lords of the three Buddha families. Nearby, there is the trunk of a wish fulfilling tree. There is a flowing river of ambrosia. There is a self-arisen stone *vajrakilaya*. To the right of the white cliff, there is a cave where Namkhai Nyingpo practiced . . .

Such features, which might also be translated as "naturally formed" or "spontaneously arisen," are miraculous and worthy of the pilgrim's attention because they are not the product of human fabrication and are instead a natural manifestation of the site's power. While objects made by artists and craftsmen are, of course, highly valued in Tibet, human-made objects bear the marks of effort and intentionality, qualities that are often denigrated in comparison to qualities of spontaneity and nonconceptuality. Self-arisen objects, by contrast, recall the self-arisen or intrinsic wisdom (*rang byung ye shes*) valorized in tantric philosophy and indicate a place where the nonconceptual and ever-creative ground underlying reality has made itself visible in the world of ordinary perception.

[36] *Indra nI la'i phung po dag dang utpala 'dab ma lta bu yi / rdo rje'i brag ri che rnams rab 'bar gzings ba'i bkod pa can / lo 'dab lhun stug rkang 'thung rnams ni rlung gis bskyod pa'i gar / rnam par mdzas shing la lar ni bsing me tog sna tshog bkra / lhung snyan sgrogs 'bab chu rnams dang mtshe'u dang lteng kar bcas / bag phab rgyu ba'i ri dwags khyu ang 'khod cing gnyis skyes tshogs rnams kyang / 'phur ba'i gshog sgra las kyang rol mo du ma sgra rnams 'byin.* Chos grags ye shes, *Dpal tsa ri tra la sogs pa'i gnas chen rnams la bstod pa*, in *Collected Works of Chos grags ye shes*, BDRC W1KG4876, 4: 269–274 (Beijing: Krung go'i bod rig pa dpe skrun khang, 2009), 242.

Already, we are starting to see a theme running through many of these recurring features: the interplay of the visible and the invisible. At times, the pilgrimage guide points to something that the pilgrim can plainly see, whether it is various landscape features or rocks with "self-arisen" images, and is told, whether explicitly or implicitly, that the visible object is a sign of some invisible underlying meaning about the site's potency. At the same time, the guide does not merely tell pilgrims what to look at and what it means but reaches out to the pilgrim and asks them to consider their own perceptual experience and then to interpret it as a sign of some otherwise invisible truth. This play of visible and invisible, as well as of superficial appearance and underlying meaning, creates a kind of depth metaphor about the site, suggesting to pilgrims that the real wonders of the pilgrimage site are not immediately visible on the surface.

Finally, guides connect the landscape of the pilgrimage site to famous spiritual masters who practiced at the site. We saw this in the above selection, which mentions the famous master Namkhai Nyingpo. Guides identify certain marks at the site as handprints left by a past master, certain caves as places where they meditated, or even retell the stories of what certain masters did at the place. These stories of past masters connect present pilgrims to the history of the holy place. Those masters recognized the site's good qualities and also added to them, leaving blessings for future pilgrims. The guide thus helps to ground the now-absent master's presence in the visible landscape, allowing pilgrims to directly encounter the place and, by extension, the master's presence. Often, guides point to handprints or footprints said to be left by the master at the rock that materialize this connection.

Such descriptions, I argue, do more than merely promote the site as wonderful; they actively *shape* pilgrims' experience of the site itself. As various scholars of space and place have pointed out, we do not merely experience the physical aspects of the place. Rather, our experience is shaped by our culturally conditioned imagination of what the place is. As such, when guides describe the holy mountain as wondrous in all these ways, it affects how pilgrims experience the place. In interpreting the landscape as meaningful and as full of signs that point to unseen realities, guides create for pilgrims the sense that what they do see is connected with all of these unseen realities. It primes them, moreover, to look for additional signs hidden behind every rock and stone.

Consider, for example, a passage that combines several of the elements discussed above. The guide to Drak Karpo reads:

> There, there is the mark of a wish-fulfilling gem. Below that, there is the image of hundreds of offering bowls offered by the dakinis. Then, when you look just beyond that, there is [the place where] long ago, when the master came, a black naga conjured up a curse. But Padmasambhava performed his yogic gaze, and the naga dissolved into the rock. There is a boulder that was split by the sword of lightning. It is a wonder visible even at present! Pray there to avoid harm from demons and spirits! Then go a bit farther and there is a self-arisen Īśvara image. Request that a child be born to you, or whatever you want! Then, go a bit farther . . .[37]

The text draws the gaze of the pilgrim from one feature to another, almost overwhelming them with the sheer amount. It barely pauses to describe individual features or where they are located. This might strike modern readers as boring and unhelpful, but that would miss the point of this type of description. Each feature it points to is a visible trace of a reality not immediately available to the pilgrim, such as the presence of *ḍākinī* spirits or the story about Padmasambhava's victory over a demon. The guide directs pilgrims' attention back and forth between perceptible and imperceptible aspects, between what they see and what they must imagine. It suggests that the mountain's solid, ordinary, physical appearance masks a world that overflows with the activity of the dharma. This primes pilgrims to search for traces of this activity overflowing into the world they can perceive and experience.

Inviting Pilgrims' Participation

In addition to denaturalizing ordinary perception and recontextualizing it in terms of an extraordinary vision of the site, pilgrimage guides explicitly reach out to the pilgrim and invite them to interpret their own visual experience. That is, guides do not merely tell pilgrims about the various sights at

[37] *Ci 'dod nor gyi zhabs rjes yod / de 'og mkha' 'gros phul ba yi / mchod ting brgya rtsa'i tshul yang yod / de nas phar la bltas tsa na / sngon tshe slob dpon byon pa'i dus / klu bdud nag pos sdig par sprul / u rgyan chen pos lha stangs mdzad / klu bdud de nyid brag tu 'thim / gnam lcags ral gris pha bong bshag / ya mtshan deng sang mjal rgyu yod / gza' klu btsan gdug bdud btsan gyi / gnod 'tshe med pa'i smon lam gdab / de nas phar tsam phyin pa dang / dbang phyug chen po rang byon yod / ci 'dod bu yi dngos grub zhus / de nas phar la phyin pa dang.* "Brag dkar po'i gnas yig dkod pa rgya mtsho'i sprin phung," 377–378.

the pilgrimage place but ask them to reflect upon how *they* see the site and to interpret what their own perception means.

This is made explicit in devices that tell the pilgrim "If you see X, it means Y, but if you see A, it means B." For instance, a guide to Bo Gangkar Mountain in eastern Tibet states:

> In the neck of the mountain is a great banner of light that appears by itself . . . if you can see it right away, that is a sign that karmic obscurations are decreasing. If you are not yet able to perceive these phenomena, this is a sign that there are still some karmic obscurations.[38]

It continues by telling pilgrims what it means if they see white, if they see yellow, or if they see red. In these cases, the pilgrim is not a passive recipient for the guide's discourse about the holy place but is *actively recruited to participate* in an act of interpreting the pilgrimage site. It is not only the pilgrimage place being interpreted, then, but also the pilgrim. In directing the pilgrim to interpret their own visual experiences, the text thus works upon the pilgrim by causing them to reflect upon their own perception and the way that it does not give transparent access to the external world. Rather, what the pilgrim experiences in perception is dependent on various factors that lie outside the immediate control of the pilgrim.

In the case just discussed, this is made explicit, but it is also communicated implicitly elsewhere. For example, a guide to Drak Karpo reads:

> If your perception is impure, and you lack faith and devotion, you will ever and always see the existence of rocks. At Tsari you will see the land empty of anything but trees, ravines, and valleys. At Kailash you will see a heap of snow.[39]

Statements like this force the pilgrim to confront the fact that they do not see the pilgrimage place as the mandala the text says it is. By extension, they are

[38] Translation by S. Brinson Aldridge, "The Seed of Devotion: A Pilgrim's Guide to Gangkar with a Synopsis of Benefits Found at Sacred Sites," in *The Incarnation from White Glacier Mountain: A Biography of Gangkar Rinpoche* (West Conshohocken, PA: Infinity Publishing, 2008), 89.

[39] *Rang snang ma dag dad mos med gyur na / kun nas kun kyang sa rdo'i rang bzhin mthong / tsa ri zhes kyang shing rong lung stong mthong / ti ser gsung yang kha ba phung zhig mthong / la phyi zer yang / chu yi rang bzhin 'dra / mtsho chen bzhi yang mjal tshe de rang tsam.* "Brag dkar po'i gnas yig bkod pa rgya mtsho'i sprin phung," 380.

forced to confront their own "impure" perception and may be led to wonder what the site would look like if they were different.

Insofar as this is framed in the second person and tailored to individual perspectives,[40] it differs from general third-person descriptions of the site that are given independent of the pilgrim's perceptions. Of course, even those third person descriptions exist in a framework that emphasizes that different sorts of beings will see the site differently, so there is always an implicit comparison with the perspective of the individual pilgrim (and thus between the pilgrim's level of accomplishment and that of the ideal viewer of the site). Nevertheless, there is an important difference between a guide saying, "This site is a mandala" and "If you see this site as a mandala, it means you have good karmic connections." The latter explicitly invokes the perception of the pilgrim, calling on them to reflect on what they see and what it means. The text thus actively recruits pilgrims to see themselves and their vision of the place as in some sense *about them* and not merely about the place.

The effect is to highlight the difference between the pilgrim's ordinary mundane perception and the extraordinary vision of the site laid forth in the text, and to focus the pilgrim's attention on the gap between the two.

Figuration: Mountain as Mandala

We will finish our examination of the tropes pilgrimage guides use to work on pilgrims by examining one that is in a sense fundamental to all the others. That is, the idea of the pilgrimage place as a mandala, a celestial palace in which the central deities of tantric texts preach the dharma. This idea occurs in almost every pilgrimage guide, even when describing a fairly minor site. The guide to Drak Karpo says, for example, that "all mandalas are contained

[40] Although this trope centers upon individual perception and reflection, it is important to remind ourselves to not fall into the trap of interpreting pilgrimage in solely individualistic terms. Many scholars of Tibetan pilgrimage have pointed out that Tibetan pilgrimages are generally social affairs, with groups of pilgrims from a particular village or family joining together for a journey, in which pilgrims generally aim to accumulate merit and rejoice in the accomplishments of advanced practitioners rather than cultivate their own individual religious experiences. In the words of Keith Basso, "senses of place, while always informed by bodies of local knowledge, are finally the possessions of particular individuals. People, not cultures, sense places . . . and they do so in varying ways." Keith H. Basso, *Wisdom Sits in Places: Landscape and Language among the Western Apache* (Albuquerque: University of New Mexico Press, 1996), xv–xvi. Nevertheless, while we must be careful not to overemphasize the individual perspective, neither should we abandon it entirely, for it can help us understand how these pilgrimage texts construct a certain kind of pilgrimage experience and contribute to the possibility of seeing the world differently.

in these rocks."[41] The guide to Tsari says that Tsari is a "great mandala all on one base."[42] Guides will sometimes phrase this in other ways by saying that the holy place is really the body of the buddha, or a buddha's pure land, but the general claim is the same: the place is really something else, visible to only a select few. It is not always a mandala, but I use that as a convenient shorthand as it is a frequently made claim. The identification of a particular place with a mandala is common across Tibetan history. The mandala is a widespread feature of Tibetan religious geography, and various places of religious significance are identified as mandalas, including, most famously, the area surrounding Lhasa.

But what does it mean for a guide to say that the mountain is a mandala? Guides say that someone with highly advanced perception would see the site as the mandala it truly is, but what does that even look like? What *work* do statements like that do on the imagined audience? Clearly, it is not a description of what the guide expects the pilgrim to actually be able to see initially. I suggest that we recall Ricoeur's work on metaphor. In his key example, the reader is confronted by the metaphor "Achilles is a lion" and tries to make sense of it in literal terms but is unable to do so. This failure opens up the possibility of the second-order *seeing-as*, in which she both sees Achilles *as* a lion and sees him *not* as a lion. These two images are in tension with one another, but it is a productive poetic tension and not a logical fallacy. This is the model on which, according to Ricoeur, poetic language functions to train people in seeing-as, and the model on which biblical texts "name" God. We might see the pilgrimage guide's assertions that the pilgrimage site is a mandala not as an expectation that ordinary pilgrims will be able to directly see the mountain as a celestial palace made of gems and populated by various gods but as a metaphor that works precisely because the pilgrim *does not* see the mountain as a literal gem-encrusted palace.

Indeed, it is difficult to imagine what it means to see the mountain as a mandala. Is the mandala inside individual rocks, or the whole mountain, or inside the practitioner? It is not clear what the pilgrim is supposed to see. However, this seeming confusion is not necessarily a flaw. For it is also not clear what it means to see Achilles as a lion. The metaphor "Achilles is a lion"

[41] *Rdo 'dir dkyil 'khor thams cad tshang.* "Brag dkar po'i gnas yig dkod pa rgya mtsho'i sprin phung," 379.

[42] *Chos can gyi ngo nas du mar snang yang / chos nyid kyi tshul nam yang 'gyur ba med pa sangs rgyas rnams kyi gzigs pas' grub pa'i phyir ro / ngo bo de ltar yin pas / gzhi gcig steng du ma lus dkyil 'khor che.* Pad+ma dkar po, *Gnas chen tsa ri tra'i ngo mtshar snang ba pad dkar legs bshad*, 209.

depends on cognitive failure; it depends on readers not knowing how to put these two things together and on those readers then scrambling to figure out a way to rectify this failure. Similarly, the pilgrimage guides' claim that the mountain is a mandala is hard to understand, but this disconnect drives the metaphor forward, compelling the audience to make sense of it.

The text clearly does not expect the ordinary pilgrim to be able to directly see the mountain as a mandala; while advanced practitioners meditating in caves might someday attain this level of perfected perception, it is clearly considered to be out of reach of most ordinary pilgrims. Identifying the mountain as a mandala, then, assumes a disconnect between what the pilgrim sees and what other, more advanced, beings might see. But it also creates the possibility of the kind of phenomenological experience Ricoeur suggests that metaphors can create, one that could possibly bridge this gap in perception, resulting in a state of seeing the object in two ways at once. In other words, it *figures* the pilgrimage place, reshaping pilgrims' experience of it by disclosing another way of seeing the site.

Conclusion

What is god
and what is stone
the dividing line
if it exists
is very thin
at jejuri
and every other stone
is god or his cousin

—Arun Kolatkar, *Jejuri*[43]

I began this chapter with a passage from Arun Kolatkar's 1974 series of poems *Jejuri*, which imagine a narrator's visit to a temple town in Maharashtra. The particular poem from which the selections are taken, "A Scratch," captures the narrator's strange feeling as he walks through the half-toppled monuments at Jejuri that every rock bursts with the potentially divine. In studying pilgrimage guides, I have tried to understand how they contribute to a similar

[43] Kolatkar, *Jejuri*, 22.

sense of charged activity underlying particular sites of Tibetan pilgrimage, and how this shapes pilgrims' experiences of the site.

The answer, I suggest, is the combined force of the various literary strategies used by guides to depict the pilgrimage site. By denaturalizing ordinary perception, recontextualizing the site in terms of a wondrous unseen landscape, inviting pilgrims' participation, and asserting that the site is a mandala, pilgrimage guides direct pilgrims' attention toward two different ways of seeing the mountain. One way is pilgrims' ordinary perception of the physical world. The other way is an extraordinary and wondrous vision of the site as a divine mandala overflowing with dharma and blessings.

In drawing attention to these two different visions of the site, guides highlight the *gap* between these two ways of seeing. They tell pilgrims that their ordinary perception is mistaken, and that they need to overcome that ordinary perception to see the site as it really is. At the same time, however, guides bring these two ways of seeing together for the pilgrim. They do so by directing pilgrims' attention back and forth between these two ways of seeing. For example, when a guide says that *this* stone is a self-arisen wonder generated by the spiritual potency of the landscape, or that *this* mark is a footprint left by a religious virtuoso who triumphed in a magical battle here long ago, the guide is connecting the landscape that the pilgrim can see with the underlying and extraordinary reality of the site that the pilgrim cannot see. In drawing a pilgrim's attention from ordinary perceptible reality to extraordinary envisioned reality and back again, the guides interweave these two worlds.[44] In seeing the pilgrimage site in front of them, the pilgrim is led to see the traces of the extraordinary world they cannot see, and that extraordinary world is made more real by being grounded in the physical landscape.

In this state of co-seeing, the pilgrim sees the site in two ways at once: the ordinary perception seen with the physical eye and the extraordinary vision seen in the mind's eye. Extraordinary vision does not replace the pilgrim's ordinary perception—recall that pilgrimage guides assume that the pilgrim sees the site in an ordinary way. Rather, ordinary perception and extraordinary vision are both present in the awareness of the pilgrim.

There are a range of possibilities for what this co-seeing can entail, ranging from simple awareness that there are two ways of seeing the site, from attention to the deficiencies of ordinary perception, to the phenomenological

[44] I adopt the language of "interwoven worlds" from Aaron Reich, "Seeing the Sacred: Daoist Ritual, Painted Icons, and the Canonization of a Local God in Ming China" (PhD Diss., The University of Wisconsin–Madison, 2018), especially 243–247.

experience of moving back and forth from the ordinary perception of the material landscape to the imagined representation of the wondrous landscape, to transformative experiences where these two visions come together in a dramatic visionary experience of the site.[45] This depends on the particular pilgrim, their background and aspirations, and the way that they engage the landscape and the pilgrimage guide itself. The text fosters co-seeing by inviting the pilgrim to consider two distinct ways of viewing the same site, but the resulting experience is produced through a collaboration of pilgrim, text, and landscape, and so it can result in a wide range of experiences.

In all of these cases, however, co-seeing shapes the way pilgrims experience the site. Guides bring the wondrous world of gods, buddhas, and bejeweled palaces into the concrete experience of the pilgrim. Other parts of the Buddhist tradition may describe or represent extraordinary pure lands, heavens, or mandalas, but in pilgrimage, that fantastic vision is grounded in the material landscape traversed by the pilgrim, grounding otherwise abstract or distant descriptions into the concrete landscape. The extraordinary world seen by the buddhas thus becomes part of the sensory and embodied experience of the pilgrim, which serves to bridge the gap between the here and now and something "beyond," thereby making the extraordinary world more proximate and real.[46]

Co-seeing also focuses pilgrims' attention on the gap between ordinary perception and the way that the guide claims that the site really is, thus highlighting the deficiencies of ordinary perception, breaking them out of habitual patterns of seeing. This is important because, as we will recall, Buddhism maintains that these habitually delusory patterns of seeing perpetuate suffering. Breaking people out of those patterns thus creates the possibility that pilgrims will act in new and hopefully better ways.

In addition, co-seeing creates the conditions for potentially transformative experiences of the site. In bringing two visions of the site together in the minds of pilgrims, co-seeing creates the possibility that these two ways of seeing converge, and pilgrims catch a *glimpse* of the wonders that lie outside

[45] See, for example, the quotation from Khatag Zamyak cited earlier.

[46] It is worth pointing out that many pilgrimage guides contain the word *dad pa* (faith) in their titles, and many explicitly state that their aim is to cultivate faith in the pilgrimage site. A full discussion of this would take us too far afield. However, we can briefly point out that Tibetan descriptions of the "three faiths" (*dad pa gsum*) include trust of unseen realities (*yid ches pa'i dad pa*), aspiration to the state of Buddhahood (*'dod pa'i dad pa*), and clear-hearted awe at the object of faith (*dang ba'i dad pa*). We might thus see pilgrimage guides as oriented toward cultivating these aspects of faith in the pilgrimage site.

their ordinary perception.[47] Such a glimpse is unstable and momentary, but it is enough to give pilgrims a taste of the world as they might someday experience it and enough to cultivate in them an affective and aspirational faith. It starts in the imagination but may then be experienced in a powerful way at the site itself. This faith, then, is not blind faith but a faith strengthened by visual experiences of the pilgrimage place.

Pilgrimage guides thus play a powerful role in facilitating meaningful encounters with the pilgrimage place. Of course, there are as many individual experiences of pilgrimage as there are individual pilgrims, and many pilgrims' experiences of the holy place differ from that envisioned by the pilgrimage guide. In the hands of an attentive pilgrim, however, pilgrimage guides and their literary strategies foster a collaboration among pilgrim, text, and landscape that has the power to shape the pilgrim's ability to see the mountain as a holy mandala and, furthermore, to cultivate meaningful and transformative pilgrimage experiences. By starting with a specific physical place as the object of transformation of perception, moreover, they provide a pathway toward the broader transformation of perception sought in Buddhism.

[47] For more on the phenomenology of the glimpse, see Edward Casey, *The World at a Glance* (Bloomington: Indiana University Press, 2007), 384 and 388–391.

6
Khatag Zamyak's Co-Seeing

Introduction

Thus far, we have mainly examined texts that try to change how pilgrims see a site. Our question throughout was how such texts promoted particular practices of seeing that would transform pilgrims' experience of the site. However, we were limited by the fact that we lacked the perspective of an ordinary pilgrim in all of this. In this chapter, we will examine a pilgrim diary that grants a valuable new perspective on the goals of transforming perception.

My main question will be how Khatag Zamyak sees on pilgrimage. What is he trying to see? How does he try to see it? How does he interpret what he does see? To put it another way, what are Khatag Zamyak's *practices of seeing*? To address these questions, I will examine the pilgrim diary of the Tibetan merchant Khatag Zamyak (1896–1961), which records his pilgrimage to central Tibet and Mount Kailash from 1944 to 1956. While Khatag Zamyak's experience cannot speak for all Tibetan pilgrims, using the diary as a case study yields insights into the structural logic of pilgrimage practice.

Based on a close reading of the diary, I suggest that Khatag Zamyak enacts a variety of practices—such as reading pilgrimage guidebooks, performing circumambulations, cultivating "pure perception" (*dag snang*), and "looking closely" (*zhib mjal*)—that cultivate co-seeing. By means of these practices, he sees the landscape and holy sites in front of him in their ordinary form with his physical eyes, and he also sees in his mind's eye the wondrous landscape depicted in scriptures, guides, and narratives. He moves back and forth between his ordinary perception—the mode of experience by which he is presented with actual things in the world—and his imagination—the mode of experience by which he represents to himself that something is possible.[1] Khatag Zamyak continually tries to bridge the disjunction between these two ways of seeing. In so doing, he constantly draws his focus back and

[1] This distinction between imagination and perception is drawn from Samuel Todes, *Body and World* (Boston: MIT Press, 2001), 130.

Making the Invisible Real. Catherine Hartmann, Oxford University Press. © Oxford University Press 2025.
DOI: 10.1093/9780197791585.003.0007

forth between ordinary perception and imaginative perception, weaving these two worlds together in his experience in a way that transforms his experience of Kailash.

The Diary of an Accidental Pilgrim

Scholars are fortunate to have Khatag Zamyak's diary, as he did not intend to publish it. He died in India in 1961, with the scrolls of his diary hidden away among his things. They sat untouched for about three decades before his nephew stumbled upon them.[2] The nephew brought the diary to a lama named Jamyang Wangyel[3] and asked if publishing the diary might be useful to the Tibetan exile community, particularly since so many in that community can no longer access holy places in Tibet. Jamyang Wangyal agreed and edited the text,[4] which was eventually published in 1997 as *Phyi lo 1944 nas 1956 bar bod dang bal po rgya gar bcas la gnas bskor bskyod pa'i nyin deb* (*A Pilgrim's Diary: Tibet, Nepal & India, 1944–1956*).[5]

The diary has received little scholarly attention since its publication in 1997.[6] This may be changing, however, for in addition to this study, Lucia M. S. Galli has also recently focused on the text for her D.Phil. dissertation.[7]

[2] Khatag Zamyak's nephew mentions that the text that he found is only part of a larger diary. When fleeing to India in 1959, Khatag Zamyak apparently left scrolls covering the years 1956–1959 behind at Shigatse.

[3] 'Jam dbyangs dbang rgyal. See also BDRC P1KG23823.

[4] The introduction says that he makes small edits, but we should be aware of the possibility that he made major emendations.

[5] Kha stag 'dzam yag, *Nyin deb*.

[6] Though the published version of the diary mentions that Karl-Heinz Everding gave a donation to support publishing the diary (*Nyin deb*, 10) as far as I can tell, Everding never discussed the diary in his scholarship. Charles Ramble discussed it in an essay entitled "The Complexity of Tibetan Pilgrimage," in *Searching for the Dharma, Finding Salvation*, ed. Christoph Cueppers and Max Deeg, 179–196 (Lumbini: Lumbini International Research Institute, 2014), 187.

[7] In this dissertation, which as of press time was not publicly available, Galli uses "two different heuristic devices, i.e. narratology and socio-economic analysis, in an attempt to capture the multilayered and complex essence of 'Dzam yak's journal." She focuses on the political, cultural, and social history of 'Dzam yak's ancestral land of Nang chen, what the information contained in the diary can tell us about practices of trade at the time, the interconnections of Khatag's pilgrimage practices and economic activities, and the power of religious communities at the time, given the large sums of money involved in pilgrimage. Galli deliberately focuses on socioeconomic analyses of the text, going so far as to question whether we should term Khatag Zamyak's travels as "pilgrimages." My work takes the approach, which I see as complementary to Galli's rather than in opposition to it, of foregrounding questions of religious practices and experiences. See an abstract for the dissertation in Lucia M. S. Galli, "The Accidental Pilgrimage of a Rich Beggar: The Account of tshong dpon Kha stag 'Dzam yag's Travels through Tibet, Nepal, and India (1944–1956)," *Études Mongoles et Sibériennes, Centrasiatiques et Tibétaines* 48 (2017): 1–5. Galli has also published several excellent articles relating to Khatag Zamyak's diary, listed in the Bibliography.

The genre of diary to which it belongs (*nyin deb*), or literally "day book," is also understudied because there are very few readily available examples of the genre.[8]

What sort of picture do we get of Khatag Zamyak from the diary? We can start with his own words, for Khatag Zamyak briefly describes himself at the very beginning of the diary:[9]

> As for myself, the one with the nickname "Zamyak" and the dharma name Ngawang Dargyay, the one who is constantly intoxicated by the afflictive emotions, I was born in the middle of the area of Rabshi, which is considered part of Ga, in Kham. Up until my 49th year, there has been success and failure, happiness and suffering, a mood inclined and disinclined to dharma—if I wrote it down, it would be like ripples on the water. Some [of these stories] give rise to compassion, some of them inspire renunciation, some show faults, some are funny, and so forth. Since there are many such [stories], I will not write them down. Now, in my 49th year, because of fortunate circumstances, I wandered alone without a leader, relying on friends from home, into all three regions of Tibet. And so, in order that the encounters (literally faces seen, *zhal mjal*) and circumambulations of the three supports and holy places may be fixed (*'jags*) in my mind, I will write down a little [of what I saw on pilgrimage].[10]

Khatag Zamyak gives almost no information about himself beyond this brief sketch—he does not elaborate on what he means by his successes and

[8] One of the few treatments of the genre, written by Janet Gyatso, relates her attempts to understand Tibetan diary-writing practices. Many of her informants are diffident and sheepish about the fact that they keep diaries, and some even deny it outright, considering the practice as pointless as "counting crows' teeth." And yet as she probes further, she realizes that, whatever their feelings about whether they ought to keep diaries, many Tibetans do in fact keep diaries. See "Counting Crows' Teeth: Tibetans and Their Diaries," in *Les Habitants Du Toit Du Monde*, ed. Samten Karmay and Phillip Sagant (Paris: Société d'Ethnologie, 1997), 159–178. For another analysis of the genre that considers Khatag Zamyak, see Lucia Galli, "The Crafting Memory of the Self: Reflections on Tibetan Diary-Keeping," *Life Writing* 17, no. 3 (2020): 347–366.

[9] It may strike us as strange that Khatag Zamyak includes an introduction of any sort to his diary, for an introduction would likely only be practically useful for an outside reader. However, Khatag Zamyak apparently never tried to publish the diary, and it remained in his effects until after his death. It would be interesting to know if other diaries contain this kind of introduction, or whether this is peculiar to Khatag Zamyak.

[10] *Nyon mongs pas rgyun du myos pa'i gces ming 'dzam yag dang chos ming ngag dbang dar rgyas sogs thogs pa'i rang nyid ni / mdo khams sga yi phyogs su brtsi ba'i rab shis zhes pa'i yul de'i dbus su skye ba blangs nas / lo ngo zhe dgu bar 'byor rgud song ba dang / bde sdug blo kha chos la phyogs ma phyogs chu yi gnyer ma lta bu yod cing bri na / la ni snying rje skye / la ni nges 'byung skye / la ni mtshang la phog.* Kha stag 'dzam yag, *Nyin deb*, 11.

failures, or discuss anything prior to his setting off on pilgrimage in 1944. At times, he mentions that he knows a place or a person from having met them previously, but for the most part, he focuses on his daily experiences on pilgrimage.

Much of what we know about Khatag Zamyak, then, comes from the introduction to the published version of the diary written by the monk Jamyang Wangyal and Khatag Zamyak's nephew. They describe Khatag Zamyak as one of the seven children—three boys and four girls—born to parents named Khatag Dranga Rabten (*kha stags drangs ga rab bstan*) and Droza Tsomo (*gro bza' mtsho mo*) in Rabshi in Kham. Lama Jamyang Wangyal paints a lovely picture of Khatag Zamyak's homeland through poetic descriptions of the various mountains, waters, and animals there. Young Khatag Zamyak received basic education at a nearby monastery but also inherited his family's profession of trade and livestock rearing, and he seems to have grown into a wealthy and important trader who patronized local Buddhist monasteries.

His life seems to have proceeded happily, until he was accused of the murder of a member of the local ruling family. He strenuously denied the charge in a hand-written statement to the judges, which Lama Jamyang Wangyal transcribes. In Khatag Zamyak's account, the lord of Rabshi, named Thuthob Namgyal (*mthu stobs rnam rgyal*), passed away in Chamdo. Amid the resulting turmoil about who would be in charge after the death of the lord, Thuthob Namgyal's eldest son, Kardor (*kar rdor*), passed away suddenly at Lüng Monastery (*klung dgon*). Khatag Zamyak seems to have been accused of murdering Kardor by poison. He claims that this unjust accusation came from the ruling family's desire to seize his extensive assets. Khatag Zamyak tells the judges how the deceased man's family sent troops to Lüng Monastery on the twelfth day of the iron male dragon year of the Sixteenth Rabjung (1940), killed a number of monks (including Tulku Jamseng (*'jam seng*), accused of being one of Khatag Zamyak's co-conspirators), and led Khatag Zamyak away in chains. His property and assets were seized, and he was kept in solitary confinement for six months. In his letter, he maintained his innocence and begged his captors for compassion. It is not clear how Khatag Zamyak ultimately secured his release, but he must have done so, for soon after, he started describing himself as a "new-born beggar and vagabond."[11]

[11] *Gsar sprang 'khyam po*. Ibid., 5.

A few years later, in 1944, Khatag Zamyak asked a lama to predict his future. The lama performed various rituals and prophesized that Khatag Zamyak must undertake pilgrimage to central Tibet (*dbus tsang*) and Kailash in the next three months. Khatag Zamyak accepted, made a great offering to the lama and the monastery, and then set off with a companion named Ba yan in the tenth month of 1944.[12] It is in this state that he began his pilgrimage, as well as the pilgrimage diary.

Soon after Khatag Zamyak set off, his diary entries take on a recognizable pattern. First, Khatag Zamyak arrives at a particular site, usually giving the name of a temple or describing its relationship to a famous practitioner. He then describes the main "supports" (*rten*) that he has seen at that site. This can include various kinds of shrine objects, statues, paintings, objects of worship, or holy texts such as the Buddhist canon. He recounts the various actions he undertakes at the site, including prostrations, worship, circumambulations, purifications, and aspirations. Sometimes he also describes the emotional state—often devotion or rejoicing—that arises when performing those actions. Descriptions of his visits to sites inevitably end with a description of the donations he makes to the monastery or to the monks, typically consisting of silver currency[13] but also a donation of tsampa[14] or daily tea.[15] Periodically, he describes buying, transporting, or selling goods, showing that for Khatag Zamyak, as with many Tibetan pilgrims, religious and economic activity are always intertwined.[16]

In between descriptions of his activities, we get notes about travel conditions and what he reads, but he rarely details his emotions. It is not nearly as juicy as some might expect a diary to be. However, there are periodic flashes of Khatag Zamyak's internal life, including his concern for the animals in his care, his disappointment at his own lack of realizations, and his difficulty coming to terms with growing older and losing physical capacity.

Over the course of the diary, Khatag Zamyak travels throughout Tibet, visiting major sites in Kham in eastern Tibet, around Lhasa and other places

[12] Ibid., 12–13.

[13] The published diary also includes an unpaginated appendix containing scans of various Tibetan coins and paper money as examples of what Khatag Zamyak uses. See Kha stag 'dzam yag, *Nyin deb*, appendix.

[14] *Rtsam pa bre gsum dang srang bcu tsam gyis zhal 'debs.* Kha stag 'dzam yag, *Nyin deb*, 102.

[15] *Mang ja dang sku 'gyed srang gang re bcas phul.* Ibid., 213.

[16] Scholars have noted that many pilgrims funded their travel by engaging in trade along the way. See, for example, Toni Huber, *The Cult of Pure Crystal Mountain: Popular Pilgrimage and Visionary Landscape in Southeast Tibet* (Oxford: Oxford University Press, 1999), 196–218.

in central Tibet, and Kailash in western Tibet, as well as visiting Buddhist sites in India and Nepal, and smaller sites on the path between the major sites he visits.

Methodological Approach

Unlike other works examined in this book, Khatag Zamyak's diary was not intended for an external audience such as pilgrims, polemical opponents, or disciples. Although this might suggest greater reliability—who lies in their own diary?—the reality is not so simple. The diary is a literary artifact that reflects complex practices of self-disclosure and self-construction, requiring careful and self-reflective reading.

One question that arises is whether Khatag Zamyak accurately documents his practices, or if it is a constructed image of himself that does not match reality. However, this framing of the issue may be unhelpful. It implies that our main goal is to uncover *what actually happened* during Khatag Zamyak's pilgrimage, and that the text merely serves as a lens through which to view this reality. At best, the language is transparent and says what happened as it happened, or at worst, the language distorts what happened, obscuring it from our view. This approach assumes that language can only warp reality. This way of approaching texts, of seeing them as documents from which we can extract useful information about the past and discard the parts that do not, has been common in historical studies.

My approach, however, has not been to view Khatag Zamyak's diary as a document from which to extract information about reality, but instead to treat it as a literary work that aims to construct a new reality. Following LaCapra's observation that texts have both "documentary" and "work-like" modes,[17] I read the diary as both describing how Khatag Zamyak sees the world and as a vehicle through which he tries to effect in himself the transformations sought on pilgrimage. In this way, the diary is an example of a "technology of the self" as theorized by Michel Foucault;[18] that is, a technique by which Khatag Zamyak works on himself to achieve a certain transformation.

[17] Dominick LaCapra, *Rethinking Intellectual History: Texts, Contexts, Language* (Ithaca, NY: Cornell University Press, 1983), 30.
[18] See Michel Foucault, *Technologies of the Self: A Seminar with Michel Foucault* (Amherst: University of Massachusetts Press, 1988).

I understand parts of the diary as having a work-like function, especially those that are repeated frequently. For instance, the diary records certain daily details and passing thoughts but also often focuses on activities and experiences oriented toward enlightenment (often the accumulation of merit). In focusing on and recording dharma activities, the diary focused Khatag Zamyak's attention on these religious goals. Despite these activities taking up a small part of his day, writing about them emphasized their centrality to his life. The act of writing allows Khatag Zamyak to represent his life to himself and amplify certain elements, such as seeing holy images, making donations, interpreting karmic signs, finding similarities between himself and Milarepa, and observing the suffering of animals. He emphasizes affective states of devotion, generosity, compassion, and emulation of holy exemplars, and directs his attention toward them, making them more salient to himself. The act of keeping a diary is not a passive documentation of events, but actively shapes Khatag Zamyak's experience by focusing his attention on religious activities that he understands to be significant.

Recognizing these work-like aspects of the text, I approach the text's descriptions of Khatag Zamyak's travels, including the places he goes, the people he meets, and, importantly, his practices of seeing, as operating in a documentary mode. That is, I read Khatag Zamyak's account as descriptive of his activities on pilgrimage. While some might recommend greater skepticism, I disagree. The diary includes random details that seem unrelated to any broader theme or message. They are simply included because they caught Khatag Zamyak's attention. Khatag Zamyak records episodes of being chased by and escaping bandits, a funny story about a horse, his encounter with an elderly Bön practitioner, encounters with Americans, his thoughts on the Golden Temple in Amritsar, the price of train tickets in India, and his thoughts on the tax policy of the Tibetan state. The diary thus blends documentary accounts of his experiences with work-like aspects that shape his memories and draw out certain religious patterns.

This understanding of Khatag Zamyak's project is supported by evidence from the dairy itself. Early in the diary, Khatag Zamyak explains why he is keeping the diary: he will write down a little of what he sees on pilgrimage "in order that the encounters (literally faces seen, *zhal mjal ba*) and circumambulations of the three supports may be fixed (*'jags*) in my mind (*yid*)." So in some sense, Khatag Zamyak thinks of the diary as having both documentary and work-like aspects, serving both to record his pilgrimage activities while also shaping his recollections of them.

The key work-like pattern that this chapter will focus on is Khatag Zamyak's engagement with visual perception. Close attention to the diary shows vision as mediating Khatag Zamyak's encounters with the places he visits. We see him adopting a variety of highly *active* modes of visual engagement. Seeing, for Khatag Zamyak, is not a passive activity, but rather creatively draws on a combination of imaginative and sensory resources to construct a particular kind of experience of the pilgrimage place. These culturally patterned ways of looking both generate certain kinds of visual experiences and grant them meaning within a broader cultural system.[19]

Khatag Zamyak's Practices of Seeing at Kailash

We will focus on Khatag Zamyak's experiences at Kailash to better understand these practices of seeing. While the diary records his experiences at many pilgrimage sites in Tibet and India, Kailash holds particular significance for him. Not only was Kailash specifically mentioned in the prophecy that led Khatag Zamyak to undertake pilgrimage,[20] but he provides more detailed descriptions of his activities there than at other sites. Appendix 1 includes an extended translation of the full text for those interested in exploring this further. The translation shows how densely references to sight and seeing occur in this section. Khatag Zamyak employs various practices of seeing during his time at Kailash, engaging both his ordinary sensory perception and his mind's eye. This affects how he encounters the physical landscape of Kailash, and it helps build an experience of the site as full of invisible wonders. I argue that this directly facilitates a visionary experience for Khatag Zamyak and deepens his experience of the reality of this invisible world.

Engaging with Pilgrimage Guides, Monastic Caretakers, and Oral History

While at Kailash, Khatag Zamyak alludes to multiple sources of information about the places he visits. He cites "the sayings of guides to the

[19] My analysis here is informed by scholars of visual culture, such as David Morgan and Birgid Meyer.
[20] Kha stag 'dzam yag, *Nyin deb*, 12.

holy place" (*gnas 'dzin kyi smra la*), likely referring to the people who lead pilgrims around the site. He also references oral tradition, such as when he reports a folk etymology for why Ngari Khorsum has the name that it does. Additionally, he discusses written pilgrimage guides, like those discussed in the previous chapter. For instance, he uses a stanza from an old inventory to explain the benefits of circumambulating Kailash a certain number of times. He says that this verse comes from old inventories (*dkar chag*), a genre term used for pilgrimage guides. He also cites inventories (*dkar chag*) when recounting the history of the Korchag Jowo images and copies a long passage into his diary.

In these examples, guides and oral traditions provide Khatag Zamyak with context for interpreting the "text" of the landscape. In "reading" what he sees in light of the narrative, historical, or identifying information given in these guides, Khatag Zamyak sees the place in a different way. Through the stories and oral traditions, he perceives the landscape in terms of a rich web of interconnections: he sees one place *as* the land spoken of in the *Lankāvatārasūtra*, another place *as* the place where the Khampa woman lost her son, and yet another place *as* the place where a hundred circumambulations mean achieving Buddhahood in this lifetime. Such connections link the physical landscape he sees with his ordinary perception with narratives he can imagine but are not otherwise immediately present to his senses. These connections render the landscape into a densely meaningful one.

Khatag Zamyak's diary, incidentally, offers insights into the discussion about pilgrimage guides in the previous chapter. One question raised in that chapter was how pilgrimage guides were used. Although Khatag Zamyak does not name specific guides or elaborate on his reactions to them, his diary indicates that he frequently consults them. He mentions reading pilgrimage guidebooks (*gnas yig*) five times[21] and inventories (*dkar chag*) eight times,[22] with an additional mention of disappointment when a particular place *lacks* an inventory for him to consult.[23]

How does he use these pilgrimage guides? Often, he copies guides' stories about places into his diary. For example, at Korchag Jowo in Purang, he writes down the story of how a dharma king came to build the central image

[21] Ibid., 76, 93, 110, 126, 156.
[22] Ibid., 36, 43, 83, 91, 95, 99, 168, 171.
[23] Ibid., 90.

of the temple, concluding the retelling with "the history of the construction is clear from the inventory."[24] Guides also describe specific practices to do at a site and the potential karmic rewards for doing so. While at Kailash, for instance, Khatag Zamyak copies down a song that tells the value of different numbers of circumambulations. "'If one circumambulates one time at the great palace of Kailash, one purifies the defilements of one life. Similarly, if one does ten circumambulations, one purifies a kalpa's worth of rebirths. If one does a hundred circumambulations, having purified the 10 signs and 8 qualities, one will attain buddhahood in one lifetime.' Thus say the previous inventories."[25] And finally, it sometimes seems that he uses the guides to identify the particular images at a site. For example, he writes, "I borrowed manuscripts of the pilgrimage guide of the holy place of Mabo Chok (*smra bo lcog*) in Lhodrak (*lho brag*) and of Ngadak Nyang (*mnga' bdag myang*) and so forth,[26] and did the identifications."[27] This is somewhat terse, but it suggests that he used the pilgrimage guide to know what images he was looking at.[28]

The diary also shows that Khatag Zamyak frequently interacted with the caretakers (*dkon gnyer*) of temples and holy places. His references to these caretakers suggest that they led him around sites and into the otherwise locked temples where important images were kept. For instance, Khatag Zamyak says that the caretakers "point out" features for him (*ngo sprod gnang ba*).[29] They provided information about the images and their special stories, powers, or qualities. Occasionally he mentions that because he could not find a caretaker, he was not able to get into the temple of a particular site to

[24] *Bzhengs pa'i lo rgyus dkar chag nas gsal.* Ibid., 168.

[25] *Pho brang chen po ti se la / bskor ba lan gcig skor gyur na / skye ba gcig gi sgrib pa dag / de bzhin rim pa bcu bskor na / bskal pa gcig gi sgrib pa dag / bskor ba brgya rtsa song ba na / rtags bcu yon tan brgyad rdzogs nas / tshe gcig sangs rgyas thob pa 'gyur / zhes dkar chag sngon ma'i gsung bzhin bskor tshad dngos yin par sems / deng sang ngag sgros su ni bskor tshad bcu gsum yin zer la.* Ibid., 170–171.

[26] I have not been able to find a pilgrimage guide to these places, but Kathog Situ visits them in his pilgrimage to central Tibet. See KaH thog si tu Chos kyi rgya mtsho, *Gangs ljongs dbus gtsang gnas bskor lam yig nor bu zla shel gyi se mo do*, 260–262.

[27] *Lho brag smra bo lcog gnas dang / mnga' bdag myang sogs kyi gnas yig phyag dpe g.yar te ngo sprod mdzad.* Kha stag 'dzam yag, *Nyin deb*, 110.

[28] Khatag Zamyak has many other references to reading texts while on pilgrimage, including the *Vessantara Jataka*, Milarepa's *Mgur 'bum* (which appears several times), Marpa's *Mgur 'bum*, the *Abhidharmakośa*, Padmasambhava's *Bka' thang shel brag ma*, Patrul Rinpoche's *Words of My Perfect Teacher*, "the best path that combines Mahamudra and Dzogchen," the *Legs bshad shel gyi me long*, Phagmodrupa's *Rnam thar*, the *Prajñāpāramitā in 8000 verses*, Milarepa's *Rnam thar*, and the *Mani Kabum*. At various points, he copies down quotations from these texts into his own diary as a way of working through his own thoughts. He quotes passages from Mipham (192), Sakya Paṇḍita's *Elegant Sayings* (193), Drakpa Gyeltsen (218), the *Mahayanasutralamkara* (219), several passages from pilgrimage guides (83, 122, 126, 170–171), and several songs from Milarepa's *Hundred Thousand Songs* (116, 130, 205).

[29] Kha stag 'dzam yag, *Nyin deb*, 128.

see the images.[30] These caretakers generally seem linked to specific temples and did not accompany him to other sites. He also references "the sayings of the pilgrimage guides" (*gnas 'dzin rnams kyi smra la*) in a way that suggests he is talking about people who guide pilgrims around the pilgrimage site.[31] Caretakers and human pilgrimage guides may then have been overlapping but separate groups.

Reporting Others' Perceptions

Khatag Zamyak also educates his perception of Kailash by citing how other people—particularly highly realized masters—see the pilgrimage place. While he describes the various sights of Kailash, he frequently invokes the superior perception of these figures. He values his own perception of the mountain, but acknowledges that buddhas, gods, and bodhisattvas can see the mountain differently (and better) than he can. His own perception exists in a hierarchy of possible perceptions of the mountain. In the relatively short section describing his stay at Kailash, he cites the vision of Atisa, Padmasambhava, various Drikung and Drukpa Kagyus, and the first Panchen Lama. Thus, Khatag Zamyak is always aware of other possible perceptions of Kailash, and particularly that more highly realized beings see it as it *truly* is. He writes, "In reality, perfected buddhas and bodhisattvas directly perceive Kailash as the palace of Cakrasaṃvara."[32] Elsewhere he cites that Milarepa has "seen it directly (*mngon sum gzigs*) in accordance with the Buddha's speech,"[33] and has consequently praised the mountain. Khatag Zamyak cannot yet see the mountain how buddhas, bodhisattvas, or Milarepa might, but he trusts their claims as a reliable source of information about how the mountain really is. His own perception is clouded, so he must rely on more advanced beings. In recollecting how such beings see it, moreover, he vicariously participates in their way of seeing.

On the grounds that advanced beings can see Kailash as it truly is, Khatag Zamyak intervenes in the dispute over Kailash's authenticity discussed in Chapter 3. Despite his lack of philosophical or monastic training, and even though he is writing about seven hundred years after Sakya Paṇḍita, Khatag

[30] Ibid., 106.
[31] Ibid., 171.
[32] Ibid., 170.
[33] Ibid., 169.

Zamyak mentions Sakya Paṇḍita by name as having maligned Kailash, and then offers his own opinion on the matter.[34] He cites the authoritative vision of masters such as Milarepa to refute Sakya Paṇḍita's claim that Kailash is not holy.[35] While Sakya Paṇḍita's took Kailash's mundane appearance to mean that it is not the holy mountain described in scripture, Khatag Zamyak argues that whether one sees the features of the mountain described in scripture is a function of one's own merit and obscurations rather than the legitimacy of the mountain. He writes, "Although there are jambu trees growing there, one [either sees or] does not see them because of the purity or impurity of one's defilements."[36] He attributes his own inability to see Jambu trees to his own obscurations, rather than, as Sakya Paṇḍita would have it, to a decisive argument against Kailash.

Khatag Zamyak also points to features of the mountain which can be seen by ordinary people like himself. Indeed, one of the most striking features of this passage is how Khatag Zamyak balances a humble deference to the advanced perception of spiritual masters with an empirical trust in what he sees with his own eyes. For instance, after arguing that advanced masters perceive Kailash directly as the palace of Cakrasaṃvara and pointing to the various signs (*rtags*) which indicate its legitimacy, Khatag Zamyak deferentially says, "I myself do not analyze it deeply."[37] Immediately after, however, he points to the fact that the four major rivers flow from the area immediately surrounding Kailash, and concludes, "All of that remains visible to all." That is, much like Chödrak Yeshe, Khatag Zamyak maintains that—regardless of the discordances between Kailash and Himavat—it is undeniable that everyone can see that the four rivers flow from Kailash. This fact, which is clearly visible to everyone, is the final argument in favor of Kailash's legitimacy. Khatag Zamyak thus strikes a balance between acknowledging the superior perception of spiritual masters and trusting his

[34] We can only speculate about how Khatag Zamyak might have known about Sakya Paṇḍita's rejection of pilgrimage to Kailash. One possible way is from having read a pilgrimage guide entitled *Gangs ri chen po ti se dang mtsho chen ma dros pa bcas kyi sngon byung gi lo rgyus mdor bsdus su brjod pa'i rab byed shel dkar me long* written by 'Bri gung chung tsang 06 Bstan 'dzin Chos kyi blo gros (1868–1906). This guidebook seems to have been popular and circulating during Khatag Zamyak's travels.

[35] Khatag Zamyak also refers to Sakya Paṇḍita's rejection of pilgrimage for ordinary people without tantric initiations, also discussed in Chapter 3. He largely takes for granted the value of pilgrimage in general, suggesting that the "ignorant, biased words" (*rmongs pa'i zhen tshig*) with which some Sakya followers have slandered Kailash "have no point beyond refuting the virtues of pilgrimage to holy places," a goal he appears to take as so ridiculous it is not worth addressing.

[36] Ibid.

[37] Ibid.

own observations of Kailash, and he draws on multiple ways of seeing to establish Kailash as holy.

Doing "Pure Perception" (*dag snang byas*)

In addition to techniques for educating or augmenting his ordinary perception, Khatag Zamyak also undertakes practices of seeing that directly alter his everyday perception. For example, he frequently describes cultivating "pure perception" (*dag snang*) at Kailash, as in the following: "Once again, I went up to Tara Slope. On top of Bonchung's giant stone, I did devotion and pure perception (*dag snang*). It was the stone which was carried by Mila after he doubled Naro Bonchung's stone."[38] Here, Khatag Zamyak references a legendary battle between the Buddhist hero Milarepa and his non-Buddhist rival Naro Bonchung. The pair duels by means of competing magical feats, and in this story, Naro Bonchung carries a heavy stone, and Milarepa bests him by carrying a stone twice the size. Already, Khatag Zamyak is reading the landscape in terms of its legendary past, seeing its events unfold in his mind's eye. However, for the moment let us focus on how he is performing pure perception on this spot.

Pure perception generally refers to the way a buddha or bodhisattva would see the world—as entirely pure and devoid of delusion or grasping. This stands in contrast to the ordinary way humans perceive the world. While pure perception can result from advanced practice, tantric Buddhists often cultivated it through visualization practices known as deity yoga (*lha'i rnal 'byor*). In deity yoga, practitioners imagine a buddha or deity in front of them and sometimes even become the deity, which helps them see the world as the deity does. Generally, these sorts of practices would have been performed in front of an image of the deity. Khatag Zamyak, however, adopts the language of cultivating pure perception even as he performs these practices outside the usual confines of deity yoga, performed in front of an image and under the supervision of an empowered master.

Where Khatag Zamyak mentions pure perception, he often pairs the phrase "pure perception" with a verb for "to do" (*byas*). The verbs "to do"

[38] *Slar yang yar bskyod pas sgrol ma la mgul du / bon chung gi gyad rdo'i thog la rje btsun rin po ches rdo de las nyis 'gyur tsam bskyal ba'i gyad rdo la mos gus dag snang byas.* Kha stag 'dzam yag, *Nyin deb*, 172.

(*byas*), "to generate" (*bskyed*), or "to train" (*sbyong*) are also used with pure perception throughout the diary, indicating that Khatag is actively working to cultivate pure perception. Intriguingly, at one point not contained in the passage above, Khatag Zamyak pairs "pure perception" with the verb "to appear" (*shar*), indicating that pure perception spontaneously arose for him after he has performed five thousand circumambulations of the *stūpas* at Ngor Monastery.[39] As was the case with Chökyi Drakpa, for whom the vision of Cakrasaṃvara both appeared to him and required effort, for Khatag Zamyak, pure perception is something that can happen spontaneously, but often also requires effort. For the most part, however, he must actively try to generate pure perception. Although it is unclear what specific practices Khatag Zamyak uses to cultivate pure perception, it is evident that he focuses on holy objects or sites encountered during his pilgrimage and uses them as supports as he tries to cultivate a new way of seeing the world.

Visualizing (*gsal btab*)

Khatag Zamyak also actively visualizes Kailash as a pure land, the perfect, celestial realm of a buddha or bodhisattva. For instance, he writes, "I went atop a cliff that was like a mandala. There, there were the footprints of the 500 *arhats* and 500 *dakinis*. . . . I visualized it (*gsal btab*) as the buddhafield of Amitabha."[40] The term *gsal btab* joins the word for clear or radiant (*gsal*) with a verbalizer (*btab*), rendering meanings such as to make radiant, to visualize, to make clear, to imagine, to picture, or to make clear in one's mind. He uses this technique on an area that he clearly thinks is special, based both on its reputation and on the footprints and signs he can see, to try to visualize it—to imagine it in his mind's eye—as the pure land of Amitabha.

Here again, we see him looking at the physical landscape and attempting to imagine it in its purified form. Given Khatag Zamyak's position that Kailash *really is* the palace of Cakrasaṃvara, even though he as an ordinary person cannot see it as such, the visualization practice he engages in here is a *way*

[39] *Chu sbrul zla 6 tshes 13 bar ngor la 'gor bas / de'i bar nangs nub rnams la bde gshegs mchod rten sogs sa yi 'bum pa bcu drug byin can la bskor ba 5000 grub pas blo bde dag snang shar.* Kha stag 'dzam yag, *Nyin deb*, 229.

[40] *Yar bskyod cing brag dkyil 'khor 'dra ba'i thog dgra bcom pa lnga brgya yi zhabs rjes / mkha' 'gro'i zhabs rjes sogs yod pa'i brag thog der / dgra bcom lnga brgya'i dur sa zhes / kun gyi skra sen dor zhing bdag nyid seng ge nyal stabs byas nas 'chi ba bsgoms te sangs rgyas 'od dpag med kyi zhing khams gsal btab.* Kha stag 'dzam yag, *Nyin deb*, 172.

of trying to see the holy place as it really is. Khatag Zamyak cannot presently see this landscape as the pure land of Amitabha with his physical eyes, but he can use his imagination to visualize it as such in his mind's eye. In other words, since his perceptual capacity is such that Amitabha's pure land does not *present* itself to his ordinary physical perception, he uses his imagination to *re-present* Amitabha's pure land to himself.

Once again, these practices of visualization would ordinarily take place within an empowered tantric lineage and in front of an image of the deity. Here, however, we see Khatag Zamyak undertaking similar practices using the material landscape as support. He is thus drawing on some of the logic of tantric visualization but applying it to pilgrimage. Both practices aim at transforming perception of the world, but Khatag Zamyak uses the material world itself as a support for his practice.

Looking for Signs

Khatag Zamyak also closely examines what he sees for signs (*rtags*, also sometimes *mtshan ma, brda'*) that can tell him about the world he cannot see. For instance, at one point he sets out to refute Sakya Paṇḍita's criticisms of Kailash's legitimacy. He justifies the legitimacy of Kailash by claiming that there are signs (*rtags*) of the descriptions given in the sutras present in the landscape, such as footprints of past masters, the presence of the four rivers, or the existence of self-arisen (*rang 'byung*) images. He cannot see Kailash in its divine form, but what he can see provides evidence that scriptural descriptions are true. These visible phenomena, Khatag Zamyak argues, point to the reality of the wondrous world lying just out of Khatag Zamyak's visual reach. He speaks of these signs as nails or points (*gzer bu*), suggesting that these signs mark places where two realms—Khatag Zamyak's ordinary visual perception or Kailash and extraordinary perceptions of the mountain—interpenetrate.

Signs can also reveal the hidden qualities of places or people. Khatag Zamyak mentions, for instance, that the geomantic signs of a particular place seem good (*rtags*),[41] that the crowds gathered to see the Panchen Lama all observed wonderful signs such as rainbow lights in the sky (*rtags*),[42] and that

[41] Ibid., 164.
[42] Ibid., 216.

the footprints around Kailash are signs (*rtags*) that it is a dwelling place of the Buddha and five hundred arhats. In each case, he moves from an externally visible sign to an ordinarily invisible quality that it indicates.

Elsewhere in the diary, Khatag Zamyak looks for signs that can tell him about himself and his place in the world.[43] In particular, he frequently notes occasions where something happens that he then interprets as telling him about his degree of realization, amount of merit, or level of spiritual attainment. He looks for these signs in the external landscape because the qualities he really wants to know about—his karmic connections and his level of realization—are not immediately knowable to Khatag Zamyak and must instead be inferred through external signs.

For instance, upon arriving at Kailash, Khatag Zamyak praises Milarepa and does a guru *sādhanā* for him and reports that he has a brief vision of Milarepa's face as a result. He writes, "I thought, 'what good karmic connections!' and immediately prostrated in a state of rejoicing."[44] He is delighted, and not only for the visionary experience itself, but for what it reveals about his good karmic connections (*rten 'brel*) to Milarepa and to Kailash. Such karmic connections might prove to be the basis of fruitful practice there. Elsewhere, Khatag Zamyak interprets the fact that a frequently closed lake is open to visitors when they arrive as a sign of good karmic connections.[45] And on yet another occasion, Khatag Zamyak sees the practice cave of Rechungpa, and the thought occurs to him, "I wonder if Precious Rechungpa was the lama I relied upon in a previous life?" and he is delighted.[46] Each of these encounters prompts him to direct his attention to his karma and past lives.

Khatag Zamyak even tries to influence events and read the results as reflective of his level of realization. This happens, for example, when the hostess in their guesthouse falls ill. Khatag Zamyak writes: "She seemed like a bird that had been hit by a stone. I gave medicine and said blessings and as forcefully as I knew how. But the sick woman did nothing but moan (*o rgyang*)

[43] For more on Khatag Zamyak's interpretation of signs, see Catherine Hartmann, "Karmic Opacity and Ethical Formation in a Tibetan Pilgrim's Diary," *Journal of Religious Ethics* 52, no. 3 (2023): 496–516.

[44] *Rje btsun mi la'i bla sgrub kha 'don bya skabs mchod pa'i 'go nas zhal mjal bas / rten 'brel legs snyam de ma thag phyag gsum btsal yid spro ba'i ngang de dgong mtsho 'gram der zhag 'dug byas.* Ibid., 166.

[45] Ibid., 172.

[46] *Phyi nyin ras chung phug la rang nyid gcig pu lam gzhan zhig nas yar bskyod pas / ras chung phug gi sgo ru slebs 'dug cing / ras chung rin po che rang gis sngon bsten bla ma yin nam snyam yid spro bar byung.* Ibid., 104.

and weep all night. So I lacked realizations, and I thus felt ashamed that I was leading others on the path."[47] Another time, he finds himself in a terrible and dangerous storm and tries to pacify it by chanting mantras.[48] When this does not work, he is left feeling depressed and writes, "I resigned myself to the fact that I have no experiences or realizations."[49] In each case, Khatag Zamyak interprets a negative external event and his inability to fix it as a sign that he lacks the realizations he either wishes he had or thinks that he should have.

Khatag Zamyak's constant search for signs shapes his visual engagement with the places he visits. He attentively scans the landscape for signs and constantly interprets the landscape, himself, and the relationship between the two in terms of such signs. As such, his experience of the landscape is colored by the belief that there is another world just outside his vision.

Looking Closely (*zhib mjal*)

Khatag Zamyak's practice of seeking signs also involves closely examining and studying things (*zhib mjal*). The term *zhib mjal* implies a detailed or fine examination, often of a high-status person or object. It indicates a more intent engagement that goes beyond simply looking or glancing quickly. Successfully performing this kind of visual engagement, moreover, is tied to the pilgrim's full appreciation of the site and ability to benefit from its blessings. For instance, Khatag Zamyak writes that "if pilgrims to the holy place and images, which are the dawning of the sun of Kadam teachings in Phen, look closely (*zhib mjal*), purify themselves, and perform prostrations and circumambulations, the entirety of the great essence [of the place] will necessarily enter into their hearts."[50] Without looking closely, the pilgrim may not be able to benefit from the entirety of the essence of the site. Elsewhere, in a passage describing his experiences at Kailash, Khatag Zamyak has already seen Gyangdrak Monastery, but he leaves his companions to return and look at it closely. This passage suggests that Khatag Zamyak thinks that he might

[47] *Byi'ur rdo phog pa ltar 'dug pas / rang gis byin rlabs dang sman bcas ci drags byas / nad pa de ni de'i nub mo mtshan nam du o rgyang dang ngu ba kho na byed 'dug pas / rang la nyams rtogs med pas gzhan gyi lam sna byed pa ngo re tsha.* Ibid., 129. It is possible "path" here means deciding what to do about the illness, or along the pilgrimage path. Thanks as well to Rory Lindsay for suggesting a much less clunky translation than my original rendering.

[48] Ibid., 166.

[49] *Bdag la nyams rtogs med pa kho thag chod.* Ibid., 166.

[50] Ibid., 41.

miss something if he looks quickly or cavalierly, and instead focuses intently at the object of his attention to make sure that if there is any trace of the thing he is looking for, he will not miss it.

Focusing (*dmigs rnam*)

Again, closely related to the idea of closely examining what one sees is *dmigs rnam* or other phrases with the term *dmigs*,[51] which Khatag Zamyak uses several times while at Kailash. The term *dmigs rnam* is not common, but some dictionaries suggest that it is a compound term formed from the focal object (*dmigs pa*) and the aspect (*rnam pa*), specifically of the mental aspect, whether pure or impure, of the observer.[52] The sense, then, is of the phenomenological meeting of subject and object, with a particular focus on how the object *appears* to the subject.

Khatag Zamyak seems to use it in the sense of actively focusing on some holy image. In the passage above, his object is the images ("supports of body, speech, and mind") at Gyangdrak temple and on his phenomenological experience of those images. He appends the term *dmigs rnam* with the words *ci shes la 'bad*, indicating something like "I endeavored as best as I knew how" with reference to the object of focus, which gives the sense that he is really trying to focus on the object and how it appears to him. This is not a simple looking, but an active and reflexive kind of seeing, recognizing that there are multiple modes of visual perception beyond an ordinary surface view.

Recognition (*ngo 'phrod*)

Khatag Zamyak frequently says that he "recognizes" (*ngo 'phrod*) some aspect of the landscape. That is, he identifies some place *as* the same place where something significant happened in the past. Once again, this practice of seeing involves moving between the physically present landscape

[51] The term *dmigs* occurs frequently in philosophical writing, where it translates Sanskrit *ālambana* and means "object of awareness," "percept," or "cause," depending on context. In less technical contexts, it can be used as a verb meaning "to be aware of" or "to observe," in nouns meaning "aim," "intention," "mental object."

[52] The *Great Tibetan Dictionary* defines the term: *Yul gzugs sogs la dmigs nas yul can sems la myong ba shar ba'i rnam pa*. Zhang Yisun, *Bod rgya tshig mdzod chen mo* (Beijing: Minzu Chubanshe, 1993), 2143.

and a reality that is not immediately visible. For instance, Khatag Zamyak writes: "I saw the rocky cliff where Bonchung lived, along with the Jetsun's footprints on the side. Bonchung also walked in that way, but he couldn't reach any farther than the lower bank of the water, so the gods and demons let out a great horse-laugh from the sky. Thus, I recognized (*ngo 'phrod*) the place where Bonchung's walking happened."[53] This connects the landscape in front of him with another episode from the life story of Milarepa.

The term *ngo 'phrod*, also spelled *ngo sprod* or *ngo sprad*, might also be translated as "to introduce" or "to point out." Elsewhere in the diary, we also find the use of the word *ngos 'dzin*, which has a similar meaning. Like many of the terms Khatag Zamyak uses, it can have technical meanings or more everyday meanings. Tantric teachers may "point out" something to a student that catalyzes a deep realization,[54] or someone might simply "recognize" another person on the street. It is not clear in which sense Khatag Zamyak is using it, but the fact that Khatag Zamyak uses so many terms for seeing that resonate with advanced meditation or teaching contexts suggests that these are important and active choices that he is making.

Recognizing connects the physical landscape to a world of history and legend. Khatag Zamyak holds multiple visionary landscapes in his mind while he travels around Kailash. One is the physical landscape in front of him that is visible to his ordinary eyes, and the other is the narrative landscape created by highly realized practitioners like Milarepa. The physical landscape is present to all travelers, and the narrative events exist in the shared imagination of Tibetans telling the story. Identifying places where the physical and narrative landscapes interpenetrate allows Khatag Zamyak to see the physical landscape in a new way and make the stories, figures, and miraculous deeds ever more real.

[53] Kha stag 'dzam yag, *Nyin deb*, 173.

[54] As Matthew Kapstein writes, "in its technical sense [the term *ngo sprod*] refers to instruction that, if skillfully delivered to an appropriately receptive disciple by an appropriately qualified master, catalyzes an immediate intuitive grasp of the instruction's content." He illustrates this admittedly technical definition with the example of a tennis pro who points out a flaw in the student's serving technique. The student immediately realizes this flaw and is able to fix it "and then deliver one that screams past Martina." Thus, the term implies both an instruction by a qualified teacher and then the student's recognition of the object taught, not merely in a way of hearing and understanding what the teacher said in a surface-level way, but of directly and deeply understanding the point of the instruction. Matthew Kapstein, "The Amnesic Monarch and the Five Mnemic Men: 'Memory' in Great Perfection (rdzogs-chen) Thought," in *In the Mirror of Memory: Reflections on Mindfulness and Remembrance in Indian and Tibetan Buddhism*, ed. Janet Gyatso (Albany: State University of New York Press, 1992), 239–268, 242.

Seeing/Meeting Face to Face (*zhal mjal*)

The final practice of seeing relevant to Khatag Zamyak's pilgrimage experience at Kailash is the notion of seeing or meeting face to face (*zhal mjal*). He uses this term multiple times in the diary, to indicate both meetings with important people but also when encountering important images. And indeed, at the beginning of the diary, he explains that the whole reason for keeping the diary is "in order that the face to face encounters (*zhal mjal ba*) and circumambulations of the three supports may be fixed in my mind."[55] So clearly these kinds of encounters are particularly meaningful to him.

The term for seeing or meeting face to face combines an honorific term for "face" (*zhal*) with a word we have already seen means "to see," "to meet," or "to encounter" (*mjal*). It is an honorific verb form that indicates respect and can be used when encountering either people or holy objects. Thus, in addition to Khatag Zamyak using the phrase as above to indicate seeing the face of a figure like Milarepa, we also find him saying elsewhere after meeting a lama named Karma Tashi, "I said a prayer that I might see his face once more in this life."[56] Or when he visits a temple, he writes "Inside the temple, as soon as I saw the face of the main image, the precious Jowo, my mind rejoiced."[57] At a few points, he even uses the term for things we might not think of as having faces, such as the great Derge printing house, about which he writes, "Then I saw the face (*zhal mjal*) of the great treasury of dharma printing house there."[58] Such usages show that *zhal mjal* does not always involve literal human faces, but rather with the outer surface of some object.

At the beginning of Khatag Zamyak's visit to Kailash, he reports a striking visionary experience of seeing Milarepa's face. It comes right after Khatag Zamyak says he recited a guru *sādhanā* for Milarepa. He interprets this experience as a very good sign—it means that there are good karmic connections, whether between himself and Milarepa or for the pilgrimage itself.

What does it mean for Khatag Zamyak to see Milarepa's face? He is not in a temple or a place where there are paintings or statues of Milarepa, so it seems unlikely that he is talking about a physical image. An encounter with a physical image, moreover, would not prompt the joy and surprise of

[55] *Gnas khyad par can dang rten gsum rnams bskor zhing / zhal mjal ba yid la 'jags pa'i ched du dbu tsam 'bri bar bya.* Kha stag 'dzam yag, *Nyin deb*, 12.

[56] *Lan cig skye ba 'di la da dung zhal mjal ba'i smon lam zhus nas.* Ibid., 14.

[57] *Lha khang nang la rten gtso jo bo rin po che zhal mjal ma thag yid spro zhing 'ong ba.* Ibid., 174.

[58] *De nas par khang chos mdzod chen po zhal mjal nas.* Ibid., 21.

saying that this was a sign of good karmic connections and then falling into three prostrations. It seems, rather, that the action of reciting a *sādhanā* to Milarepa at a place that is particularly associated with Milarepa triggers a kind of visionary experience. Here, then, we see a moment where the gap between Khatag Zamyak's ordinary perception and imagined vision collapses for a small while, allowing a pilgrim like Khatag Zamyak to experience Milarepa as immediately present and real.

Conclusion: Co-Seeing

In this chapter, I have pointed to the various practices of seeing by which Khatag Zamyak does two things. First, he directs his attention at two different ways of seeing the mountain. One way is pilgrims' ordinary perception of the physical world. The other way is an extraordinary and wondrous vision of the site as a divine mandala overflowing with dharma and blessings.

The second thing he does is try to bridge this gap between his own ordinary perception and the extraordinary vision of the mountain. For example, when Khatag Zamyak looks closely (*zhib mjal*), visualizes (*gsal btab*), cultivates pure perception (*dag snang*), reads guidebooks, cites advanced beings' modes of seeing, or focuses on how the object appears to him (*dmigs rnam*), he is denaturalizing his ordinary way of perceiving the world and effortfully adopting some other way of seeing. When Khatag Zamyak reads pilgrimage guidebooks about Milarepa's exploits at a site and recognizes (*ngo 'phrod*) places as part of that narrative, he is interpreting his ordinary sense perceptions in terms of the imaginative landscape constructed by the narrative. When he looks for signs (*rtags*), he is examining his ordinary perception for traces of an extraordinary reality he cannot see directly.

All these practices of seeing constitute a way of paying attention. That is, by constantly interrogating, comparing, and reimagining his ordinary perception, he is continually directing his attention to the nature of that ordinary perception and to the idea that this ordinary perception is not the only way to see the world. Because he believes that there is a world just outside his ordinary perception, he is always looking for signs of that world, and he is consequently paying more attention than he normally would to that which he is trying to see. In addition, the fact that he writes these activities in the diary is itself a practice of seeing that amplifies the impact of these other practices by directing his attention to them over and over again.

The cumulative effect is that Khatag Zamyak co-sees the landscape in front of him. He sees it in terms of his ordinary perception but is always aware of another way of seeing. That is, he sees ordinary reality present to his ordinary sense perception and thinks about, searches for evidence for, visualizes, or imagines the elevated reality that lies just outside his ordinary perception.

It may help here to draw on Samuel Todes's ideas about the phenomenology of the imagination. He contrasts perception—"that form of experience by which we are presented with something actual"[59]—with imagination—"that form of experience by which we represent to ourselves that something is possible."[60] Where perception involves objects that are directly present to the senses, imagination involves *re-presentation* of objects to ourselves by means of the creative imagination. The objects represented in imagination may be of objects we have previously seen, or they may be of things we have never seen, such as the classic Buddhist example of a horned rabbit. However, we cannot imagine that which is impossible, such as the round square Todes gives as an example. Thus, while our perceptions provide evidence about what is in the world, imaginations provide "proxy-evidence" about what is *possible* in the world.

Todes argues that humans are characterized by the ability to move between these two modes of perception and imagination. In the perceptual mode, humans are their bodies, and they gain nonconceptual but objective perceptual knowledge as they move about the world trying to satisfy their needs. In the imaginative mode, humans are their minds, and they use their imaginations to engage abstract categories and can gain objective conceptual knowledge. As such, he writes, "we are individuals who belong to two worlds."[61]

This account of humans shifting between the perceptual mode and the imaginative mode can help in thinking about Khatag Zamyak. Using practices of seeing, Khatag Zamyak moves back and forth between perception and imagination while on pilgrimage at Kailash. He sees the landscape with his ordinary perception, but he imagines what highly realized people perceive, narratives of Milarepa's exploits, and descriptions of Kailash as the wondrous palace of Cakrasaṃvara. This creates tension between the two visions, and it motivates him to bridge the gap between the world he perceives and the world he imagines. Or to put it another way, he attempts to bridge the gap

[59] Todes, *Body and World*, 130.
[60] Ibid., 130.
[61] Ibid., 132.

between the world he perceives and the world he wants to be able to perceive. Thus, Khatag Zamyak *co-sees* Kailash in both modes.

Not all of Khatag Zamyak's attempts to bridge the gap between the world he sees and the world he wants to be able to see fail, but neither do all of them succeed. He sometimes has breakthrough moments, such as the occasion where he has a vision of Milarepa's face as he approaches Kailash, after which he falls to the ground in amazement. Much of the time, however, he finds himself disappointed.

In either case, however, we might say that the pilgrimage *works.* When Khatag Zamyak fails to see what he hopes to, he is led to reflect on perception, and about the gaps between his perception and the perception of divine beings; however, the way Khatag Zamyak is led to juxtapose two "visions" of the landscape and constantly moves between them helps facilitate moments where he has these experiences of bridging the gap. In both cases, we can say that, by drawing his attention back and forth from ordinary perception to extraordinary vision, he *interweaves* these worlds into his own experience, inscribing the extraordinary vision of the site into his material experience.

These practices enable Khatag Zamyak to have a visionary experience of Milarepa and also to cultivate his general sense of the reality of the invisible world present at Kailash. When Khatag Zamyak affirms Kailash's legitimacy, it is not merely based on blind faith but also on his own experience of the landscape. For Khatag Zamyak, these practices of seeing *build* and *rebuild* the sacred landscape of Kailash anew so that it is experienced as real and materially present.

Conclusion

A Glimpse of the Mandala

> Between me and the night sky, Mount Kailash glowed as if lit from within. To so many, it was the navel of the world, home to the divine, an unscalable pyramid with a mythic scar down its side. From its base, I saw the veins of the Indus River, the mighty Yarlung, and even the river that flows before our camp in Pokhara. As I walked the ancient, footworn path in the twilight, I realized that I had been endowed with all the knowledge of the mountain and the land. I knew the story of each saint, pilgrim, and beggar who had laid their body on the rocky trail encircling the mountain. I knew the name of every blossom they admired, the songs of the lonesome birds that have lived in this valley through the ages, the faithful patterns of breath from the sky in each season, and the eternal sorrows of the rivers splitting into streams around me. I understood this place completely, as though I had always been there. As though I had never been anywhere else. When I woke up, I felt something harden inside me.
>
> —Tsering Yangdzom Lama, *We Measure the Earth with Our Bodies*[1]

In the novel *We Measure the Earth with Our Bodies*, the character Dolma, born in exile and living in Canada while she attends university, dreams of the land her mother fled as a child. She doubts if she will ever see it herself and dreams of being *home*. She longs to "measure the earth with my body, to know our country with my skin. It seemed like the only way to fathom such a land."[2] But though she cannot see or touch it herself, the land will not let go of her, and its pull shapes the difficult choices she and other characters must

[1] Tsering Yangzom Lama, *We Measure the Earth with Our Bodies* (New York: Bloomsbury, 2022), 89.

[2] Ibid., 88. Dolma thinks this as she listens to a Tibetan studies professor, kindly but also somewhat condescendingly, tell her about his trip to Kailash as she sits silently.

Making the Invisible Real. Catherine Hartmann, Oxford University Press. © Oxford University Press 2025.
DOI: 10.1093/9780197791585.003.0008

make in the course of the novel. At the end, she realizes, "This land will remain. Long after our own brief, flickering lights fade, these mountains, these plains, this wind will persist. And because this land is the source of everything that makes us, we will still be here."[3] She speaks of "the land," and not in the denuded sense of bare earth. The land, for her, contains memories, hopes, and ancestral ties. It contains gods, spirits, and sacred channels. She stands before it not as an isolated individual, but as a *we.*

Tsering Yangdzom Lama's novel explores family, colonization, displacement, and exile, but it also demonstrates the power of place to situate people in a world of shared meaning. Individuals encounter a world already full of meaning, where we are always connected to the stories, cultural habits, and wisdom embedded in the land around us. Places tells us who we are and how we should live. Far from being the mute backdrops to human activity, places shape how we understand and operate in the world. In the words of Keith Basso, "We *are*, in a sense, the place-worlds we imagine."[4] Some places are more or less thick with meaning—this book explores pilgrimage places, which are especially dense with significance—but this is only a difference of degree, and not kind.

But how are these places created? How do people make landscapes that feel real—real enough to ground you, to sustain you, to orient you in the world? Even when people come to recognize the power and meaning of landscape, we may think that those meanings are established at some point in the past and simply exist thereafter. But meaningful landscapes do not simply exist without communities who create and sustain them. People make places. Whether by building structures, telling stories, performing rituals, or any number of other actions, people layer meanings onto places. No one act creates a place where there was none before. But collectively, many practices of place-making bring a world into existence so that it is powerful enough to shape the people who go there.

The situation of Tibetan pilgrimage, where pilgrims are invited to learn to see the pilgrimage mountain as other than their ordinary senses present it to them—as a mandala—raises new questions about how places are made. In particular, it raises the question of how the ordinarily invisible landscapes described by the pilgrimage tradition become real for the pilgrim.

[3] Ibid., 345.
[4] Keith H. Basso, *Wisdom Sits in Places: Landscape and Language among the Western Apache* (Albuquerque: University of New Mexico Press, 1996), 7.

Overall, the goal of this book has been to show how ordinarily invisible landscapes have been created and sustained through deliberate practices of seeing. In the process, I first made the case that seeing is neither passive nor given, and that there are many types of activity that are included in the broad category of seeing, including looking, watching, understanding, imagining, glimpsing, and more. Seeing mediates between material and immaterial, present and possible, external and internal, and active and passive. Because it bridges these boundaries, and because seeing is connected with ideas, imagination, affect, emotion, and bodily comportment, seeing breaks down the duality of body and mind. Attention to seeing thus raises questions about agency, about constructivism versus materialism, and about faith, imagination, literature, and the material world. Recognizing that seeing is an active and therefore malleable process, religious traditions have long used perception as a site to reshape human experience of the world. For all of these reasons, perception merits increased attention in religious studies scholarship.

Second, I showed how multiple genres of Tibetan writing about pilgrimage thematize and work with perception to cultivate particular ways of seeing, and I gave an interpretive account for how these genres functioned to produce meaningful pilgrimage experiences. I considered advice texts, pilgrimage guides, founding narratives, and pilgrim diaries, and a variety of other minor genres to consider the topic of pilgrimage from multiple angles. These texts exhorted pilgrims to cultivate ethical bodily discipline and a faithful attitude, related stories about what happened at holy sites in the past, and promised pilgrims what benefits would result from a successful pilgrimage.

Most importantly for my account, I argued that these texts cultivate a variety of practices of seeing—effortful practices of looking at and interpreting the world. These include reading the landscape for signs, closely looking at specific objects, visualizing pure lands, recognizing places from narrative, and reading pilgrimage guides, among other activities. These practices direct the attention toward two different ways of seeing the same landscape. One is the ordinary way of seeing the landscape, available to ordinary perception, and the other is an extraordinary way of seeing the landscape, ordinarily seen in the mind's eye. Within this state of co-seeing, there are a range of possibilities for what the pilgrim might experience. For instance, simple awareness that there are two ways of seeing the site, awareness of the deficiencies of ordinary perception, moving back and forth from the ordinary perception of the material landscape to the imagined representation of the wondrous landscape, or even transformative experiences where these two visions come together in a dramatic visionary experience of the site, as was the case for Chökyi Drakpa and Khatag Zamyak. This depends on the pilgrim, their background and aspirations, and the way that the pilgrim collaborates with the text to produce an experience. Ultimately, while scholars can try to interpret how texts structure pilgrimage experiences, there are as many individual experiences of pilgrimage as there are individual pilgrims.

In all of these cases, however, co-seeing shapes the way pilgrims experience the site. Guides bring the wondrous world of gods and buddhas and bejeweled palaces into the concrete experience of the pilgrim. Other parts of the Buddhist tradition may describe or represent extraordinary pure lands, heavens, or mandalas, but in pilgrimage, that fantastic vision is grounded in the material landscape traversed by the pilgrim, grounding otherwise abstract or distant descriptions into the concrete landscape. The extraordinary world seen by gods and buddhas thus becomes part of the sensory and embodied experience of the pilgrim, which serves to bridge the gap between the here and now and something "beyond," thereby making the extraordinary world more proximate and real.

Co-seeing also focuses pilgrims' attention on the gap between ordinary perception and the way that the guide claims that the site really is, thus highlighting the deficiencies of ordinary perception, breaking them out of habitual patterns of seeing. This is important because, as we will recall, Buddhism maintains that these habitually delusory ways of seeing perpetuate suffering. Breaking people out of those patterns thus creates the possibility that pilgrims will act in new and hopefully better ways.

In addition, co-seeing creates the conditions for potentially transformative experiences of the site. In bringing two visions of the site together in the minds of pilgrims, co-seeing creates the possibility that these two ways of seeing converge, and pilgrims catch a glimpse of the wonders that lie outside their ordinary perception. Such a glimpse is unstable and momentary, but it can give pilgrims a taste of the world as they might someday experience it, and it is enough to cultivate an affective and aspirational faith. It starts in the imagination, but it may then be experienced in a powerful way at the site itself. This faith, then, is not a blind faith, but a faith strengthened by experiences of the pilgrimage place.

Third, I argued that all these practices of seeing functioned collectively to create the conditions in which the invisible, extraordinary landscape of the pilgrimage place feel *real* to pilgrims—not true in the abstract, but real for the individual pilgrim. Analyzing the practices through which this real-making occurs helps us to understand that the seemingly fantastical claims of pilgrimage guides are not simply believed or taken for granted, but actively constructed and reconstructed for new generations of practitioners.

One of the reasons that pilgrimage in Tibet has been somewhat overlooked in academic scholarship is that scholars sometimes see it as a superstitious practice that is beneath the lofty aims of Buddhist philosophy. But Tibetan pilgrims are not credulous, and they do not live in an enchanted world by virtue of their birthright. Pilgrimage texts are not confused about the material world and ordinary perception, and they can clearly distinguish between ordinary and extraordinary in the appropriate context. But they deliberately interweave different ways of looking at the world to bring about the same transformation of experience sought by Buddhist philosophy. What is more, they do so in a way that is more accessible, by starting with a specific physical place as the object of a transformation of perception. The fact that Tibetan pilgrimage guides develop such sophisticated methods of engaging and attempting to transform perception suggests affinities between pilgrimage practice and the more well-known Buddhist practices of meditation and philosophy. Though these different sets of practices adopt different ways of engaging the human body and mind, each shares the larger goal of reshaping the fundamentally flawed perception that perpetuates suffering.

In the end, this book is a call to appreciate the creativity and sophistication of Tibetan pilgrimage, and the ways the tradition recruits text, imagination, and landscape to collaborate with pilgrims to envision new worlds. Taken in isolation, the texts and practices examined in this book may seem small. And it is true that practices of seeing are one small part of pilgrimage, which is one small part of Tibetan culture. But I hope that taking pilgrimage texts seriously can help us understand how small practices, performed by individuals and communities over a long time, make a meaningful world. Most individual pilgrims probably did not literally see a mountain as a mandala. But in traveling, in searching, in looking, in imagining, and in hoping, perhaps they got a glimpse of a more perfect world, and a land that could unite and inspire.

APPENDIX 1

Full Translation of *Guidebook to Gyangme: Vajradhāra's Feast*

'Bri gung chung tsang Rig 'dzin Chos kyi grags pa. "Rgyang me'i gnas yig rdo rje 'dzin pa'i dga' ston." In *Collected Works of Chos kyi grags pa*. BDRC W22082. 2: 449–469. Kulhan: Drikung Kagyu Institute, 1999.

I prostrate to my lama and exalted deity!

The splendid sun of highest compassion,
mounted atop the chariot of mighty prayers,
plays in sky of purified minds.
I prostrate to my illuminating lotus teacher!

The great method "E" of limitless great bliss
and the great wisdom "VAM" of superior union
weave the net of innate nonduality.
I prostrate to the ever-present Heruka!

In the channels and elements one's own body are gods and goddesses,
They miraculously appear as stones, earth, and the like.
Here I will write a presentation of this holy place
which is a center of emanation in the external world.

This concise presentation of the layout of the holy place of Gyangme and detailed guidebook to the holy place of Sarma Yangdzö is as follows:

In the great land of Tibet, in upper Kham, there is a valley called Ngö (BDRC G4880), which is no different from the holy land of India. On the right side of the upper part of the valley, there is another valley called Gyangme. The valley is limitless, with a wide upland, and contains hidden bundles of sutras. It is surrounded by ranges of snow-capped mountains and is full of snow-capped mountains itself. It is no different from Mount Kailash!

Those with fortunate destinies may travel there easily, but those without are blocked from traveling there by their wrong views. Those who have not planted the seed of their own liberation are few among the travelers there. It is a holy place which is no different from the wisdom mandala Tsari!

I had a firm resolve to go to such a place. There were also some prophecies that if I went, and open the doors of exceedingly holy places, my lifespan would grow longer. So I took up the burden of the mountain and came, and when I did, I stayed for a night near the auspicious snow mountain. Then, I began the process of going to this holy place.

At first, the karmic connections for traveling there were not suitable because I did not have the right travel companions. But recently, I renewed my desire to go, and so undertook to do so with great effort. Although there were some small difficulties in terms of the karmic connections for going, I arrived there without obstacle. I will tell [the story] of our travels step by step.

This holy place has a round shape that is encircled by snow-capped mountains—this is a sign of the accomplishment of pacifying. There are many streams of *sindura* and square shapes—this is a sign of increasing. There are many red crags resembling half-moons—this is a sign of magnetizing. All of the rocks are rough and triangular in shape, and all the rivers sound like fierce roars—this is a sign of subjugating.

Gri demons in the shape of camels guard the doors [to the holy place], and there are countless other guardian deities. If you wish to know about those, or the mountain faces which were there previously, they can be known from other pilgrimage guides.

As we continued on to see the previously unseen mountain faces, there was a great waterfall to the left of a rainbow cave. Below that, there were clearly self-arisen images of the Four Great Executioners: Yama Raja, Arya Marpo, Ralpa Tsalgu, and Nyoche Barwa. There were deep pits in six places, moreover, which I understood to symbolize the six realms of existence.

Then, gradually proceeding, there is the Blissful Protector's spirit-lake, and below that there is a protectors' temple that no one had previously visited. In the lower part of the protector temple, you can see a clear "HUM" syllable, as well as the many specific elements of charnel ground ornamentation, including a mat made of human skin and a tiger skin. Beneath a waterfall nearby, there is a small cave where there is an image of Lodan Chogse (one of the eight incarnations of Padmasambhava). When we went there, everyone [in the group] saw me disappear and be encircled by a rainbow.

We went to Bliss-Protector's spirit-lake, performed a tantric feast offering, then returned. We went back to the uppermost chapel at the protectors' temple. It was a little difficult to reach it, so we went to put up a ladder as a way to climb up, but then all of a sudden, a magical ladder appeared effortlessly. We went inside, and there was a great cache of treasures! These included many tantras of Mahakala, the lord of wisdom, and *sādhanā* texts. The task of protecting that treasure had been entrusted to the demon Rahula.

Furthermore, there were very clear images, including a mandala of the *Gathered Intention*, an image with Mahakala's head and a brahmin's body, a black Manjusri, the goddess Remati, and images of black Hayagriva, who protects the teachings of the *Gathered Intention*.

My nephew Konchok Drakpa said that we should make handprints there like the ones in Kharak. Although I generally see making modern handprints and miracles as a cause of vow-breaking and slanderous criticism, so that my nephew did not lose face, there is now a clear imprint of my own hand as well.

By visiting that uppermost protector chapel once, all obstructions are cleared away and favorable conditions for achieving ordinary and extraordinary goals are created. This *stūpa* is no different than Dharma Cloud Fortress! Those who have the proper karmic destiny and act without doubts achieve ordinary and extraordinary boons. The unlucky, however, have incorrect views, and so have their life-veins cut instantly by wisdom *dakinis* and karma protectors just for going there. Without a doubt, this will eventually be known by all.

Then, moving on, we arrived at a protectors' temple in a cave on the far side of a mountain by Hunchback Palace Lake. Outside the door to the cave, there was a cliff face with a very clear image of black Zhambala.

Next, we reached Turquoise Lake. That night, we made a supplication to the great master Padmasambhava. We intended to go to sleep afterward because it was after sunset, but local gods and demons magically made the lake waters roar up. The earth, rocks, and stones all shook back and forth as if a great earthquake was happening.

I made a resolution in my own mind, and thereby calmed myself. Immediately, right at that very moment, I had a vision that I was at Trolung. In my vision, a monk spoke to me, saying, "I am Lama Rabgye."

"Where did you come from?" I asked.

"I am Master Padmasambhava," he said. "At present I live at Glorious Copper-Colored Mountain, so I have come from there."

"What have you come to do?" I asked.

"It is you who have needed to come here since last year," he said. "However, you fell under the influence of your vow-breaking students and their wrong views, so now you absolutely need to go to the peak [of this mountain]."

I responded, "But it seems like I cannot get through to the peak [of this mountain]. The path is difficult, there is so much snow, and I am weak and inadequate. Besides, even Jedrung Rabjampa did not have the proper karmic connections for opening the doors of this holy place at the peak [of the mountain]. So how could I? In any case, all of my dharma companions seem to be pure. Tonight I will supplicate to Padmasambhava—I am at a loss for what to do. Although it is good that you have come, how could there be the proper karmic connections for me to open the doors of this holy place?"

He said, "Although you are weak, rely on the help and guidance of Padmasambhava's compassion. Although the path seems difficult and full of snow, in reality, [the difficulty] depends on the ease or dis-ease of your own mind. So don't concern yourself with external stones and earth! Jetsun Rabjampa didn't have the karmic connections for opening the doors of this holy place. Consider how all of your companions have given up their lives and traveled [with you] across the highest reaches of the sky and the lowest depths of the oceans just for the sake of food and drink. So what is your problem with coming here? It is for the sake of your own liberation!"

I said, "Well, if it's important and there's no option but to go, what way should I take to get there? What sort of holy place is it?"

The monk was delighted, and said, "Even though there is no difference between Padmasambhava and myself, and there is no difference between myself and the minds of sentient beings, it is difficult for people to truly understand this. Leave here early tomorrow. Although you will have difficulties traversing the lower part, the hardship won't be too great. This holy place is extremely powerful and sensitive, so generate faith and devotion toward Padmasambhava, and go with loving compassion for sentient beings. At the door to the holy place, there will be a boulder with the four *Śvana* sisters acting as protectors.

Continue on from there. Be aware that there are many forms of gods on the mountain faces, and they will show you the crossing points. Continue on, and there will be a cave where the great master Padmasambhava attained identity with many Secret Mantra deities. This place is difficult for ordinary people to reach, like a celestial city. Climb up the rock face. You will need to keep going. Inside, there will be a clear three-dimensional mandala. Climb into the entrance of a small cave above that, and at the peak, you will find a pleasant meadow. Therefore, the name of this cave is "Durgākāshagrāmanam," or in Tibetan, "Dröka Namkhé Drongkhyer" (Difficult to Traverse Sky City).

Continue up from there, and in the middle of a ringed enclosure of glaciers, under a mottled rock, there will be a very pure cave. In it, there will be the mark of Guru Rinpoche's golden vajra, the mark of his hat, a mantra from the *Eight Pronouncements* written by Padmasambhava's own hand, Mandarava's handprint, and the syllable "A" made by Yeshe Tsogyal's thumb. Padmasambhava did a long-life ritual in that cave, and so its name is "Amarasiddhidhāna," or in Tibetan, it is called "Chimé Drupjin" (Granting the Boon of Deathlessness). This newly discovered holy place above where the *Śvana* sisters are door-guardians is generally known to people as "Sarma Yangdzö" (New Treasury)."

He also said that if the karmic connections were not properly aligned, then obstacles may appear. He told me at length how to pacify such obstacles, but I will explain that below.

The next morning, I intended to begin at dawn. However, the protector of the holy place welcomed us with a great snowfall, so we were temporarily blocked. A few of my companions, however, led the way and we set out. Just as the monk [from the vision] had said, there was a boulder with clear images of the four *Śvana* sisters acting as door guardians. We continued on, and on another boulder, there was the oath-bound protector Tiger-Mounted Lord who was guarding the inner door.

As we went, there was a great rock face to our right. On it, there were clear images of the Buddha Dipamkara's palace, Padmasambhava, Vajrapani holding an arrow, the great *yaksa* demon Tsi Marpo, and a right-coiling conch shell. We went upward, and on the rocky face of the mountain nearest to us, there was a cave that was a practice place for Yamantaka. On the innermost part of what seemed like a door, there was an image of a seal affixed on Yamantaka's mouth.

There was also a treasure chest marked with the syllable "Hum." On it was the sign of treasures—the outline of a six-spoked wheel. Inside the chest, there were many dharma teachings, including cycles of *sādhanās* for Yama. The protection of that Treasure had been entrusted to naga demons and black *candālas*. I showed [the Treasures] to my companions.

On the rock face to our right, there was a boulder. Hidden within that boulder was a cave that was extremely difficult to get into. The entire rock face was narrow and well-formed, in the shape of a wish-fulfilling jewel. There was only a single rocky set of steps up. I was terrified, but I led the way and went on with two or three companions. It was like the dream.

The door to the three-dimensional mandala and everything was extremely clear. It was realistic, and the inner part of the three-dimensional mandala was huge, with a covered gateway. It had a square column which seemed to flow out of a wishing vase, and which was not resting on anything. It had a very handsome four-cornered pillar ornament. The threshold had many layers of eaves and pediments. The walls were made of five layers, which were adorned with blue *bakuli* and studded with white precious pills. There were pictures of blooming lotuses on white parapets, and a layer of black wall hangings on top of which white wall hangings hung.

Behind the pillar ornaments on one side of a wall, there was a four-sided treasure chest in which I found a stone box that was vibrating. Inside, there were Treasures—many profound dharma teachings called *The Treasury of the Lama's Pronouncement*, which is in the class of Atiyoga. This holy place had been entrusted to *nagas*, demons, and spirits as protectors. It goes without saying that each time a person goes there, all of their ordinary obstacles will be pacified.

The great Padmasambhava, who pacifies obstacles, promised that it would even clear away the obstacles that would surely have led to death within the year. I myself would have had a very harsh obstacle in my twenty-fifth year, but because I discovered this cave, it was clear that I had met the requirements of the prophecy and was able to clear away this obstacle by doing a minor ritual.

We continued climbing up from atop a small cave, eventually arriving at a meadow above the cave called "Wondrous Turquoise Array." There was an obstacle because someone had committed a minor violation of their vows, so we did a tantric feast offering and did a confession to pacify the obstacle.

Right then, on the side of a far-off mountain that looked like a stack of books, we saw Vairocana surrounded by bodhisattvas of the four families.

We traveled on gradually, hoping to find the "Granting the Boon of Deathlessness" cave [Padmasambhava had described in the vision]. But the sun was slipping away, and it was starting to get dark, so we rested for a little while. As we were resting, on a mottled rock face to our left, we saw a perfect buddha that was surrounded by the sixteen *sthavīras*.

Furthermore, on a rock face to our right, we saw Padmasambhava surrounded by his eight emanated forms. Although that vision was shown to all, because of the darkness, some in our group seemed unable to see it. One or two of them to whom this vision was not shown stopped their own minds, and then the vision occurred for them. It was clear that their karma had been purified.

Eventually we found "Granting the Boon of Deathlessness" cave. The rear part of the cave was surrounded by glaciers, so we sat happily on top of a mottled rock that was shaped like a helmet. Those caves, which appeared clearly in our perception, were pleasant to travel through. Inside, as well, they were comfortable and nice. Inside the cave there was an imprint made by the five-pointed vajra of Padmasambhava's hand, marks of deer and melodious birds, thirty-seven mantras from the *Eight Commands: Assemblage of Sugatas* written in Padmasambhava's own hand, the handprint of Mandarava's left hand, and the syllable "A" written by Yeshe Tsogyal. There were also various symbols and many images of gods. Their protection was entrusted to Conch-Crowned Brahma.

Padmasambhava had promised that if I found [another] cave, I would extend my lifespan by three years, and each person who went there with me would also extend their lifespan by a year. Since the night had gotten dark, we couldn't find it. So we returned down to our camp by Turquoise Lake. We tried later to go back and find the cave, but there was a great snowstorm, and there were no signs that we would find it. Because of that, I felt very unsatisfied.

I had a vision in which Padmasambhava clearly made a prophecy while we were at Turquoise Lake. The prophecy that my own lifespan would be diminished by a year, so to clear away this obstacle, in the first month of this horse year, I should perform an offering ritual: I offered a hundred *tormas* in an enriching fire pujas to a mandala of Amitayus with his nine-fold retinue, a hundred *tormas* in a wrathful fire pujas to the mandala of Manjusri Yamantaka, four monks marked a hundred thousand *tormas* with the name of Amitayus, seven monks performed a hundred thousand Long Life Rituals of the Northern Continent, a thousand rituals of the supreme wisdom body, a hundred tantric feast offerings, a thousand benedictions, a thousand mending and confession rituals, a thousand *tsatsa* images, an expiation rite in front of the mandala of *The Summary of the Guru's Intention*, and many more rituals of expiation. It was prophesied that if I did all that, it would correct the diminishment of my lifespan, that my lifespan would be increased again, and that I would clear away the obstacle of my twenty-fifth year.

Then Turquoise Lake truly manifested itself as the dwelling place of Cakrasaṃvara in the *yab yum* form. In the lake, there were two round white boulders that symbolize wisdom and method of the *yab yum* form of Cakrasaṃvara. Those boulders were not resting on anything, whether earth, rock, mountain, or cliff, but rather they were moving back and forth on top of the lake.

I and a few others had a shared vision (*mthong bar mthun snang byung*), so it became a holy site (*gnas*) of extreme astonishment and wonder.

This new holy place is called "Sarma Yangzo." Its general dharma protector is Yamaraja, the lord of karma, but each cave and treasure site has its own particular protector. The mountain faces of the holy place of Sarma Yangzo are simply much brighter and purer than others, generating sincere faith. There is not a single feature at Sarma Yangzo that, lacking bright white, dark blue, or brilliant red, or lacking the heads, hands, and legs of images, requires imagination [to see].

Everyone who reaches the point where the four *Śvana* sisters guard the doors to this holy place of Sarma Yangzo are cheerful, with light and happy hearts. Then, when they clearly understand [the holy place], they are struck with fear, and instantly even ordinary people are led to realize one-pointed mind. If such pilgrims recite mantras and supplicate to Padmasambhava, there is no doubt that they will obtain boons. If they complete the rituals explained above on the first month of the year, moreover, any declines in their lifespan over the course of a year will be reversed.

Furthermore, I will find the "Boon of Deathlessness" cave again before my thirty-seventh year. If I hadn't completed those rituals on the first month, my lifespan would have deteriorated and many obstacles would have come, but since I found the cave, this will not happen. Still, there weren't any special features of a holy place, such as self-appearing images or syllables, above the "Boon of Deathlessness" cave.

The benefits of going to see (*mjal*) the holy place Sarma Yangzo that naturally come to whoever goes on the tenth day of each of the twelve months are in accord with condensed mantra at the end of the fierce holy place of the *Profound Intention of the Holy Dharma*.

Then, gradually we returned down. On the path down, I had a dream that I was in an auspicious valley. I dreamed that a group of *dakinis* encircled some vow-breaking beings and liberated them, and then gave me the blessings. I saw a cliff face of the Treasure of a Hundred Thousand *Dakinis* Rock, and the great king Vaishravana was posed majestically on top, mounted on a lion.

Then we went on top of the Treasure of a Hundred Thousand *Dakinis* Rock and performed a tantric feast offering. While all of us were on top of the Treasure of the Hundred Thousand *Dakinis* Rock, Manjusri revealed himself twice, and on the second occasion he was the shining central figure among 2,800 glorious gods. Then Guru Padmavajra appeared at the peak of the mountain, surrounded by eight attendants. He gave us the empowerment and initiation into the *Summary of the Guru's Intention*, and five-colored rays of light emanated from his heart. At the ends of the rays of light, Padmasambhava appeared brandishing a golden vase in his right hand and sounding a silver-white bell in his left hand. He placed a vase on the crown of each of our heads and performed an ablution. I was struck with wonder.

We did a dedication, and then recited a mantra from the *Summary of the Guru's Intention*. Then a manifestation of Padmasambhava appeared—he was gently swaying in a dancing pose surrounded by his retinue. And it appeared that the manifestation of Padmasambhava and his retinue dissolved into me. In that instant, I felt limitless great joy. I had countless memories of when Padmasambhava had given me many empowerments and prophecies in the Turquoise Room at the central chapel of Samye long ago in past lives. But I have not recorded [these accounts], for fear of putting them down in writing.

All of our group were gathered atop the Treasure of a Hundred Thousand *Dakinis* Rock, but the great master Padmasambhava only manifested himself to those who has the karmic destiny to receive the empowerment.

Right then, I saw that mountain [Gyangme], which is Cakrasaṃvara's palace, as the palace of Glorious Cakrasaṃvara in actuality.

At that time, there was no obscuring cover of mist. Then, from the midst of rainbow lights, there appeared that god who nobody had recognized before. For a long time, many miraculous bodily forms—great and small, thick and thin—appeared. At that time, I was carefully examining and analyzing, and so I saw the mountain as the sixty-two-deity mandala of Cakrasaṃvara.

Cakrasaṃvara manifests himself at different times as the eight heroes of the Underground Realm: Ratnavajra, Hayagriva, Akashagarbha, Sri Heruka, Padma lord of dancers, Vairocana, and Vajrasattva.

Furthermore, I saw all the rocks and stones of this holy place of Gyangme as the essence of gods and goddesses. All of the waters there exist solely as the chanted mantras of profound secret tantra. This will be realized by all those with the correct karmic destiny.

However, writing more here would not be appropriate. This brief description is merely an introduction to the general layout of the holy place of Gyangme. In particular, it mainly gives a pilgrimage guide to the holy place of Sarma Yangzo.

Afterward, we gradually went down, staying for a day at a pleasant spot between [rocks shaped like] a camel's face and a conch. While we stayed there, the place spirit Gyanglha Mugbe sent down an avalanche as a welcome. There was also a great deal of snow and rain as though the protectors of the holy place were delighted. The mountain behind the field where we were staying was surrounded by forest, like the king of mountains Tanaduk, and the mountain crags in front of us looked like wish-fulfilling jewels.

To our east, the unending chain of rivers and snow-capped mountains were like a great rocky tiger bridge. To our south, the central river looked like a turquoise thunder dragon. To our west, the red cliffs looked like a red she-bird. To our north, there was a great rocky edge at the peak of a forested mountain which looked like a dark turtle flipped on its back. What is more, all the mountains, forests, and rivers in the plain [where we were staying] seemed to be prostrating and praying. The geomancy of the site was very auspicious and had many wonderfully auspicious signs.

If you looked at it from the east, the plain was round in shape. If you looked from the south, it was square. If you looked from the west, it was half-moon shaped. And if you looked from the north, it was simply triangle shaped. This means that the four types of enlightened activities can be accomplished there without hindrance.

Practicing there, a person can attain enlightenment, destroy the ten kinds of enemies, or perform other activities. If that person practiced at another holy place, it would go slowly, but if they practice at this holy place, they will quickly accomplish [their aims]. [Gyangme] has many such wonders. In general, whoever makes it their special residence will realize the precious teachings of the Buddha.

In particular, several signs were seen indicating karmic connections for the supreme flourishing of the teaching of the victorious Drikung Kagyu, the holy crown ornament of all practice lineages. Based on that, that night, we saw a great rainstorm. [That place] is Potalaka, the foundation of the supreme vehicle, emerge. [Whoever practices there,] the flowers of auspiciousness will bloom, and he will directly perceive the palace of great compassion of the noble lord of the world. The protectors of that great holy place,

Potalaka, the foundation of the supreme vehicle, are the planetary demon Rahula and the naga demon black Candala.

[Colophon]

This is the condensed pilgrimage guide to Gyangme. It explains in detail the story of the previously unseen mountain faces at the old holy place, some new caves there, and the arrangement of the holy place of Sarma Yangzo.

There are also pure perception *dakini* Treasures which are a supplement to that, but although those Treasures are very detailed and pure, I was not able to record them, out of fear of putting them into writing.

Not even the smallest part of the meaning has been misunderstood, so understand this amount. I have written the full meaning so that it is all easy to understand, without too much proliferation of words, and without it being obscured through metrics and verse. Let that much explanation be sufficient.

Mangalam!

APPENDIX 2

Translation of Khatag Zamyak's *Nyindeb*, pages 166–174

[We arrived at] the mansion palace of Cakrasaṃvara which is called Kailash, is praised by the Buddha, and is the dwelling place of five hundred *arhats*. There was no obscuring cover of clouds or darkness. I worshipped and recited the guru *sādhanā* for Milarepa, and so saw his face (*zhal mjal bas*), and I thought, "What good karmic connections!" and immediately prostrated three times in a state of joy. I stayed at the edge of the lake that night.

The next day, we went to see and worship at the small monastery founded by Ngor Evam Konchok Lundrup (*ngor evam dkon mchog lhun 'grub*) known as the "South-East Cleansing Door."[1] I offered a mandala of three *zho* coins and did prostrations, circumambulations, and prayers. The next day, we went to the authentic and unrivaled "Southern Thaw Door," which has a monastery connected with Riwo Ganden. The three supports were swept, clean, and pure, and whatever mandala or butter lamp you looked at, it seemed as if it were trimmed with pure gold. I thought, "Who is like master Losang Drakpa (*rje blo bzang grag pa*), who holds the teachings and whose blessings are most extraordinary?" I made an offering of seven *zho* coins to the Southern Thaw Door Monastery, where faith arises naturally. I did prostrations, circumambulated, and made prayers. At this real Southern Thaw Door, south of Lake Anavatapta, my friends and I, together with horses and mules, washed and cooked food, and then settled nearby for the night.

The following day, [we crossed] a mountain pass called "Song Pass" (*mgur la*). Long ago, when the precious, venerable Milarepa was arriving at the holy place of Lake Manasarovar and Kailash, he was welcomed and feasted there by *dakinis* and local spirits. Since this was the pass sung about by the precious, venerable one, I thought, "This really (*don du*) is the pass from the Song!" There were, moreover, visible (*mjal rgyu*) footprints in the stone.

Having crossed over that mountain pass, we stayed and rested for two days at a household called Gongmo Baro Butsang (*gong mo ba rod bu tsang*). Then we went straight, via Purang Zam (*spu hrengs zam*), and spent a night at a village near Jangchub Gompa.

The next day, we saw the Korchag Jowo (*'khor chags jo bo*), the lord of the three buddha families. I made a mandala by replenishing the butter lamps and offered a *zupchi* scarf[2] and three *srang* coins. I diligently performed extensive prostrations and circumambulations.... [Gives story of how the Korchag Jowo image was discovered].[3] ... This story is clear from the inventory (*dkar chag*) of that place.

[1] Kailash has eight "doors" on the cardinal and subcardinal directions. For more information on the specific doors, their names, and their histories, see the notes in chapter 11 of "At Mount Kailash," in Matthieu Ricard et al., *The Life of Shabkar: The Autobiography of a Tibetan Yogin* (Albany: State University of New York Press, 1994), 275–348.

[2] *Zub phyi*, a medium quality of silk scarf.

[3] For a version of this story, see note 86 on page 347 of Źabs-dkar Tshogs-drug-raṅ-grol, *The Life of Shabkar: The Autobiography of a Tibetan Yogin*, trans. Matthieu Ricard (Albany: State University of New York Press, 1994). I have excluded it here for reasons of space.

Nearby, there was a small Sakya monastery. In the innermost chapel of the monastery, there was precious Maitreya image. To its left corner, there was an assembly hall with images of a dharma protector and a goddess. In a room nearby, there were images of the seven buddhas [before Shakyamuni]. I prostrated, circumambulated, and respectfully paid reverence to the supports contained there, and then returned.

I visited a Kagyu monastery called "Jangchub Monastery." Its main images were a Jetsun Milarepa with a self-arisen "A" on the heart, and [images] of the excellent patriarchs of the Kagyu lineage in the assembly hall. I worshipped by prostrating, circumambulating, and offering a mandala of eight *zho*. Then we arrived at Dongmo Zamkar Tsongral and stayed there for two nights.

In general, it is said that Purang is surrounded by mountains, Ruthok is surrounded by lakes, and Guge is surrounded by slate, so the name Ngari Khorsum (*mnga' ris bskor gsum*) was formed. Some assert that in ancient times, Purang was connected to the demon Lanka, so it was known as Lanka Purang (*lang ka spu hrangs*). It was known, too, as being the place where the precious Buddha preached the *Lankavatara Sutra*. [It was also reputed to have] the palace of Prince Sudhana, the cave of the two thousand queens, and the rock cave known as Asura Cave where Manohara flew into the sky. Also, if you cross Trakla Pass, there is also a spring that naturally liberates those who see it. Previously, it was known as Brahmasabha pool. It is said to be a place of practice where sages dwell. There are also the palaces of the four *naga* kings, and [there] is the Manasarovar lake where the hunter Phalaka rested, having eaten the fish.[4]

Although there are *jambu* trees growing there, one [either sees or] does not see them because of the purity or impurity of one's defilements. There are many scriptures and supporting citations where these distinctive features are described.

According to the narrative accounts of the Buddha and his teachings by Jetsun Marpa and Jetsun Milarepa, Kailash and Manasarovar are praised by the buddhas, and they are recognized as the source of the four flowing rivers. Jetsun Milarepa, moreover, overpowered Naro Bonchung with his magical power there, and thus brought Kailash and Manasarovar under his control.

Milarepa saw Kailash directly just as it was described by the Buddha, and he joyfully scattered flowers of praise in all directions. After that,[5] when Atisa came to upper Ngari, he heard the sound of drumbeats arose from Kailash right when it was time for the five hundred arhats' noon meal. [Hearing that,] Atisa said, "We too should make preparations, because it's time for lunch!" The *Gathered Intention of Padmasambhava* also says that some distance to the east of Kailash, the chicks of the *shang shang* bird are raised. Later, the Drikung and Drukpa Kagyus praised Kailash and gave many reasons why it is [Himavat, the mountain of Buddhist scriptures]. Still later, the first Panchen Lama, Lobsang Chökyi Gyaltsen (1569–1662), praised this very Kailash. Furthermore, it is clear that authentic Indian *mahasiddhas* said that this very Kailash is real (*dngos*).

Sakya Paṇḍita shot an arrow of words [saying that] Manasarovar and Kailash, which are spoken of in the sutras, are not [really] the medicine mountain described in treatises of medicine and other scriptures,[6] and so smeared all beings with uncertainty. This is

[4] The references to Sudhana, Manohara, Brahmasabha pool, and Palaka are from the story of Sudhāna and Manohāra, which can be found in multiple versions across the Buddhist tradition.

[5] This timeline seems to be confused because Atiśa (980–1054) should come before Milarepa (1052–1135).

[6] It is unclear what Khatag Zamyak means here, because Sakya Paṇḍita does not mention any medical texts. It is possible he is thinking of Tanaduk (*lta na sdug*), the mountain mentioned in Buddhist medical texts. However, his overall point is clearly that Sakya Paṇḍita questioned the legitimacy of Kailash.

probably a sign that detailed analysis of sutras and tantras is necessary. Some followers of the Sakya tradition use biased and ignorant words to refute [the authenticity of Kailash], but there is no point to those fuzzy refutations [by the Sakyas] apart from refuting the virtue of pilgrimage to holy places.

In reality, the perfected buddhas and bodhisattvas directly perceive Kailash as the palace of Cakrasaṃvara. Also, the signs (*rtags*) of it being a dwelling place of buddhas and the five hundred arhats are unchanging nails (*gzer bu*) all around. And one can see (*mjal*) the visible phenomena (*mthong chos*) of the Buddha's footprints. Although there are countless self-arisen and subsequently formed images in the rocks and stones, at present I cannot write them all down. I myself do not analyze it deeply.

In actuality, the four great rivers flow from the four directions around Kailash and Manasarovar. They flow from four hills which are like animals. To the east, a river flows from the mouth of a great horse toward Drogshog. The river flowing from the mouth of the peacock goes to Purang. The river flowing from the mouth of the lion goes toward Ladakh. The river flowing from the mouth of the elephant goes toward Guge. This is and remains visible to all.

Furthermore, as for the benefits of pilgrimage to this holy place, and the value of circumambulating it, according to Tsangpa Gyare (1161–1211):

> If one circumambulates once
> at the great palace of Kailash,
> the defilements of one life are purified.
> Similarly, if one does circumambulates ten times,
> the defilements of one aeon are purified.
> If one completes a hundred circumambulations,
> having purified the ten signs and eight qualities,
> one will attain buddhahood in one lifetime.

Thus it is said according to the old inventories (*dkar chag*), and so that seems to be the real value of a circumambulation.

The present oral tradition says that the most valuable number of circumambulations is thirteen. The reason for this is because there was once a Khampa woman who was carrying her son on her back at the small lake atop Tara Pass. Her body was hunched over, and so when she bent to drink water, the son [fell out] and was killed. As penance, she accumulated circumambulations. It is said that after she did thirteen circumambulations, there were footprints in stone as a sign that she had purified her obscurations. The guides to the holy place (*gnas 'dzin*) say that it is wise to do the full measure of circumambulations [and look] for signs of if your defilements are purified or not.

The established route for pilgrimage is from Purang Zam [to] Bugda. We went via the peacock-mouthed hill, which is the source of the great river, and then crossed a pass to the upper central valley. Then we cooked a meal at the Tsongral market and stayed three nights at Khargog Tshora. The path [normally takes] about three days, [but we took longer] since we took a leisurely pace.

Then, after coming through Karleb Chuka, we saw the Dharmakaya cave. We made mandalas [i.e., donations], prostrations, circumambulations, and purifications of sins in front of the many holy images, such as the main image of Choku Ö. We moved along gradually, endeavoring in the protectors' practice together with supplications. We did prostrations and circumambulations, and made donations at the divine images and scriptures at Ralung monastery in the Drilung valley. We continued upward, and we spent the night at the slope of Tara Pass.

The next day, at the cave in which twenty-one Taras had dissolved, we did extensive prostrations and circumambulations. Then we crossed that pass and headed down. The purifying lake at which the Khampa woman had lost her child had been closed. This year, however, it was opened, just in time for us to be able to purify ourselves and worship there. I thought "the karmic connections are extremely good!" and went down. When we arrived at Magical Powers Cave, we cooked and saw the cave. I generated devotion and pure perception (*mos gus dag snang bskyed*), and made a mandala, did prostrations, circumambulated, and purified defilements.

Then, on the evening of the fourteenth day of the seventh month, we stayed at Gyangdrak (*rgyang grags*) Monastery. On the fifteenth day, I refilled a few silver butter lamps which were clean and beautiful, as well as a few copper and brass lamps. Then I worshipped the main image, which was about the size of twelve fingers of the Buddha and was called "Rippled Water Sage." It had been offered by the great *nāgas* of Lake Manasarovar, and there were also many other supports of body, speech, and mind. I endeavored in terms of whatever visualizations I knew (*dmigs rnam ci shes la 'bad*). I made prostrations and circumambulations.

I took just a few things with me and left people, horses, and mules behind to look closely (*zhib mjal*) at the holy place again and went on a circumambulation.

I went via Gyangdrak. I saw the Serlung gompa, then I prostrated to the mountain pass and went down. I saw the great gold prayer flag and circumambulated it. I went atop a cliff that was like a mandala. There, there were the footprints of the five hundred *arhats* and five hundred *dakinis*. That cliff peak is known as the charnel ground of the five hundred *arhats*. I left my hair and nail clippings there, and I took up the sleeping lion posture and mediated on death. I visualized (*gsal btab*) the charnal ground as the buddhafield of Amitabha.

Then I got up, and in the lower valleys to the right of that cliff, there was a cave. Inside that cave, there are traces left behind of Naro Bonchung's meditation practice. In the high awning of the western cliff on the other side of that, the Jetsun master [Milarepa] dwelled with his disciples. Through his magical power, Milarepa extended his legs [across the valley]. I saw the rocky cliff where Bonchung lived, along with the Jetsun's footprints on the side. Bonchung also attempted to stretch his legs [across the valley], but he couldn't reach any farther than the lower bank of the water, so the gods and demons let out a great horse-laugh from the sky. Thus I recognized (*ngo 'phrod*) the place where Bonchung's humiliation took place.

I was there in Dharmakaya Hollow for a day and prostrated and did circumambulations. I went up in the morning and then offered a mandala at night to the precious snow mountain [Kailash]. Then I passed through Drilung valley. I cooked at Drira hollow. With single-pointed focus (*phur tsug*) on Kailash, I performed prostrations, offered mandalas, and made offerings.

Once again, I went up to Tara Slope. On top of Bonchung's giant stone, I did devotion and pure vision (*mos gus dag snang byas*). It was the stone which was carried by Milarepa after he [carried a stone] double the size of Naro Bonchung's stone. Then I went up to the pass where twenty-one forms of Tara dissolved into a rock. I performed full-body prostrations and circumambulations. In a state of reverence, I performed a tantric feast offering and gave a portion of the offering to pilgrims.

Then I went down to Tara Lake to bathe and worship. At the cliff where Milarepa and Naro Bonchung took water for ablutions and debated Bön versus Dharma, there were many footprints. And I recognized (*ngo 'phrod*) the crag where Milarepa, through the potency of the precious Jetsun, taught the Bönpo about dharma. Then we went down, and at the peak of the pass, and at the top of a rocky cairn, I saw that there were footprints of the Buddha.

Then, at the foot of the mountain, on the sunny side of Menlung valley, I stayed for a night at Magical Illusion Cave. At the monastery, there were good images of Jetsun Milarepa and so forth, and there was a cache of treasures [and] fruit of the *jambu* tree. Two lineage gurus from Ü did tantric feast offerings, so I rejoiced in that and contributed a donation.

The next day I went to Gyangdrak and stayed for two nights to rest. I saw a footprint of the Buddha located at the monastery. In general, there is a footprint of the Buddha on each of the four sides of Kailash. I was unable to go in order to see two footprints [i.e., on two of the sides].

Then, on the nineteenth day of the seventh month, there was a proper universal incense-offering ritual at Gyangdrak Monastery. I offered a mentally emanated mandala as a thanks for kindness at Kailash, which is the palace of the sixty-two deity mandala of Cakrasaṃvara, the dwelling place of the five hundred arhats such as the *sthavira* Angiraja, and has an wealth of deities, images, and scriptures.

I cooked and bought some provisions from the market. I made offerings again and again to the great holy place. It was the beginning of returning to my own country.

Bibliography

Asian-Language Sources

Bcom ldan rig pa'i ral gri. *Chos mngon pa kun las btus pa'i rgyan gyi me tog.* BDRC W24700. No publisher, no date.

Bod rang skyong ljongs spyi tshogs tshan rig khang gi bod yig dpe rnying dpe skrun khang, ed. *Bod kyi snga rabs khrims srol yig cha bdams bsgrigs.* BDRC W00KG09682. Lhasa: Bod ljongs bod yig dpe rnying dpe skrun khang, 1989.

Bod rang skyong ljongs yig tshangs khang, ed. *Bca' yig phyogs bsgrigs.* BDRC W21612. Lhasa: Bod ljongs mi dmangs dpe skrun khang, 2001.

'Bri gung chung tsang 01 Rig 'dzin Chos kyi grags pa. *Brag dkar lha chur tshe sgrub bgyis dus mthong snang byung tshul.* In *Collected Works of Chos kyi grags pa.* BDRC W22082. 1: 525–530. Kulhan: Drikung Kagyu Institute, 1999.

'Bri gung chung tsang 01 Rig 'dzin Chos kyi grags pa. *Bye ri stag rtser zla gsang gi bsnyen sgrub zhig bgyis pa'i tshe 'khrul snang du byung ba bden par bzung nas bris pa.* In *Collected Works of Chos kyi grags pa.* BDRC W22082. 1: 469–478. Kulhan: Drikung Kagyu Institute, 1999.

'Bri gung chung tsang 01 Rig 'dzin Chos kyi grags pa. *Gzhan gyi rgol ngal 'joms pa'i legs bshad lung rigs smra ba'i mgul rgyan.* In *Collected Works of Chos kyi grags pa.* BDRC W22082. 2: 385–446. Kulhan: Drikung Kagyu Institute, 1999.

'Bri gung chung tsang 01 Rig 'dzin Chos kyi grags pa. *Kha rag bde chen thar pa gling gi gnas bstod dad ldan snying la dga' ster ku ma da'i phreng ba.* In *Collected Works of Chos kyi grags pa.* BDRC W22082. 2: 447–456. Kulhan: Drikung Kagyu Institute, 1999.

'Bri gung chung tsang 01 Rig 'dzin Chos kyi grags pa. *Me sprel zla ba drug pa'i tshes bco lnga'i nyin ti sgro'i zhing skyong sna tshar du lung bstan sa stod smad bar gsum gyi skad cha sna tshogs.* In *Collected Works of Chos kyi grags pa.* BDRC W22082. 1: 573–582. Kulhan: Drikung Kagyu Institute, 1999.

'Bri gung chung tsang 01 Rig 'dzin Chos kyi grags pa. *Mthong snang phran bu sgyu ma'i grong khyer lta bu.* In *Collected Works of Chos kyi grags pa.* BDRC W22082. 1: 385–460. Kulhan: Drikung Kagyu Institute, 1999.

'Bri gung chung tsang 01 Rig 'dzin Chos kyi grags pa. *Rang gi gnas tshul nyams mtshar du bkod pa'i tho.* In *Collected Works of Chos kyi grags pa.* BDRC W22082. 1: 461–468. Kulhan: Drikung Kagyu Institute, 1999.

'Bri gung chung tsang 01 Rig 'dzin Chos kyi grags pa. *Rang gi tshul gyi rtogs pa brjod pa'i gtam rang bzhin brjod pa'i rgyan kho nas smras pa gsong po'i dga' ston.* In *Collected Works of Chos kyi grags pa.* BDRC W22082. 1: 19–264. Kulhan: Drikung Kagyu Institute, 1999.

'Bri gung chung tsang 01 Rig 'dzin Chos kyi grags pa. *Rgyang me'i gnas yig rdo rje 'dzin pa'i dga' ston.* In *Collected Works of Chos kyi grags pa.* BDRC W22082. 2: 457–477. Kulhan: Drikung Kagyu Institute, 1999.

'Bri gung chung tsang 01 Rig 'dzin Chos kyi grags pa. *Snyan ngag me long gi rgyan gyi dper brjod gzhon nu dga' ba'i gtam ngag gi 'dod 'jo.* In *Collected Works of Chos kyi grags pa.* BDRC W22082. 15: 105–164. Kulhan: Drikung Kagyu Institute, 1999.

'Bri gung chung tsang 06 Dkon chog bstan 'dzin Chos kyi blo gros. *Gangs ri chen po ti se dang mtsho chen ma dros pa bcas kyi sngon byung gi lo rgyus mdor bsdus su brjod pa'i rab byed shel dkar me long.* In *Gnas yig phyogs bsgrigs*, edited by Dge 'dun chos 'phel. BDRC W20828. 114–219. Chengdu: Si khron mi rigs dpe skrun khang, 1998.

'Brug chen 04 Kun mkhyen Pad+ma dkar po. *Bod yul lho de wi ko Ta'i gnas bshad mdor bsdus ya mtshan gyi 'dod 'jo*. In *Collected Works of Padma dkar po*. BDRC W10736. 4: 283–288. Darjeeling: Kargyud sungrab nyamso khang, 1973–1974.

'Brug chen 04 Kun mkhyen Pad+ma dkar po. *Gnas chen mkhar chu'i bstod pa bden pa'i gnas la dga' ba'i ngang pa rnams dga' ba bskyed pa'i padma can*. In *Collected Works of Padma dkar po*. BDRC W10736. 9: 543–548. Darjeeling: Kargyud sungrab nyamso khang, 1973–1974.

'Brug chen 04 Kun mkhyen Pad+ma dkar po. *Gnas chen tsa ri tra'i ngo mtshar snang ba pad dkar legs bshad*. In *Collected Works of Padma dkar po*. BDRC W10736. 4: 215–282. Darjeeling: Kargyud sungrab nyamso khang, 1973–1974.

'Brug chen 04 Kun mkhyen Pad+ma dkar po. *Tsa ri tra zhes pa'i gnas la bstod pa pad dkar legs bshad*. In *Collected Works of Padma dkar po*. BDRC W10736. 9: 537–542. Darjeeling: Kargyud sungrab nyamso khang, 1973–1974.

Bzhad pa'i rdo rje. *Gsal dwangs ri bo che'i gnas zhal gsar du phye ba'i lo rgyus*. In *Collected Works of Bzhad pa'i rdo rje*. BDRC W22130. 9: 237–262. Leh: T. Sonam and D.L. Tashigang, 1983–1985.

Bzhad pa'i rdo rje. *Ltal chung mkha' 'gro'i dga' tshal gyi gnas sgo gsar du phye ba'i lam yig*. In *Collected Works of Bzhad pa'i rdo rje*. BDRC W22130. 9: 213–229. Leh: T. Sonam and D.L. Tashigang, 1983–1985.

Chos rje Sgam po pa Zla 'od gzhon nu. *Dam chos yid bzhin nor bu thar pa rin po che'i rgyan*. BDRC W1KG5451. Kathmandu: Gam-po-pa Library, 2005.

Chos sde chen po dpal ldan 'bras dkar spungs pa'i dgon gyi bca' yig tshul 'chal sa srung 'dul ba'i lcags kyo kun sel me long. In *Bod kyi snga rabs khrims srol yig cha bdams bsgrigs*, edited by Bod rang skyong ljongs spyi tshogs tshan rig khang gi bod yig dpe rnying dpe skrun khang. BDRC W00KG09682. 275–323. Lhasa: Bod ljongs bod yig dpe rnying dpe skrun khang, 1989.

Dge 'dun chos 'phel, ed. *Gnas yig phyogs bsgrigs*. BDRC W20828. Chengdu: Si khron mi rigs dpe skrun khang, 1998.

Dri ma med par grags pas bstan pa'i mdo. In *Bka' 'gyur (dpe bsdur ma)*. BDRC W1PD96682. 60: 476–635. Beijing: Krung go'i bod rig pa'i dpe skrun khang, 2006–2009.

'Dul ba phran tshegs. In *Bka' 'gyur (dpe bsdur ma)*. BDRC W1PD96682. 11: 20–822. Beijing: Krung go'i bod rig pa'i dpe skrun khang, 2006–2009.

Go rams pa Bsod nams seng ge. *Sdom gsum rab dbye'i kha kong legs bshad 'od kyi snang ba*. In *Sdom gsum rab dbye dang sdom gsum gtan 'bebs 'jam dbyangs bla ma'i dgongs rgyan gyi rnam 'grel*. BDRC W29981. 1: 158–210. Beijing: Mi rigs dpe skrun khang, 2004.

Grags pa rgyal mtshan. *Gnas bstod kyi nyams dbyangs*. In *Sa skya gong ma rnam lnga'i gsung 'bum dpe bsdur ma las grags pa rgyal mtshan gyi gsung*. BDRC W2DB4569. 5: 344–347. Beijing: Krung go'i bod rig pa dpe skrun khang, 2007.

'Jam mgon Kong sprul Blo gros mtha' yas. *Thugs kyi gnas mchog chen po de bI ko TI tsA 'dra rin chen brag gi rtog pa brjod pa yid kyi rgya mtsho'i rol mo*. In *Rgya chen bka' mdzod*. BDRC W21808. 11: 489–558. Paro: Ngodup, 1975–1976.

'Jigs med gling pa Mkhyen brtse 'od zer. *Gnas bskor ba la spring ba'i gtam*. In *The Collected Works of 'Jigs med gling pa Mkhyen brtse 'od zer*. BDRC W27300. 4: 575–579. Gangtok: No Publisher, 1985.

KaH thog Si tu 03 Chos kyi rgya mtsho. *Dbus gtsang gi gnas yig*. BDRC W9668. Palampur, H.P.: Sungrab nyamso gyunphel parkhang, 1972.

KaH thog Si tu 03 Chos kyi rgya mtsho. *Gangs ljongs dbus gtsang gnas bskor lam yig nor bu zla shel gyi se mo do*. BDRC W27524. Chengdu: Si khron mi rigs dpe skrun khang, 2001.

KaH thog Si tu 03 Chos kyi rgya mtsho. "Gnas skor pa rab 'bring mtha' gsum gyi rnam dbye." In *Gnas yig phyogs bsgrigs*. BDRC W20828, 1–2. Chengdu: Si khron mi rigs dpe skrun khang, 1998.

Karma chags med. *Gnas mjal ba'i tshul*. In *Collected Works of Karma chags med*. BDRC W22933. 43: 637–638. Chengdu: Si khron zhing chen mi rigs zhib 'jug su'o bod kyi rig gnas zhib 'jug khang, 1999.

Karma rgyal mtshan, ed. *Mdo khams gnas yig phyogs bsgrigs dad bskul lha dbang rnga sgra.* BDRC W29295. Beijing: Mi rigs dpe skrun khang, 2005.

Kha stag 'dzam yag. *Bod dang Bal-po Rgya-gar bcas la gnas bskor bskyod pa'i nyin deb: phyi lo 1944 nas 1956 bar.* BDRC W1KG23814. Dharamsala, India: Acharya Jamyang Wangyal, 1997.

Lcang skya 03 Rol pa'i rdo rje. *Ri bo rtse lnga'i gnas yig.* BDRC W2CZ6238. Lhasa: Bod ljongs bod yig dpe rnying dpe skrun khang, 1992.

Nā ro pa. *Rdo rje'i tshig gi snying po bsdus pa'i dka' 'grel* (S. *Vajrapādasārasaṃgraha*). In *Bstan 'gyur (dpe bsdur ma).* BDRC W1PD95844. 2: 914–1137. Beijing: Krung go'i bod rig pa'i dpe skrun khang, 1994–2008.

'Phags pa yongs su mya ngan las 'das pa chen po'i mdo. In *Bka' 'gyur (dpe bsdur ma).* BDRC W1PD96682. 52: 17–802. Beijing: Krung go'i bod rig pa'i dpe skrun khang, 2006–2009.

Rang byung rdo rje. *Dgyes pa rdo rje'i brtag pa gnyis pa'i 'grel pa dri ma med pa'i 'od.* In *Collected Works of Rang byung rdo rje.* BDRC W30541. 8: 497–636. Zi ling: Mtshur phu mkhan lo yag bkra shis, 2006.

Rgyal mtshan bzang po. *Mdo khams gnas chen nyer lnga'i gnas yig phyogs bsgrigs.* BDRC W1AC435. Zi ling: Mtsho sngon mi rigs dpe skrun khang, 2013.

Rigs ldan Pad + ma dkar po (S. Puṇḍarīka). *Bsdus pa'i rgyud kyi rgyal po dus kyi 'khor lo'i 'grel bshad rtsa ba'i rgyud kyi rjes su 'jug pa stong phrag bcu gnyis pa dri ma med pa'i 'od* (S. *Vimalaprabhā*). In *Bstan 'gyur (dpe bsdur ma).* BDRC W1PD95844. 6: 706–1482. Beijing: Krung go'i bod rig pa'i dpe skrun khang, 1994–2008.

Sa skya Paṇḍita Kun dga' rgyal mtshan. *A Clear Differentiation of the Three Codes: Essential Distinctions among the Individual Liberation, Great Vehicle, and Tantric Systems: The Sdom Gsum Rab Dbye and Six Letters.* Translated by Jared Rhoton. Albany: State University of New York Press, 2002.

Sa skya Paṇḍita Kun dga' rgyal mtshan. *Mkhas pa rnams 'jug pa'i sgo.* In *Sa skya bka' 'bum.* BDRC W22271. 10:333–456. Dehra Dun: Sakya Center, 1992–1993.

Sa skya Paṇḍita Kun dga' rgyal mtshan. *Sdom pa gsum gyi rab tu dbye ba.* In *Sa skya bka' 'bum.* BDRC W22271. 12:15–110. Dehra Dun: Sakya Center, 1992–1993.

Shākya mchog ldan. *Sdom pa gsum gyi rab tu dbye ba'i bstan bcos kyi 'bel gtam rnam par nges pa legs bshad gser gyi thur ma.* In *The Works of Pen-Chen Shakya Mchog-Lden.* BDRC W00EGS1016899. 7:7–244. Kathmandu: Sachen International, 2006.

Shākya mchog ldan. "Sdom pa gsum gyi rab tu dbye ba'i bstan bcos kyi 'bel gtam rnam par nges pa legs bshad gser gyi thur ma." In *The Works of Pen-Chen Shakya Mchog-Lden*, vol. 7, 7–244. Kathmandu: Sachen International, 2006.

Spos khang pa Rin chen rgyal mtshan. *Sdom pa gsum gyi rab tu dbye ba'i gzhung lugs legs par bshad pa.* In *Dpal sa skya'i sdom gsum phyogs bsgrigs*, edited by Si khron bod yig dpe rnying bsdu sgrig khang. BDRC W3CN5910. 1: 222–695. Chengdu: Rgyal khab dpe mdzod khang dpe skrun khang, 2015.

Sras mkhar dgu thog gtsug lag khang, gro bo lung, zangs phug stag gnya' bcas kyi gnas yig rna ba'i bdud rtsi dad pa'i shing rta. BDRC W15649. No publisher, No date.

Sras mkhar dgu thog sogs bod kyi gnas yig khag cig. BDRC W00EGS1016705. Dharamsala: Library of Tibetan Works and Archives, 1985.

Tā ra nā tha. *Las stod kyi gnas skor ba 'dra la gdams pa.* In *Collected Works of Tāranātha* BDRC W1PD45495. 3: 79–80. Beijing: Krung go'i bod rig pa dpe skrun khang, 2008.

Tshe ring dpal 'byor, ed. *Bod kyi gnas yig bdams bsgrigs.* BDRC W22019. Lhasa: Bod ljongs bod yig dpe rnying dpe skrun khang, 1995.

Vajragarbha. *Rdo rje snying po'i 'grel pa* (S. *Hevajrapiṇḍārthaṭīkā*). In *Bstan 'gyur (dpe bsdur ma).* BDRC W1PD95844. 1: 940–1144. Beijing: Krung go'i bod rig pa'i dpe skrun khang, 1994–2008.

Vasubandhu, *Abhidharmakośabhāṣyam of Vasubandhu.* Edited by P. Pradhan. K. P. Jayaswal Research Institute, 1975.

Zhang, Yisun. *Bod rgya tshig mdzod chen mo.* Ti 1 pan., Min tsu ch'u pan she, 1993.

Zhi ba 'od. *Byang chub sems dpa'i spyod pa la 'jug pa*. In *Bstan 'gyur (dpe bsdur ma)*. BDRC W1PD95844. 61: 970–1067. Beijing: krung go'i bod rig pa'i dpe skrun khang, 1994–2008.

Zhwa dmar 04 Chos grags ye shes. *Dben par bsngags pa'i gtam ku mu da'i dga' ston sogs*. In *Collected Works of Chos grags ye shes*. BDRC W1KG4876. 3: 70–75. Beijing: Krung go'i bod rig pa dpe skrun khang, 2009.

Zhwa dmar 04 Chos grags ye shes. *Dge ba'i 'bras bu gsal bar ston pa'i me long*. In *Collected Works of Chos grags ye shes*. BDRC W1KG4876. 3: 76–94. Beijing: Krung go'i bod rig pa dpe skrun khang, 2009.

Zhwa dmar 04 Chos grags ye shes. *Dpal bde chen yangs pa can gyi gnas la bstod pa*. In *Collected Works of Chos grags ye shes*. BDRC W1KG4876. 4: 284–286. Beijing: Krung go'i bod rig pa dpe skrun khang, 2009.

Zhwa dmar 04 Chos grags ye shes. *Dpal tsa ri tra la sogs pa'i gnas chen rnams la bstod pa*. In *Collected Works of Chos grags ye shes*. BDRC W1KG4876. 4: 269–274. Beijing: Krung go'i bod rig pa dpe skrun khang, 2009.

Zhwa dmar 04 Chos grags ye shes. *Gnas chen po g.ya' bu la bstod pa*. In *Collected Works of Chos grags ye shes*. BDRC W1KG4876. 4: 277–278. Beijing: Krung go'i bod rig pa dpe skrun khang, 2009.

Zhwa dmar 04 Chos grags ye shes. *Gnas kyi rnam par bzhag pa rdo rje 'dzin pa'i zhal gyi lung*. In *Collected Works of Chos grags ye shes*. BDRC W1KG4876. 3: 49–64. Beijing: Krung go'i bod rig pa dpe skrun khang, 2009.

Zhwa dmar 04 Chos grags ye shes. *Jo mo kha rag gi gnas la bstod pa*. In *Collected Works of Chos grags ye shes*. BDRC W1KG4876. 4: 281–283. Beijing: Krung go'i bod rig pa dpe skrun khang, 2009.

Zhwa dmar 04 Chos grags ye shes. *Lha zhol gyi gnas bstod*. In *Collected Works of Chos grags ye shes*. BDRC W1KG4876. 4: 275–275. Beijing: Krung go'i bod rig pa dpe skrun khang, 2009.

Zhwa dmar 04 Chos grags ye shes. *Phyag rgya chen po thig le dang ye shes thig le'i 'grel par gnas kyi rnam bzhag bshad pa'i gsal byed*. In *Collected Works of Chos grags ye shes*. BDRC W1KG4876. 3: 65–69. Beijing: Krung go'i bod rig pa dpe skrun khang, 2009.

Zhwa dmar 04 Chos grags ye shes. *Ri bo gangs chen dang mtsho ma dros pa chu bo bzhi dang bcas pa gtan la dbab pa mkhas pa'i rna rgyan*. In *Collected Works of Chos grags ye shes*. BDRC W1KG4876. 6: 440–463. Beijing: Krung go'i bod rig pa dpe skrun khang, 2009.

Zhwa dmar 04 Chos grags ye shes. *Ri bo gangs can dang mtsho ma dros pa chu bo bzhi dang bcas pa gtan la dbab pa mkhas pa'i rna rgyan*. BDRC W1CZ886 (Mtshur phu, No date).

Zhwa dmar 04 Chos grags ye shes. *Ri bo gangs can dang mtsho ma dros pa chu bo bzhi dang bcas pa gtan la dbab pa mkhas pa'i rna rgyan*. BDRC W00KG09824 (Dharamsala: Mnga' ris gzhung gces skyong khang, 1984).

Zhwa dmar 04 Chos grags ye shes. *Rtogs pa brjod pa'i tshigs su bcad pa utpala'i phreng ba*. In *Collected Works of Chos grags ye shes*. BDRC W1KG4876. 6: 959–1024. Beijing: Krung go'i bod rig pa dpe skrun khang, 2009.

Zhwa dmar 04 Chos grags ye shes. *Rtsa ri 'ja' tshon phug gi gnas bstod*. In *Collected Works of Chos grags ye shes*. BDRC W1KG4876. 4: 276–276. Beijing: Krung go'i bod rig pa dpe skrun khang, 2009.

European-Language Bibliography

Aitkin, Molly Emma, ed. *Meeting the Buddha: On Pilgrimage in Buddhist India*. New York: Riverhead Books, 1995.

Ambros, Barbara. *Emplacing a Pilgrimage: The Oyama Cult and Regional Religion in Early Modern Japan*. Cambridge, MA: Harvard University Asia Center, 2008.

Anālayo, Bhikkhu. "Visualization in Early Buddhism." *Mindfulness* 13, no. 9 (2022): 2155–2161.

Arnold, Dan. *Buddhists, Brahmins, and Belief: Epistemology in South Asian Philosophy of Religion*. New York: Columbia University Press, 2008.

Audi, Robert. *Moral Perception*. Princeton, NJ: Princeton University Press, 2013.

Bailey, Cameron. *A Feast for Scholars: The Life and Works of Sle Lung Bzhad Pa'i Rdo Rje*. Oxford: University of Oxford, 2017.

Bareau, André. "III. La composition et les étapes de la formation progressive du Mahàparinirvânasûtra ancien." *Bulletin de l'Ecole française d'Extrême-Orient* 66, no. 1 (1979): 45–103.

Basso, Keith H. *Wisdom Sits in Places: Landscape and Language among the Western Apache*. Albuquerque: University of New Mexico Press, 1996.

Bennett, Jane. *Vibrant Matter: A Political Ecology of Things*. Durham, NC: Duke University Press, 2010.

Berger, John. *Ways of Seeing*. London: Penguin, 1972.

Bhardwaj, Surinder M. *Hindu Places of Pilgrimage in India: A Study in Cultural Geography*. Berkeley: University of California Press, 1983.

Bianchi, Robert. *Guests of God: Pilgrimage and Politics in the Islamic World*. Oxford: Oxford University Press, 2008.

Birnbaum, Raoul. "Secret Halls of the Mountain Lords: The Caves of Wu-t'ai Shan." *Cahiers d'Extrême-Asie* 5, no. 1 (1989): 115–140.

Bitton-Ashkelony, Brouria. *Encountering the Sacred: The Debate on Christian Pilgrimage in Late Antiquity*. Berkeley: University of California Press, 2005.

Bjerken, Zeff. "On Mandalas, Monarchs, and Mortuary Magic: Siting the Sarvadurgatipariśodhana Tantra in Tibet." *Journal of the American Academy of Religion* 73, no. 3 (2005): 813–841.

Blackburn, Anne M. *Buddhist Learning and Textual Practice in Eighteenth-Century Lankan Monastic Culture*. Princeton, NJ: Princeton University Press, 2001.

Blair, Heather. *Real and Imagined: The Peak of Gold in Heian Japan*. Cambridge, MA: Harvard University Asia Center, 2015.

Blondeau, Anne-Marie, and Ernst Steinkellner. *Reflections of the Mountain: Essays on the History and Social Meaning of the Mountain Cult in Tibet and the Himalaya*. Wien: Verlag de Österreichischen Akademie der Wissenschaften, 1996.

Bloom, Phillip E. "Ghosts in the Mists: The Visual and the Visualized in Chinese Buddhist Art, ca. 1178." *The Art Bulletin* 98, no. 3 (2016): 297–320.

Bodhi, Bhikkhu, trans. *The Connected Discourses of the Buddha: A Translation of the Saṃyutta Nikāya*. Somerville, MA: Wisdom Publications, 2000.

Boer, Wietse de, and Christine Göttler. *Religion and the Senses in Early Modern Europe*. Leiden: Brill, 2013.

Bogel, Cynthea J. *With a Single Glance: Buddhist Icon and Early Mikkyō Vision*. Seattle: University of Washington Press, 2009.

Bourdieu, Pierre. *Outline of a Theory of Practice*. Translated by Richard Nice. Cambridge: Cambridge University Press, 2013.

Braun, Erik. *The Birth of Insight: Meditation, Modern Buddhism, and the Burmese Monk Ledi Sayadaw*. Chicago: University of Chicago Press, 2013.

Briscoe, Robert Eamon. *Superimposed Mental Imagery: On the Uses of Make-Perceive*. Oxford: Oxford University Press, 2018.

Broido, Michael. "Sa-Skya Paṇḍita, the White Panacea and the Hva-Shang Doctrine." *The Journal of the International Association of Buddhist Studies* 10, no. 2 (1987): 27–68.

Brown, David. *God and Enchantment of Place: Reclaiming Human Experience*. Oxford: Oxford University Press, 2006.

Buddhaghosa. *The Path of Purification: Visuddhimagga*. Translated by Bhikkhu Ñāṇamoli. Kandy: Buddhist Publication Society, 1991.

Buffetrille, Katia. "The Blue Lake of A-Mdo and Its Island: Legends and Pilgrimage Guide." In *Sacred Spaces and Powerful Places in Tibetan Culture: A Collection of Essays*, edited by Toni Huber, 105–124. Dharamsala: The Library of Tibetan Works and Archives, 1999.

Buffetrille, Katia. "The Evolution of a Tibetan Pilgrimage: The Pilgrimage to A Myes RMa Chen Mountain in the 21st Century." In *Symposium on Contemporary Tibetan Studies*,

21st Century Tibet Issue, Collected Papers, 325–363. Taipei: Mongolian and Tibetan Affairs Commission, 2003.

Buffetrille, Katia. "The Great Pilgrimage of A Myes RMa-Chen: Written Traditions, Living Realities." In *Mandala and Landscape*, edited by A. W. Macdonald, 75–132. New Delhi: D.K. Printworld, 1997.

Buffetrille, Katia. "One Day the Mountains Will Go Away . . . Preliminary Remarks on the Flying Mountains of Tibet." In *Reflections of the Mountain: Essays on the History and Social Meaning of the Mountain Cult in Tibet and the Himalaya*, edited by A. M. Bondeau and E. Steinkellner, 77–90. Wien: Verlag der Österreischiche Akademie der Wissenschaften, 1996.

Buffetrille, Katia. "The Pilgrimage to Mount Kha Ba Dkar Po: A Metaphor for Bardo?" In *Searching for the Dharma, Finding Salvation: Buddhist Pilgrimage in Time and Space. Proceedings of the Workshop "Buddhist Pilgrimage in History and Present Times" at the Lumbini International Research Institute (LIRI), Lumbini, 11–13 January 2010*, edited by Christoph Cueppers and Max Deeg, 197–220. Lumbini: Lumbini International Research Institute, 2014.

Buffetrille, Katia. "Reflections on Pilgrimages to Sacred Mountains, Lakes and Caves." In *Pilgrimage in Tibet*, edited by Alex McKay, 18–34. London: Curzon Press, 1998.

Buffetrille, Katia. "The RTsib Ri Pilgrimage: Merit as Collective Duty?" In *Nepalica-Tibetica: Festgabe for Christoph Cüppers*, edited by Franz-Karl Ehrhard and Petra Maurer, vol. 1, 37–64. Andiast: International Institute for Tibetan and Buddhist Studies, 2013.

Buswell, Robert E., and Donald S. Lopez. *The Princeton Dictionary of Buddhism*. Princeton, NJ: Princeton University Press, 2014.

Cabezón, José Ignacio. *Buddhism and Language: A Study of Indo-Tibetan Scholasticism*. Albany: State University of New York Press, 1994.

Cabezón, José Ignacio, and Roger R. Jackson, eds. *Tibetan Literature: Studies in Genre*. Ithaca, NY: Snow Lion, 1996.

Cardman, Francine. "The Rhetoric of Holy Places: Palestine in the Fourth Century." *Studia Patristica* 17 (1982): 18–25.

Casey, Edward S. *The Fate of Place: A Philosophical History*. Berkeley: University of California Press, 1997.

Casey, Edward S. *Getting Back into Place: Toward a Renewed Understanding of the Place-World*. Bloomington: Indiana University Press, 2009.

Casey, Edward S. *Imagining: A Phenomenological Study*. Bloomington: Indiana University Press, 1976.

Casey, Edward S. *The World at a Glance*. Bloomington: Indiana University Press, 2007.

Castoriadis, Cornelius. *The Imaginary Institution of Society*. Translated by Kathleen Blamey. Cambridge: Polity Press, 1987.

Chou, Wen-shing. *Mount Wutai: Visions of a Sacred Buddhist Mountain*. Princeton, NJ: Princeton University Press, 2018.

Chou, Wen-shing. "Reimagining the Buddhist Universe: Pilgrimage and Cosmography in the Court of the Thirteenth Dalai Lama (1876–1933)." *The Journal of Asian Studies* 73, no. 2 (2014): 419–445.

Classen, Constance, et al. *A Cultural History of the Senses*. London: Bloomsbury Academic, 2014.

Coleman, Simon, and John Eade, eds. *Reframing Pilgrimage: Cultures in Motion*. London: Routledge, 2004.

Coleman, Simon, and John Elsner. *Pilgrimage: Past and Present in the World Religions*. Cambridge, MA: Harvard University Press, 1997.

Collins, Steven. *Nirvana and Other Buddhist Felicities: Utopias of the Pali Imaginaire*. Cambridge: Cambridge University Press, 1988.

Collins, Steven. "On the Very Idea of the Pali Canon." *Journal of the Pali Text Society* XV (1990): 89–126.

Collins, Steven. *Selfless Persons: Imagery and Thought in Theravada Buddhism.* Cambridge: Cambridge University Press, 1990.

Coole, Diana H., and Samantha Frost. *New Materialisms: Ontology, Agency, and Politics.* Durham, NC: Duke University Press, 2010.

Coster, Will, and Andrew Spicer, eds. *Sacred Space in Early Modern Europe.* Cambridge: Cambridge University Press, 2011.

Csordas, Thomas J. "Somatic Modes of Attention." *Cultural Anthropology* 8, no. 2 (1993): 135–156.

Cüppers, Christoph, and Max Deeg, eds. *Searching for the Dharma, Finding Salvation: Buddhist Pilgrimage in Time and Space: Proceedings of the Workshop "Buddhist Pilgrimage in History and Present Times."* Lumbini: Lumbini International Research Institute, 2014.

Currie, Gregory, and Ian Ravenscroft. *Recreative Minds: Imagination in Philosophy and Psychology.* Oxford: Oxford University Press, 2002.

Dalton, Jacob P. *The Taming of the Demons: Violence and Liberation in Tibetan Buddhism.* New Haven, CT: Yale University Press, 2011.

Davidson, Ronald M. *Indian Esoteric Buddhism: A Social History of the Tantric Movement.* New York: Columbia University Press, 2002.

Davidson, Ronald M. "The Kingly Cosmogonic Narrative and Tibetan Histories: Indian Origins, Tibetan Space, and the BKa' 'chems Ka Khol Ma Synthesis." *Lungta* 16 (2004): 64–83.

Davidson, Ronald M. *Tibetan Renaissance: Tantric Buddhism in the Rebirth of Tibetan Culture.* New York: Columbia University Press, 2005.

Davis, Richard H. *Ritual in an Oscillating Universe: Worshipping Siva in Medieval India.* Princeton, NJ: Princeton University Press, 2014.

de la Vallée-Poussin, Louis, trans. *L'Abhidharmakośa de Vasubandhu.* Paris: Geuthner, 1923–1932.

De Rossi Filibeck, Elena. *Two Tibetan Guide Books to Ti Se and La Phyi.* Bonn: VGH Wissenschaftsverlag, 1988.

Debreczeny, Karl. "Wutai Shan: Pilgrimage to Five-Peak Mountain." *Journal of the International Association of Tibetan Studies* 6 (2011): 1–133.

Dhammajoti, Kuala Lumpur. *Abhidharma Doctrines and Controversy on Perception.* Hong Kong: Centre of Buddhist Studies, 2007.

Dodin, Thierry. "The Observatory Hill in Darjeeling: Some Remarks on Space, Time, Power, and Religions." *Tibetan Studies: Proceedings of the 7th Seminar of the International Association of Tibetan Studies, Graz 1995*, edited by H. Krasser et al., 213–235. Wien: Verlag der Österreischiche Akademie der Wissenschaften, 1997.

Dōgen. *Treasury of the True Dharma Eye: Zen Master Dogen's Shobo Genzo.* Translated by Kazuaki Tanahashi. Boulder, CO: Shambhala, 2012.

Dotson, Brandon. "At the Behest of the Mountain: Gods, Clans and Political Topography in Post-Imperial Tibet." In *Old Tibetan Studies Dedicated to the Memory of Professor Ronald E. Emmerick (1937–2001)*, edited by Christina Scherrer-Schaub, 157–202. Leiden: Brill, 2012.

Dowman, Keith. *The Power-Places of Central Tibet: The Pilgrim's Guide.* London: Routledge, 1988.

Dreyfus, Georges. *Recognizing Reality: Dharmakirti's Philosophy and Its Tibetan Interpretations.* Albany: State University of New York Press, 1997.

Dreyfus, Georges. *The Sound of Two Hands Clapping: The Education of a Tibetan Buddhist Monk.* Berkeley: University of California Press, 2003.

Dubisch, Jill. *In a Different Place: Pilgrimage, Gender, and Politics at a Greek Island Shrine.* Princeton, NJ: Princeton University Press, 1995.

Duckworth, Douglas S., Malcolm David Eckel, Jay L. Garfield, John Powers, Yeshes Thabkhas, and Sonam Thakchoe. *Dignāga's Investigation of the Percept: A Philosophical Legacy in India and Tibet.* Oxford: Oxford University Press, 2016.

Duncan, James S. *The City as Text: The Politics of Landscape Interpretation in the Kandyan Kingdom*. Cambridge: Cambridge University Press, 2005.

Dzongsar Jamyang Khyentse. *Best Foot Forward: A Pilgrim's Guide to the Sacred Sites of the Buddha*. Boulder, CO: Shambala, 2018.

Eade, John, and Michael J. Sallnow. *Contesting the Sacred: The Anthropology of Christian Pilgrimage*. Eugene, OR: Wipf & Stock, 2013.

Eck, Diana L. *Darśan: Seeing the Divine Image in India*. New York: Columbia University Press, 1996.

Eckel, Malcolm David. *To See the Buddha: A Philosopher's Quest for the Meaning of Emptiness*. San Francisco: Harper, 1992.

Eco, Umberto. *Six Walks in the Fictional Woods*. Cambridge, MA: Harvard University Press, 1994.

Edelgass, William, and Jay L. Garfield. *Buddhist Philosophy: Essential Readings*. Oxford: Oxford University Press, 2009.

Edwards, Philip. *Pilgrimage and Literary Tradition*. Cambridge: Cambridge University Press, 2009.

Eickelman, Dale F., and James Piscatori, eds. *Muslim Travellers: Pilgrimage, Migration, and the Religious Imagination*. Berkeley: University of California Press, 1990.

Ellingson, Ter. "Tibetan Monastic Constitutions: The BCa' Yig." In *Reflections on Tibetan Culture: Essays in Memory of Turrell V. Wylie*, edited by Lawrence Epstein and Richard F. Sherburne, 205–229. Lewiston, NY: Edward Mellen Press, 1990.

Elsner, Jas, and Ian Rutherford, eds. *Pilgrimage in Graeco-Roman and Early Christian Antiquity: Seeing the Gods*. Oxford: Oxford University Press, 2008.

Elverskog, Johan. *Buddhism and Islam on the Silk Road*. Philadelphia: University of Pennsylvania Press, 2013.

Enfield, N. J., and Paul Kockelman. *Distributed Agency*. Oxford: Oxford University Press, 2017.

Faxian. *A Record of Buddhistic Kingdoms*. Translated by James Legge. Oxford: Clarendon Press, 1886.

Fedele, Anna. *Looking for Mary Magdalene: Alternative Pilgrimage and Ritual Creativity at Catholic Shrines in France*. Oxford: Oxford University Press, 2012.

Feldhaus, Anne. *Connected Places: Region, Pilgrimage, and Geographical Imagination in India*. London: Palgrave Macmillan, 2003.

Ferrari, Alfonsa. *Mk'yen BrTse's Guide to the Holy Places of Central Tibet*. Roma: Istituto Italiano per il Medio ed Estremo Oriente: 1958.

Flores, Ralph. *Buddhist Scriptures as Literature: Sacred Rhetoric and the Uses of Theory*. Albany: State University of New York Press, 2009.

Fodor, Jerry A. *Modularity of Mind: An Essay on Faculty Psychology*. Cambridge, MA: MIT Press, 1983.

Fogelin, Lars. *An Archaeological History of Indian Buddhism*. Oxford: Oxford University Press, 2015.

Foucault, Michel. "Of Other Spaces." Translated by Jay Miskowiec. *Diacritics* 16, no. 1 (1986): 22–27.

Foucault, Michel. *Technologies of the Self: A Seminar with Michel Foucault*. Edited by Luther H. Martin, Huck Gutman, and Patrick H. Hutton. Amherst: University of Massachusetts Press, 1988.

Frankfurter, David, ed. *Pilgrimage and Holy Space in Late Antique Egypt*. Leiden: Brill, 1998.

Galli, Lucia. "The Accidental Pilgrimage of a Rich Beggar. The Account of Tshong Dpon Kha Stag 'Dzam Yag's Travels through Tibet, Nepal, and India (1944–1956)." *Études Mongoles & Sibériennes, Centrasiatiques & Tibétaines* 48 (2017): 1–5.

Galli, Lucia. "Giving Meaning to an Illusory Wealth: A Trader's Pilgrimage." *Revue d'Etudes Tibétaines* 58 (2021): 5–59.

Galli, Lucia. "Money, Politics, and Local Identity: An Inside Look at the 'Diary' of a Twentieth-Century Khampa Trader." In *Frontier Tibet: Patterns of Change in the Sino-Tibetan*

Borderlands, edited by Stéphane Gros, 313–335. Amsterdam: University of Amsterdam Press, 2019.
Galli, Lucia. "Next Stop, Nirvana: When Tibetan Pilgrims Turn into Leisure Seekers." *Études Mongoles & Sibériennes, Centrasiatiques & Tibétaines* 51 (2020): 1–26.
Garfield, Jay L. *Buddhist Ethics: A Philosophical Exploration.* Oxford: Oxford University Press, 2021.
Garfield, Jay L. *Engaging Buddhism: Why It Matters to Philosophy.* Oxford: Oxford University Press, 2015.
Garrett, Frances, Elizabeth McDougal, and Geoffrey Samuel, eds. *Hidden Lands in Himalayan Myth and History: Transformations of* Sbas Yul *through Time.* Leiden: Brill, 2020.
Gentry, James Duncan. *Power Objects in Tibetan Buddhism: The Life, Writings, and Legacy of Sokdokpa Lodrö Gyeltsen.* Leiden: Brill, 2017.
Gentry, James Duncan. "Tibetan Religion and the Senses." *Revue d'Etudes Tibétaines* 50 (2019): 5–12.
Gifford, Julie. *Buddhist Practice and Visual Culture: The Visual Rhetoric of Borobudur.* London: Routledge, 2011.
Gold, Jonathan C. *The Dharma's Gatekeepers: Sakya Paṇḍita on Buddhist Scholarship in Tibet.* Albany: State University of New York Press, 2007.
Gold, Jonathan C. *Paving the Great Way: Vasubandhu's Unifying Buddhist Philosophy.* New York: Columbia University Press, 2014.
Goldstein, Melvyn C. *The New Tibetan-English Dictionary of Modern Tibetan.* Berkeley: University of California Press, 2001.
Gombrich, Richard F. *Theravada Buddhism: A Social History from Ancient Benares to Modern Colombo.* London: Routledge, 1988.
Grapard, Allan. "Flying Mountains and Walkers of Emptiness: Towards a Definition of Sacred Space in Japanese Religions." *History of Religions* 21, no. 3 (1982): 195–221.
Grapard, Allan. "Geosophia, Geognosis, and Geopiety: Orders of Significance in the Japanese Representation of Space." In *NowHere: Time, Space and Modernity*, edited by D. Boden and R. Friedland, 372–401. Berkeley: University of California Press, 1994.
Grapard, Allan. *Mountain Mandalas: Shugendō in Kyushu.* London: Bloomsbury Academic, 2016.
Gray, David. *The Cakrasamvara Tantra.* New York: American Institute of Buddhist Studies, 2007.
Greene, Eric M. "Visions and Visualizations: In Fifth-Century Chinese Buddhism and Nineteenth-Century Experimental Psychology." *History of Religions* 55, no. 3 (2016): 289–328.
Gyatso, Janet. *Apparitions of the Self: The Secret Autobiographies of a Tibetan Visionary: A Translation and Study of Jigme Lingpa's Dancing Moon in the Water and Ḍākki's Grand Secret-Talk.* Princeton, NJ: Princeton University Press, 1998.
Gyatso, Janet. *Being Human in a Buddhist World: An Intellectual History of Medicine in Early Modern Tibet.* New York: Columbia University Press, 2015.
Gyatso, Janet. "Counting Crows' Teeth: Tibetans and Their Diaries." In *Les Habitants Du Toit Du Monde*, edited by Samten Karmay and Philippe Sagant, 159–178. Nanterre: Société d'Ethnologie, 1997.
Gyatso, Janet. "Down with the Demoness: Reflections on a Feminine Ground in Tibet." *The Tibet Journal* 12, no. 4 (1987): 38–53.
Gyatso, Janet. "Healing Burns with Fire: The Facilitations of Experience in Tibetan Buddhism." *Journal of the American Academy of Religion* 67, no. 1 (1999): 113–147.
Gyatso, Janet. "The Logic of Legitimation in the Tibetan Treasure Tradition." *History of Religions* 33, no. 2 (1993): 97–134.
Haberman, David L. *Journey through the Twelve Forests: An Encounter with Krishna.* Oxford: Oxford University Press, 1994.
Hahn, Thomas. "The Standard Taoist Mountain and Related Features of Religious Geography." *Cahiers d'Extrême-Asie* 4 (1988): 145–156.

Halkias, Georgios T. *Luminous Bliss—A Religious History of Pure Land Literature in Tibet.* University of Hawaii Press, 2012.

Hargett, James M. *Stairway to Heaven: A Journey to the Summit of Mount Emei.* Albany: State University of New York Press, 2007.

Hartmann, Catherine. "Against Pilgrimage: Materiality, Place, and Ambivalence in Tibetan Pilgrimage Literature." *Revue d'Etudes Tibétaines* 65, no. 5 (2022): 127–158.

Hartmann, Catherine. "How to See the Invisible: Attention, Landscape, and the Transformation of Vision in Tibetan Pilgrimage Guides," *History of Religions* 62, no. 4 (2023): 313–339.

Hartmann, Catherine. "Karmic Opacity and Ethical Formation in a Tibetan Pilgrim's Diary," *Journal of Religious Ethics* 52, no. 3 (2023): 496–516.

Hartmann, Catherine. *To See a Mountain: Writing, Place, and Vision in Tibetan Pilgrimage Literature.* PhD Diss., Harvard University, 2020.

Harvey, Susan Ashbrook. *Scenting Salvation: Ancient Christianity and the Olfactory Imagination.* Berkeley: University of California Press, 2006.

Hatchell, Christopher. "Buddhist Visual Worlds II: Practices of Visualization and Vision." *Religion Compass* 7, no. 9 (2013): 349–360.

Hatchell, Christopher. *Naked Seeing: The Great Perfection, the Wheel of Time, and Visionary Buddhism in Renaissance Tibet.* Oxford: Oxford University Press, 2014.

Havnevik, Hanna. "On Pilgrimage for Forty Years in the Himalayas: The Female Lama Jetsun Lochen Rinpoche's (1865-1951) Quest for Sacred Sites." In *Pilgrimage in Tibet*, edited by Alex McKay, 85–107. London: Curzon Press, 1998.

Hirsch, Eric, and Michael O'Hanlon. *The Anthropology of Landscape: Perspectives on Place and Space.* Oxford: Oxford University Press, 1995.

Holt, John C. "Pilgrimage and the Structure of Sinhalese Buddhism." *Journal of the International Association of Buddhist Studies* 5, no. 2 (1982): 23–40.

Howard, Donald R. *Writers and Pilgrims: Medieval Accounts of the Jerusalem Pilgrimage.* Berkeley: University of California Press, 1980.

Huber, Toni. *The Cult of Pure Crystal Mountain: Popular Pilgrimage and Visionary Landscape in Southeast Tibet.* Oxford: Oxford University Press, 1999.

Huber, Toni. "Guide to La-Phyi Mandala: History, Landscape, and Ritual in Western Tibet." In *Mandala and Landscape*, edited by A. W. Macdonald, 233–286. New Delhi: D.K. Printworld, 1997.

Huber, Toni. *The Holy Land Reborn: Pilgrimage and the Tibetan Reinvention of Buddhist India.* Chicago: University of Chicago Press, 2008.

Huber, Toni. "Putting the Gnas Back into Gnas-Skor: Rethinking Tibetan Pilgrimage Practice." In *Sacred Spaces and Powerful Places in Tibetan Culture: A Collection of Essays*, edited by Toni Huber, 77–104. Dharamsala: The Library of Tibetan Works and Archives, 1999.

Huber, Toni, ed. *Sacred Spaces and Powerful Places in Tibetan Culture: A Collection of Essays.* Dharamsala: Library of Tibetan Works and Archives, 1999.

Huber, Toni. "Where Exactly Are Caritra, Devikota and Himavat? A Sacred Geography Controversy and the Development of Tantric Buddhist Pilgrimage Sites in Tibet." *Kailash: A Journal of Himalayan Studies* 16, no. 3–4 (1990): 121–164.

Huber, Toni. "Why Can't Women Climb Pure Crystal Mountain? Remarks on Gender, Ritual, and Space in Tibet." *Tibetan Studies: Proceedings of the 6th Seminar of the International Association for Tibetan Studies, Fagernes, 1992*, edited by Per Kvaerne, 350–371. Oslo: Institute for Comparative Research in Human Culture, 1994.

Huber, Toni, and Tsepak Rigzin. "A Tibetan Guide for Pilgrimage to Ti-Se (Mount Kailas) and MTsho Ma-Pham (Lake Manasarovar)." In *Sacred Spaces and Powerful Places in Tibetan Culture: A Collection of Essays*, edited by Toni Huber, The Library of Tibetan Works and Archives, 1999, pp. 125–153.

Huntington, Eric. *Creating the Universe: Depictions of the Cosmos in Himalayan Buddhism.* Seattle: University of Washington Press, 2019.

Jackson, David P. "Commentaries on the Writings of Sa-Skya Paṇḍita." *The Tibet Journal* 8, no. 3 (1983): 3–23.

Jackson, David P. *The Mollas of Mustang: Historical, Religious, and Oratorical Traditions of the Nepalese-Tibetan Borderland.* Dharamsala: Library of Tibetan Works and Archives, 1984.

Jackson, David P. "Several Works of Unusual Provenance Ascribed to Sa Skya Paṇḍita." In *Tibetan History and Language: Studies Dedicated to Uray Géza on His Seventieth Birthday*, edited by Ernst Steinkellner, 233–254. Wien: Universität Wien, 1991.

Jaini, Padmanabh S. "The Story of Sudhana and Manoharā: An Analysis of the Texts and the Borobudur Reliefs." *Bulletin of the School of Oriental and African Studies, University of London* 29, no. 3 (1966): 533–558. http://www.jstor.org/stable/611473.

Jansen, Berthe. "How to Tame a Wild Monastic Elephant: Drepung Monastery According to the Great Fifth." In *Tibetans Who Escaped the Historian's Net: Studies in the Social History of Tibetan Societies*, edited by Charles Ramble, Peter Schwieger, and Alice Travers, 111–139. Kathmandu: Vajra Books, 2013.

Jansen, Berthe. *The Monastery Rules: Buddhist Monastic Organization in Pre-Modern Tibet.* Berkeley: University of California Press, 2018.

Jayatilleke, Kulatissa Nanda. *Early Buddhist Theory of Knowledge.* London: G. Allen & Unwin, 1963.

Kapstein, Matthew. "The Amnesic Monarch and the Five Mnemic Men: "Memory" in Great Perfection (rdzogs-chen) Thought." In *In the Mirror of Memory: Reflections on Mindfulness and Remembrance in Indian and Tibetan Buddhism*, edited by Janet Gyatso, 239–268. Albany: State University of New York Press, 1992.

Kapstein, Matthew. "The Guide to Crystal Peak." *Religions of Tibet in Practice*, edited by Donald S. Lopez Jr., 103–119. Princeton, NJ: Princeton University Press, 1997.

Kapstein, Matthew. *The Tibetan Assimilation of Buddhism: Conversion, Contestation, and Memory*. Oxford: Oxford University Press, 2002.

Karlsson, Klemens. "The Formation of Early Buddhist Visual Culture." *Material Religion* 2, no. 1 (2006): 68–96.

Karmay, Samten. "The Cult of Mount Murdo in Gyalrong." *Kailash* 18, no. 1–2 (1996): 1–16.

Karmay, Samten. "The Cult of Mountain Deities and Its Political Significance." *The Arrow and the Spindle: Studies in History, Myths, Rituals and Beliefs in Tibet*, edited by Samten Gyaltsen Karmay, 432–450. Kathmandu: Mandala Book Point, 1998.

Karmay, Samten. "Mount Bon-Ri and Its Association with Early Myths." In *The Arrow and the Spindle: Studies in History, Myths, Rituals, and Beliefs in Tibet*, edited by Samten Karmay, 211–227. Kathmandu: Mandala Book Point, 1998.

Karmay, Samten. "The Pilgrimage to Kong Po Bon Ri." In *Tibetan Studies: Proceedings of the 5th Seminar of the International Association of Tibetan Studies: Narita 1989*, edited by S. Ihara and Z. Yamaguchi, 2: 527–539. Narita: Naritasan Shinshoji, 1992.

Karmay, Samten, and Jeff Watt, eds. *Bon: The Magic Word: The Indigenous Religion of Tibet.* London: Philip Wilson Publishers, 2007.

Kieschnick, John. "Material Culture." In *The Oxford Handbook of Religion and Emotion*, edited by John Corrigan, 223–237. Oxford: Oxford University Press, 2008.

Kind, Marietta. *The Bon Landscape of Dolpo: Pilgrimages, Monasteries, Biographies and the Emergence of Bon.* Lausanne: Peter Lang, 2012.

Kinnard, Jacob N. *Imaging Wisdom: Seeing and Knowing in the Art of Indian Buddhism.* London: Curzon, 1999.

Kolaṭakara, Aruṇa. *Jejuri.* New York: New York Review Books, 2005.

Kramer, Jowita. *A Noble Abbot from Mustang: Life and Works of Glo-Bo MKhan-Chen (1456–1532).* Wien: Universität Wien, 2008.

Kvaerne, Per. "A g.Yung Drung Bon Description of Mount Kailāśa (Gangs Ti Se)." *Revue d'Etudes Tibétaines* 51 (2019): 171–187.

LaCapra, Dominick. *Rethinking Intellectual History: Texts, Contexts, Language*. Ithaca, NY: Cornell University Press, 1983.

Lama, Tsering Yangzom. *We Measure the Earth with Our Bodies*. London: Bloomsbury Publishing, 2022.

Lamminger, Navina. *Der Sechste Zhva Dmar Pa Chos Kyi Dbang Phyug (1584–1630) Und Sein Reisebericht Aus Den Jahren 1629/1630*. Munich: Ludwig-Maximilians-Universität München, 2013.

Latour, Bruno. *Reassembling the Social: An Introduction to Actor-Network Theory*. Oxford University Press, 2005.

Latour, Bruno. *Science in Action: How to Follow Scientists and Engineers through Society*. Cambridge, MA: Harvard University Press, 1987.

Latour, Bruno. "Thou Shall Not Freeze-Frame: Or How Not to Misunderstand the Science and Religion Debate." In *Science, Religion and the Human Experience*, edited by James D. Proctor, 27–48. Oxford: Oxford University Press, 2005.

Le Breton, David. *Sensing the World: An Anthropology of the Senses*. London: Bloomsbury Academic, 2017.

Lefebvre, Henri. *The Production of Space*. Translated by Donald Nicholson-Smith. Oxford: Blackwell, 1991.

Lewis, Todd. "A History of Buddhist Ritual." In *The Buddhist World*, edited by John S. Strong, 318–337. London: Routledge, 2016.

Liang, Lisa, and Brianna K. Morseth. "Aesthetic Emotions: The Existential and Soteriological Value of Saṃvega/Pasāda in Early Buddhism." *Journal of Buddhist Ethics* 28 (2021): 205–239.

Lin, Wei-Cheng. *Building a Sacred Mountain: The Buddhist Architecture of China's Mount Wutai*. Seatlle: University of Washington Press, 2014.

Lochtefeld, James. *God's Gateway: Identity and Meaning in a Hindu Pilgrimage Place*. Oxford: Oxford University Press, 2009.

Loseries-Leick, A. "On the Sacredness of Mount Kailasa in the Indian and Tibetan Sources." In *Pilgrimage in Tibet*, edited by Alex McKay, 143–164. London: Curzon Press, 1998.

Luhrmann, T. M. *How God Becomes Real: Kindling the Presence of Invisible Others*. Princeton, NJ: Princeton University Press, 2020.

Luhrmann, T. M. *When God Talks Back: Understanding the American Evangelical Relationship with God*. New York: Knopf, 2012.

Maclean, Kama. *Pilgrimage and Power: The Kumbh Mela in Allahabad, 1765–1954*. Oxford: Oxford University Press, 2008.

Macpherson, Fiona, and Fabian Dorsch, eds. *Perceptual Imagination and Perceptual Memory*. Oxford: Oxford University Press, 2018.

Makley, Charlene. "Gendered Practices and the Inner Sanctum: The Reconstruction of Tibetan Sacred Space in 'China's Tibet.'" *Tibet Journal* XIX, no. 2 (1994): 61–94.

Markus, R. A. "How on Earth Could Places Become Holy?: Origins of the Christian Idea of Holy Places." *Journal of Early Christian Studies* 2, no. 3 (1994): 257–271.

Matilal, Bimal Krishna. *Perception: An Essay on Classical Indian Theories of Knowledge*. Oxford: Oxford University Press, 1986.

Maurer, Petra. *Die Grundlagen Der Tibetischen Geomantie Dargestellt Anhand Des 32. Kapitels Des Vaiḍūrya Dkar Po von Sde Srid Sangs Rgyas Rgya Mtsho (1653–1705): Ein Beitrag Zum VerstAndnis Der Kultur-Und Wissenschaftsgeschichte Tibets Zur Zeit Des 5. Dalai Lama Ngag Dbang Blo Bzang Rgya Mtsho (1617–1682)*. Halle: International Institute for Tibetan and Buddhist Studies, 2009.

Maurer, Petra. "Landscaping Time, Timing Landscapes: The Role of Time in the Sa Dpyad Tradition." In *Glimpses of Tibetan Divination: Past and Present* , edited by Petra Maurer, Donatella Rossi, and Rold Scheuermann, 89–117. Leiden: Brill, 2019.

Maurer, Petra. "Sa Dpyad and the Concept of Bla Ri." In *This World and the Next: Contributions on Tibetan Religion, Science and Society*, edited by Charles Ramble and Jill Sudbury, 67–79. Andiast: International Institute for Tibetan and Buddhist Studies GmbH, 2012.

Maurer, Petra. "When the Tiger Meets Yul 'khor Srung, or How to Protect a Construction Site." *Etudes Mongoles et Sibériennes*, no. 50 (2019): 1–36.

McGinn, Colin. *Mindsight: Image, Dream, Meaning*. Cambridge, MA: Harvard University Press, 2004.

McKay, Alex. "The British Imperial Influence on the Kailas-Manasarovar Pilgrimage." *Sacred Spaces and Powerful Places in Tibetan Culture: A Collection of Essays*, edited by Toni Huber, 305–321. Dharamsala: The Library of Tibetan Works and Archives, 1999.

McKay, Alex. *Kailas Histories: Renunciate Traditions and the Construction of Himalayan Sacred Geography*. Leiden: Brill, 2015.

McKay, Alex, ed. *Pilgrimage in Tibet*. London: Curzon Press, 1998.

McMahan, David L. *Empty Vision: Metaphor and Visionary Imagery in Mahāyāna Buddhism*. London: RoutledgeCurzon, 2002.

Meyer, Birgit. *Aesthetic Formations: Media, Religion, and the Senses*. London: Palgrave Macmillan, 2009.

Meyer, Birgit. "Picturing the Invisible: Visual Culture and the Study of Religion." *Method & Theory in the Study of Religion* 27, no. 4–5 (2015): 333–360.

Meyer, Birgit. *Sensational Movies: Video, Vision, and Christianity in Ghana*. Berkeley: University of California Press, 2015.

Mills, Martin A. *Identity, Ritual and State in Tibetan Buddhism: The Foundations of Authority in Gelukpa Monasticism*. London: Routledge, 2010.

Mills, Martin A. "Re-Assessing the Supine Demoness: Royal Buddhist Geomancy in the Srong Btsan Sgam Po Mythology." *Journal of the International Association of Tibetan Studies*, no. 3 (2007): 1–47.

Mishra, Saurabh. *Pilgrimage, Politics, and Pestilence: The Haj from the Indian Subcontinent, 1860–1920*. Oxford: Oxford University Press, 2011.

Moerman, D. Max. *Localizing Paradise: Kumano Pilgrimage and the Religious Landscape of Premodern Japan*. Cambridge, MA: Harvard University Press, 2006.

Monius, Anne E. "Literary Theory and Moral Vision in Tamil Buddhist Literature." *Journal of Indian Philosophy* 28, no. 2 (2000): 195–223.

Morgan, David. *The Embodied Eye: Religious Visual Culture and the Social Life of Feeling*. Berkeley: University of California Press, 2012.

Morgan, David. "Religion and Media: A Critical Review of Recent Developments." *Critical Research on Religion* 1, no. 3 (2013): 347–356.

Morgan, David. *The Sacred Gaze: Religious Visual Culture in Theory and Practice*. Berkeley: University of California Press, 2005.

Morgan, David. *Visual Piety: A History and Theory of Popular Religious Images*. Berkeley: University of California Press, 1998.

Mrozik, Susanne. *Virtuous Bodies: The Physical Dimensions of Morality in Buddhist Ethics*. Oxford: Oxford University Press, 2007.

Mus, Paul. "Buddhism and World Order." *Daedalus* 95, no. 3 (1966): 813–827.

Nakza, Drolma. *Pilgrimage to Drakar Dreldzong: The Written Tradition and Contemporary Practices among Amdo Tibetans*. M.Phil Thesis, University of Oslo, 2008.

Naquin, Susan, and Chün-Fang Yü, eds. *Pilgrims and Sacred Sites in China*. Berkeley: University of California Press, 1992.

Nattier, Jan. "The Indian Roots of Pure Land Buddhism: Insights from the Oldest Chinese Versions of the Larger Sukhāvatīvyūha." *Pacific World* 5 (2003): 179–201.

Nattier, Jan. "The Realm of Akṣobhya: A Missing Piece in the History of Pure Land Buddhism." *Journal of the International Association of Buddhist Studies* 23, no. 1 (2000): 71–102.

Nebesky-Wojkowitz, René de. *Oracles and Demons of Tibet: The Cult and Iconography of the Tibetan Protective Deities*. Graz: Akademische Druck-uVerlagsanstalt, 1975.

Newman, John. "Itineraries to Sambhala." In *Tibetan Literature: Studies in Genre*, edited by José Ignacio Cabezón and Roger R. Jackson, 485–499. Ithaca, NY: Snow Lion, 1996.

Newman, John. *The Outer Wheel of Time: Vajrayāna Buddhist Cosmology in the Kālacakra Tantra*. PhD Diss., University of Wisconsin, 1987.

Ngawang, Zangpo. *Sacred Ground: Jamgon Kongtrul on "Pilgrimage and Sacred Geography."* Ithaca, NY: Snow Lion, 2001.

Norbu, Namkhai, and Ramon Prats. *Gaṅs Ti Se'i Dkar c'ag: A Bon-Po Story of the Sacred Mountain Ti-Se and the Blue Lake Ma-Paṅ.* Roma: Istituto Italiano per il Medio ed Estremo Oriente, 1989.

Nugteren, Albertina. *Belief, Bounty, And Beauty: Rituals Around Sacred Trees in India.* Leiden: Brill, 2005.

Orsi, Robert. *History and Presence.* Cambridge: Belknap Press, 2018.

Orsi, Robert. "Material Children: Making God's Presence Real Through Catholic Boys and Girls." In *Religion, Media and Culture: A Reader*, edited by Gordon Lynch, Jolyon Mitchell, and Anna Strhan, 147–158. London: Routledge, 2012.

Pecchia, Cristina. "Seeing as Cognizing: Perception, Concepts and Meditation Practice in Indian Buddhist Epistemology." *Asiatische Studien - Études Asiatiques* 74, no. 4 (2020): 771–796.

Pink, Sarah. "The Future of Sensory Anthropology/The Anthropology of the Senses." *Social Anthropology* 18, no. 3 (2010): 331–333.

Proser, Adriana G. *Pilgrimage and Buddhist Art.* New Haven, CT: Yale University Press, 2010.

Pruden, Leo M., trans. *Abhidharmakosabhasyam* by Vasubandhu. Berkeley: Asian Humanities Press, 1988–1990.

Quintman, Andrew, trans. *The Life of Milarepa* by Gtsang smyon he ru ka. New York: Penguin Books, 2010.

Quintman, Andrew. "Toward a Geographic Biography: Mi La Ras Pa in the Tibetan Landscape." *Numen* 55, no. 4 (2008): 363–410.

Radich, Michael. *The Mahaparinirvana-Mahasutra and the Emergence of Tathagatagarbha Doctrine.* Maburg: Hamburg University Press, 2015.

Rambelli, Fabio. *Buddhist Materiality: A Cultural History of Objects in Japanese Buddhism.* Redwood City, CA: Stanford University Press, 2007.

Ramble, Charles. "The Complexity of Tibetan Pilgrimage." *Searching for the Dharma, Finding Salvation: Buddhist Pilgrimage in Time and Space*, edited by Christoph Cueppers and Max Deeg, 179–196. Lumbini: Lumbini International Research Institute, 2014.

Ramble, Charles. "The Creation of the Bon Mountain of Kongpo." In *Maṇḍala and Landscape*, edited by Alexander W. MacDonald, 133–231. New Delhi: D.K. Printworld, 1996.

Ramble, Charles. "Gaining Ground: Representations of Territory in Bon and Tibetan Popular Tradition." *The Tibet Journal* 20, no. 1 (1995): 83–124.

Ramble, Charles. "A Nineteenth-Century Bonpo Pilgrim in Western Tibet and Nepal: Episodes from the Life of DKar Ru Grub Dbang BsTan 'dzin Rin Chen." *Revue d'Etudes Tibétaines* 15, no. 12 (2011): 481–501.

Ramble, Charles. "The Politics of Sacred Space in Bon and Tibetan Popular Tradition." In *Sacred Spaces and Powerful Places in Tibetan Culture: A Collection of Essays*, edited by Toni Huber, 3–33. Dharamsala: The Library of Tibetan Works and Archives, 1999.

Ramble, Charles. "Tsewang Rigdzin and The Bon Tradition of Sacred Geography." In *Bon: The Magic Word: The Indigenous Religion of Tibet*, edited by Samten Karmay, 125–146. London: Philip Wilson Publishers, 2007.

Reader, Ian. "Local Histories, Anthropological Interpretations, and the Study of a Japanese Pilgrimage." *Japanese Journal of Religious Studies* 30, no. 1–2 (2003): 119–132.

Reader, Ian. *Making Pilgrimages: Meaning and Practice in Shikoku.* Honolulu: University of Hawaii Press, 2005.

Reader, Ian. *Pilgrimage in the Marketplace.* London: Routledge, 2013.

Reich, Aaron K. *Seeing the Sacred: Daoist Ritual, Painted Icons, and the Canonization of a Local God in Ming China.* PhD Diss., University of Wisconsin, 2018.

Rettler, Bradley. "Analysis of Faith." *Philosophy Compass* 13, no. 9 (2018): e12517.

Rhoton, Jared, trans. *A Clear Differentiation of the Three Codes: Essential Distinctions among the Individual Liberation, Great Vehicle, and Tantric Systems: The Sdom Gsum Rab Dbye and Six Letters.* Albany: State University of New York Press, 2002.

Ricard, Matthieu. *The Life of Shabkar: The Autobiography of a Tibetan Yogin*. Albany: State University of New York Press, 1994.

Ricoeur, Paul. *Interpretation Theory: Discourse and the Surplus of Meaning*. Translated by Ted Klein. Forth Worth: Texas Christian University Press, 1976.

Ricoeur, Paul. "The Metaphorical Process as Cognition, Imagination, and Feeling." *Critical Inquiry* 5, no. 1 (1978): 143–159.

Ricoeur, Paul. "Naming God." In *Figuring the Sacred: Religion, Narrative, and Imagination*, edited by Mark Wallace, translated by Donald Pellauer, 217–235. Minneapolis: Fortress Press, 1995.

Ricoeur, Paul. *The Rule of Metaphor: Multi-Disciplinary Studies of the Creation of Meaning in Language*. Translated by Robert Czerny. Toronto; University of Toronto Press, 1981.

Ricoeur, Paul. *Time and Narrative*. Translated by Kathleen McLaughlin et al. Chicago: University of Chicago Press, 1984.

Rieger, Joerg, and Edward Waggoner. *Religious Experience and New Materialism: Movement Matters*. London: Palgrave Macmillan, 2016.

Robson, James. *Power of Place: The Religious Landscape of the Southern Sacred Peak*. Cambridge, MA: Harvard University Asia Center, 2009.

Rogers, Brian J. *Perception: A Very Short Introduction*. Oxford: Oxford University Press, 2017.

Rotman, Andy. *Thus Have I Seen: Visualizing Faith in Early Indian Buddhism*. Oxford: Oxford University Press, 2009.

Saraccandra, Edirivīra. *Buddhist Psychology of Perception*. Colombo, Sri Lanka: Ceylon University Press, 1958.

Sardar-Afkhami, Abdol-Hamid. *The Buddha's Secret Gardens: End Times and Hidden-Lands in Tibetan Imagination*. PhD Diss., Harvard University, 2001.

Sax, William S. *Mountain Goddess: Gender and Politics in a Himalayan Pilgrimage*. Oxford: Oxford University Press, 1991.

Schaeffer, Kurtis R. *The Culture of the Book in Tibet*. New York: Columbia University Press, 2014.

Schaeffer, Kurtis R., and Leonard W. J. van der Kuijpl, eds. *An Early Tibetan Survey of Buddhist Literature: The Bstan Pa Rgyas Pa Rgyan Gyi Nyi 'od of Bcom Ldan Ral Gri*. Cambridge, MA: Harvard University Press, 2009.

Schaeffer, Kurtis R. "Tibetan Poetry on Wutai Shan." *Journal of the International Association of Tibetan Studies* 6 (2011): 215–242.

Schaik, Sam Van, and Imre Galambos. *Manuscripts and Travellers: The Sino-Tibetan Documents of a Tenth-Century Buddhist Pilgrim*. Berlin: Walter de Gruyter, 2011.

Schmid, Karl. "Knowing How to See the Good: Vipaśyanā in Kamalaśīla's The Process of Meditation." *Wilfrid Sellars and Buddhist Philosophy: Freedom from Foundations*, edited by Jay Garfield, 200–218. London: Routledge, 2019.

Schopen, Gregory. "Archaeology and Protestant Presuppositions in the Study of Indian Buddhism." *History of Religions* 31 (1991): 1–23.

Schopen, Gregory. *Bones, Stones, and Buddhist Monks: Collected Papers on the Archaeology, Epigraphy, and Texts of Monastic Buddhism in India*. Honolulu: University of Hawai'i Press, 1997.

Selby, Martha Ann, ed. *Tamil Geographies: Cultural Constructions of Space and Place in South India*. Albany: State University of New York Press, 2009.

Seligman, Adam B., Robert P. Weller, Michael Puett, and Bennett Simon. *Ritual and Its Consequences: An Essay on the Limits of Sincerity*. Oxford: Oxford University Press, 2008.

Sharf, Robert H. *Visualization and Mandala in Shingon Buddhism*. Redwood City, CA: Stanford University Press, 2001.

Shimada, Akira, and Jason Hawkes, eds. *Buddhist Stupas in South Asia: Recent Archaeological, Art-Historical, and Historical Perspectives*. Oxford: Oxford University Press, 2009.

Shulman, David Dean. *More than Real: A History of the Imagination in South India*. Cambridge, MA: Harvard University Press, 2012.

Skilling, Peter. "The Advent of Theravada Buddhism to Mainland South-East Asia." *Journal of the International Association of Buddhist Studies* 20, no. 1 (1997): 93–107.

Smith, Jonathan Z. *Map Is Not Territory: Studies in the History of Religions.* Chicago: University of Chicago Press, 1993.

Smith, Jonathan Z. *To Take Place: Toward Theory in Ritual.* Chicago: University of Chicago Press, 1987.

Snellgrove, David. *The Hevajra Tantra: A Critical Study.* Oxford: Oxford University Press, 1971.

Strong, John S. "The Beginnings of Buddhist Pilgrimage: The Four Famous Sites in India." In *Searching for the Dharma, Finding Salvation: Buddhist Pilgrimage in Time and Space*, edited by Christoph Cueppers and Max Deeg, 49–63. Lumbini: Lumbini International Research Institute, 2014.

Sturken, Marita, and Lisa Cartwright. *Practices of Looking: An Introduction to Visual Culture.* Oxford: Oxford University Press, 2001.

Stutchbury, Elisabeth. "Perceptions of Landscape in Karzha: 'Sacred' Geography and the Tibetan System of 'Geomancy.'" In *Sacred Spaces and Powerful Places in Tibetan Culture: A Collection of Essays*, edited by Toni Huber, 154–186. Dharamsala: The Library of Tibetan Works and Archives, 1999.

Tagliacozzo, Eric. *The Longest Journey: Southeast Asians and the Pilgrimage to Mecca.* Oxford: Oxford University Press, 2013.

Taves, Ann. "History and the Claims of Revelation: Joseph Smith and the Materialization of the Golden Plates." *Numen* 61, no. 2–3 (2014): 182–207.

Taves, Ann. *Religious Experience Reconsidered: A Building Block Approach to the Study of Religion and Other Special Things.* Princeton, NJ: Princeton University Press, 2009.

Taves, Ann. *Revelatory Events: Three Case Studies of the Emergence of New Spiritual Paths.* Princeton, NJ: Princeton University Press, 2016.

Thondup, Tulku. *Hidden Teachings of Tibet: An Explanation of the Terma Tradition of Tibetan Buddhism.* Somerville, MA: Wisdom Publications, 1997.

Thurman, Robert A. F, trans. *The Holy Teaching of Vimalakīrti: A Mahāyāna Scripture.* Philadelphia: Pennsylvania State University Press, 1976.

Tian, Xiaofei. "Seeing with the Mind's Eye: The Eastern Jin Discourse of Visualization and Imagination." *Asia Major: Third Series* 18, no. 2 (2005): 67–102.

Tilley, Christopher Y., and Kate Cameron-Daum. *Anthropology of Landscape: The Extraordinary in the Ordinary.* London: UCL Press, 2017.

Todes, Samuel. *Body and World.* Cambridge, MA: MIT Press, 2001.

Turner, Victor, and Edith Turner. *Image and Pilgrimage in Christian Culture: Anthropological Perspectives.* New York: Columbia University Press, 1978.

Tweed, Thomas A. *Crossing and Dwelling: A Theory of Religion.* Cambridge, MA: Harvard University Press, 2006.

van der Kuijp, Leonard. "Two Early Reactions to Sa Skya Paṇḍita's Rejection of the Ti Se Ri Bo." Unpublished Manuscript.

van Leeuwen, Neil. "Religious Credence Is Not Factual Belief." *Cognition* 133, no. 3 (2014): 698–715.

van Spengen, Wim. "On the Geographical and Material Contextuality of Tibetan Pilgrimage." In *Pilgrimage in Tibet*, edited by Alex McKay, 35–51. London: Curzon Press, 1998.

van Spengen, Wim. *Tibetan Border Worlds: A Geohistorical Analysis of Trade and Traders.* London: Routledge, 1999.

Venturi, Frederica. "A Gnas Yig to the Holy Place of Pretapuri." *Revue d'Etudes Tibetaines* 51 (2019): 415–447.

Waldschmidt, Ernst. *Das Mahaparinirvanasutra: Text in Sanskrit und tibetisch, verglichen mit dem Pāli; nebst einer Übersetzung der chinesischen Entsprechung im Vinaya der Mūlasarvāstivādins; auf Grund von Turfan-Handschriften.* Berlin: Akademie-Verlag, 1950.

Wallace, Vesna A. *The Inner Kalacakratantra: A Buddhist Tantric View of the Individual.* Oxford: Oxford University Press, 2001.

Walshe, Maurice, trans. *Long Discourses of the Buddha: A Translation of the Digha Nikaya.* Somerville, MA: Wisdom Publications, 2005.

Wedemeyer, Christian K. *Making Sense of Tantric Buddhism: History, Semiology, and Transgression in the Indian Traditions.* New York: Columbia University Press, 2013.

Wittgenstein, Ludwig. *Philosophical Investigations.* Translated by G. E. M. Anscombe. New York: Macmillan, 1953.

Wolfson, Elliot R. *Through a Speculum That Shines: Vision and Imagination in Medieval Jewish Mysticism.* Princeton, NJ: Princeton University Press, 1994.

Wollein, Andrea. "Tibetan Pilgrimage Guides to Bhaktapur." *Himalaya* 41, no. 2 (2022): 54–69.

Wynn, Mark R. *Faith and Place: An Essay in Embodied Religious Epistemology.* Oxford: Oxford University Press, 2009.

Zahler, Leah. "Meditation and Cosmology: The Physical Basis of the Concentrations and Formless Absorptions According to DGe-Lugs Tibetan Presentation." *Journal of the International Association of Buddhist Studies* 13, no. 1 (1990): 53–78.

Index

For the benefit of digital users, indexed terms that span two pages (e.g., 52–53) may, on occasion, appear on only one of those pages.

Ananda, 24, 25–26

Buddha, 1, 77, 78–79, 82
body of, 61
and Buddhahood, 2, 151
and death, 27n.10
and "dharma eye," 48–49
dwelling place of, 157–58
enjoyment body, 94
life of, 24–25, 38
and perception, 3, 128
and pilgrimage, 26, 75–76
primordial, 111
and Śāriputra, 2, 3–5
and Shakyas, 64
and significant sites, 39
and suffering, 27–28
tantric, 33–34, 102, 117
teachings of, 48–49, 61–62, 90–91
Buddhism, 26, 80–81
and Anagarika Dharmapāla, 38–39
and China, 35–36
and Chödrak Yeshe, 87, 88
and communities, 24, 26–27
and cosmology, 130
and eye, 54
and frameworks, 32–33
history of, 79–80
and India, 30, 38–39, 72, 101, 147–48
and interdependent arising, 41–42
and languages, 47
and literature, 52
and Milarepa, 155
and monasteries, 146
and Nepal, 147–48
and perception, 20, 53–54, 57–58, 64–65, 84, 142
and philosophers, 14–15, 49–50, 56n.37
and philosophy, 22, 170
and pilgrimage sites, 38–39
and pilgrims, 23, 55–56
project, 2–3
scholars of, 5
scriptures of, 69–71, 76–77, 81
spread of, 29–30
and suffering, 169
and tantras, 101
tantric, 6, 28, 37–38, 53, 155
and texts, 3–4, 6, 20, 24–27, 35, 48–49, 50–52, 88–89
and Tibet, 30, 31–33, 36–37, 45
traditions of, 2–4, 19–20, 48, 52, 53, 65, 132, 141, 169
Buddhist pilgrimage, 19–20, 23–24, 25–26, 29–30, 45–46, 65
and Ananda, 25–26
and Buddhist thought, 20
and holy mountains, 4–5
and India, 30, 38
practices of, 27–28, 46, 47–48
sites of, 27
and Tibet, 30, 38–39, 61

Cakrasaṃvara, 6, 21, 32, 114–15, 116, 117–18, 127, 153, 154–55
Buddha, 111
and Chökyi Drakpa, 104, 108–9, 111, 112–13, 155–56
and Kailash, 156–57, 164–65
and mandala, 21, 96–97, 98, 104–5, 111
palace of, 33, 102, 112
and pilgrimage, 101
and tantra, 34–35, 69–70
Cakrasaṃvara Tantra, 12–13, 28, 101
Chökyi Drakpa, 73–74, 78–79, 96–97, 99–100, 104–5, 113–14, 118–19
and Cakrasaṃvara, 21, 108–9, 155–56
and *Guidebook to Gyangme: Vajradhāra's Feast*, 98, 99, 100, 103–4, 105, 106, 107, 108, 109–13, 114–15
and Gyangme, 116, 117–18
and perception, 97, 107–8

Chökyi Drakpa (*cont.*)
and pilgrimage, 100
and pilgrims, 97
and "opening the doors" *sgo phye*, 101, 102
and vision, 116–17, 118, 168–69
co-seeing, 9, 10, 93, 94, 140–42
and Chödrak Yeshe, 71, 94, 117
and Chökyi Drakpa, 113
and Kailash, 93
and Khatag Zamyak, 143–44
and pilgrimage guides, 21, 121, 126–27
and pilgrims, 68, 168–69
and texts, 120

direct perception (*pratyakṣa*), 19n.46, 55n.30, 83, 96
and Chödrak Yeshe, 79–80, 81, 82, 84–85, 95
and Chökyi Drakpa, 98n.4, 102n.18, 104, 111, 114, 114n.49, 115, 117–18
definition of, 56, 57
and Kailash, 83
and Sakya Paṇḍita, 84

extraordinary (*thun mong ma yin pa*), 6–7, 79–80
extraordinary perception, 6–7, 19, 20, 71, 79–81, 82, 84, 90, 93–94, 129–30, 157

Gyangme: Vajradhāra's Feast, 96–98, 99, 101, 103, 104–5, 108–9, 111, 114–15, 116, 117–19
Gyeltsen, Drakpa, 12–13

holy mountains, 4–5, 91n.75
and Chödrak Yeshe, 70
and Chökyi Drakpa, 98
cult of, 34
and guides, 134
and Gyangme, 96–97, 112, 114, 116
and Kailash, 34–35, 72, 105, 153–54
and lakes, 36
as mandalas, 6, 21, 45–46
and open doors, 37, 98, 101
and pilgrimage guides, 121
and pilgrimages, 30, 39, 69
and pilgrims, 5, 15, 47, 120, 128
and practices, 32
as residences, 33
and temple complex, 13
in Tibet, 17–18, 31–32, 34, 37–38, 117
and Tsari, 105
Huber, Toni, 7, 27, 32–33, 39–40, 124–25

India, 12–13, 26, 28, 29–30, 35–36, 37–39, 45, 105, 144, 147–48, 149, 150
invisibility, 3–4, 10–11
invisible beings, 1, 18–19
invisible realities, 4–5, 9–10, 68, 69, 79–80, 134
and Buddha, 157–58
and Chökyi Drakpa, 105
and landscapes, 96, 167–68, 170
and mountains, 90, 115
and pilgrims, 97, 118–19
invisible wonders, 150
invisible worlds, 18–19, 165

jingyi lap (*byin gyis brlabs*), 40
Jokhang, 36–37

Kailash, 13–14, 36, 69, 70–73, 74–75, 89–90, 92–93, 127, 136
authenticity of, 20, 69–70, 153–54
and Cakrasaṃvara, 32, 34–35
and Chödrak Yeshe, 77–79, 80–81, 82–84, 85–87, 93–94
and Chökyi Drakpa Yeshe Pal Zagpo, 74, 78–79
and dharma, 92
and divine perception, 90
experience of, 21–22
and Himavat, 35, 37–38, 76–77, 78–79, 84
and Jigten Gonpo, 34
and Khatag Zamyak, 147–48, 150–52, 153–55, 156–57, 158, 159–60, 161–62, 164–65
and Meru, 35
and ordinary perception, 85
and pilgrimage, 72, 88, 91–92, 101, 143, 164–65
and pilgrimage guide, 33
and pilgrimage sites, 45
and Sakya Paṇḍita, 75–77, 79, 93
and tantric practice, 38
and Tibetan Buddhist pilgrims, 23, 30
and Tsari, 99–100, 105

Lake Anavatapta, 76–77
Lake Manasarovar, 84
lakes, 31, 36, 39, 43–44, 67, 70, 78–79, 81, 85–86, 91–92, 103, 127, 132–33
and Chökyi Drakpa, 104, 107, 108–9
and Himavat, 87n.58
and islands, 100
and Khatag Zamyak, 158
spirit, 107

landscape, 21, 38, 111, 113, 120, 140–41, 167, 168–69
and Buddha, 128, 130
and Chökyi Drakpa, 104, 105–6, 107, 116, 118–19
and dharma, 32–33
and Kailash, 150
and Khatag Zamyak, 143–44, 151, 155, 158, 159, 160–61, 163, 164–65
material, 157
natural, 36, 131–32
physical, 93–94, 102, 123, 140, 150, 156–57
and pilgrimages, 134, 170
and pilgrims, 10–11, 94–95, 96–97, 140, 142
reading, 21–22
sacred, 29, 45–46, 96
and sutras, 157
Tibetan, 31–32, 93–94
visible, 7
language, 10, 14–15, 19, 21, 97, 126, 138, 148, 155
and perception, 47–48, 53–54
and pilgrimage guides, 126–27
Tibetan, 11, 20, 70–71

Maheśvara, 7, 9
mandala, 4–5, 6, 28, 33, 102, 127n.22, 140, 141, 169
and Cakrasaṃvara, 21, 96–97, 98, 104–5, 111, 112–13, 114n.49
and Chödrak Yeshe, 94
and Chökyi Drakpa, 104–5, 115, 116, 117
and Gyangme, 116
and Kailash, 156
and Khatag Zamyak, 163
and mountains, 6–7, 16, 21, 33–34, 45–46, 47, 68, 70, 96–97, 112, 113–14, 120, 137–39, 142, 170
and pilgrimages, 39, 63, 136–37, 167
materialism, 168
Milarepa, 21–22, 34, 36, 42–43, 69–70, 75, 82, 102, 117, 149, 153–55, 158, 160–63, 165
monasteries, 26–27, 31–32, 36–37, 39, 44, 59, 75, 100, 146
Mount Himavat, 20, 35, 37–38, 69–71, 76–79, 81, 82, 83–86, 90–91, 93–94, 154–55

objects, 14–15, 18–19, 39, 40–41, 52, 78–80, 168–69
and Chödrak Yeshe, 88
external, 50–52, 53, 57, 63, 88, 89–90
holy, 66, 155–56, 162
and holy places, 90–91
human-made, 133
and perception, 164
physical, 58n.43, 67
pilgrimage tradition of, 66–67, 121
powerful, 65–66
and religion, 10
visual, 52–53
and visual encounters, 47–48, 87
of worship, 147
ordinary (*thun mong*), 2–3, 6–7, 10–11, 79–80, 85
ordinary perception, 2–3, 6–7, 8–9, 10, 19, 20–22, 49, 66, 68, 121, 126–27, 128, 133
and Buddhahood, 151
and Chödrak Yeshe, 55–80, 82–84, 85–86, 93–94
and Chökyi Drakpa, 108–9, 110, 111
and co-seeing, 168–69
deficiencies of, 140–41
denaturalization of, 128, 135–36, 140
and Kailash, 84–85, 143–44
and Khatag Zamyak, 143–44, 155, 162–65
and landscape, 168–69
and mountain, 130
and pilgrimage guides, 140, 170
and pilgrimages, 129–30
and pilgrims, 140, 141–42, 169
and Sakya Paṇḍita, 79
and sanctity, 70
and scriptures, 78–79
value of, 71

Padmasambhava, 82, 102, 103–4, 108, 110–11, 112, 113, 114, 117, 135, 153
Paṇḍita, Sakya, 20, 69–73, 74
and Chödrak Yeshe, 93
and *Clear Differentiation*, 75–77
and holy places, 92
and Kailash, 77, 78–79, 84, 153–54, 157
and Khatag Zamyak, 153–54
philosophy of perception, 48, 50, 50n.7, 89n.66
pilgrim diaries, 11–12, 21–22, 44, 123–24, 146, 147–53, 155–56, 158, 161, 162, 163
pilgrimage guides (*gnas yig*), 13, 15–16, 21, 37, 121, 122–25, 126–27, 135–36, 150–51, 152–53, 168–69, 170
and holy places, 98
and Khatag Zamyak, 151–52
and literary strategies, 21, 142
and mandala, 140
and mountains, 34, 130, 138–39
and oral traditions, 13
and perception, 66, 94, 128, 140

pilgrimage guides (*gnas yig*) (*cont.*)
and Pema Karpo, 12–13
and Sexed Rocks, 7
and tropes, 137–38
practices of seeing, 10–11, 45–46, 95, 168–69
as active practice, 68
and Buddhism, 47–48, 65
and Chökyi Drakpa, 96–97, 113
and Gyangme, 104–5
and invisible landscapes, 18–19, 168, 170
and Khatag Zamyak, 21–22, 143, 149, 150, 155, 163, 164–65
and pilgrimages, 9, 170
and pilgrims, 66–67, 94, 143
and sacred worlds, 118

real-making practices, 9, 18–19, 22, 95
religious culture, 3–4, 10–11
religious experiences, 10, 137n.40, 144n.7
religious geography, 137–38
religious leaders, 30–31
religious motivations, 44
religious texts, 126
religious traditions, 1, 2–4, 6n.10, 18, 44, 168
and local deities, 29–30
and Tibetan pilgrimage, 5, 10

sacred geography, 29–30, 36, 37, 89–90, 93–94, 105
sacred landscapes, 3–4, 11, 45–46, 105–6n.28, 118–19, 165
sacred mountains, 31, 34, 39, 69–70, 102
sacredness, 21, 40, 114–15, 166–67
sacred palaces, 4–5
sacred sites, 26, 37–38, 44–45, 75–76, 87–88n.60, 96–97, 117–18
sacred traces, 26–27, 29
sacred trees, 26–27
Śāriputra, 1, 2–5, 6

Tibet, 8, 16, 17–18, 71–72, 92–93, 99–100, 122–23, 137–38
and advice literature, 58
and artists, 133
and Buddhism, 23–24, 29–30, 31–33, 36–37, 38–39, 45–46, 47–48, 88
and communities, 19
and dictionaries
and India, 38–39, 150
and Kailash, 13–14, 20, 69–70
and Khatag Zamyak, 149
and landscapes, 31–32
and language, 54, 56, 57, 64–65, 70–71
and medical tradition, 105
and mountains, 33–36, 117, 136
and mountain pilgrimages, 3–4, 34, 46, 97, 113–14, 116
and pilgrimage texts, 6–7, 19, 48, 57, 61
and pilgrims, 15, 17, 23–24, 35–36, 38, 44, 143
and religion, 129–30
and Sexed Rocks, 7–8, 43–44
and society, 30–31, 42–43
and tantra, 37–38
and tantric texts, 12–13, 37–38
and Tengyur, 12–13
and Treasure tradition, 114–15
and vision, 53
and visual perception, 53–55
Western, 20
and writing, 11, 13–14, 47–48, 74–75, 104–5, 121–22, 168
Tibetan pilgrimages, 15–16, 19–20, 21–22, 25–26, 31, 43, 44, 59–60, 65–66, 68, 69–70, 147–48
accounts of, 93–94
and Buddhist, 30
and destinations, 34, 45–46
and guides, 170
and holy places, 55
and modernity, 45
and mountains, 167
and "opening doors," 97
and perception, 10, 20
and Sexed Rocks, 7
sites of, 139–40
study of, 5
texts of, 5, 6–7, 10, 17, 19, 20–21, 48, 57, 61, 63
and traditions, 20, 22, 34, 45–46, 47, 68, 69, 70, 96, 170
transformation of perception, 2–3, 5, 68, 69, 82, 93, 94, 96–97, 113–14, 142, 170
Tsari, 7–8, 9, 34–35, 37–38, 67, 128–29
beauty of, 133
and Cakrasaṃvara, 101
guidebooks to, 132
and Gyangme, 105
and Jigten Sumgön, 99–100
as mandala, 137–38
and perception, 136
Pilgrimage Guide to Tsari, 41
Rongkor pilgrimage, 44
and Tibetan pilgrimage, 6
and Toni Huber, 7, 124
walking sticks, 44
wildlife at, 133
Turquioise Lake, 108–10

visual culture, 14–15, 52n.17, 150n.19
and Chökyi Drakpa, 113
and Khatag Zamyak, 157
and pilgrim diary, 144
visualization, 6n.10, 15n.37, 18–19, 40, 53, 155, 156–57

Zamyak, Khatag, 21–22, 143–44, 145–48, 157–59, 164, 168–69
and *dmigs rnam*, 160
and Kailash, 150–55, 156–57
and *ngo 'phrod*, 160–61
and perception, 153, 163, 164–65
and pilgrimage, 13–14, 162–63
and pilgrim diary, 44, 123–24, 127, 148–50
and pure perception, 155–56
and Sakya Paṇḍita, 72n.7
and *zhib mjal*, 159–60